ZHOU ENLAI

ZHOU ENLAI

The Last Perfect Revolutionary

A BIOGRAPHY

GAO WENQIAN

Translated by

PETER RAND

and

LAWRENCE R. SULLIVAN

PublicAffairs
New York

Copyright © 2007 by Gao Wenqian. Translated by Peter Rand and Lawrence R. Sullivan.

Published in the United States by PublicAffairs™, a member of the Perseus Books Group.

PublicAffairs books are available at special discounts for bulk purchases in the U.S. by corporations, institutions, and other organizations. For more information, please contact the Special Markets Department at the Perseus Books Group, 2300 Chestnut Street, Suite 200, Philadelphia, PA 19103, or call (800) 255-1514, or e-mail special.markets@perseusbooks.com.

Text design by Jeff Williams

Cataloging-in-Publication Data is available from the Library of Congress
ISBN-13: 978-1-58648-415-6
ISBN-10: 1-58648-415-x

First Edition
10 9 8 7 6 5 4 3 2 1

To the memory of
my mother Fu Xiu,
who had encouraged me
to tell the truth
to the Chinese people.

Contents

Contents

INTRODUCTION

Andrew J. Nathan

OF ALL THE MYTHS OF THE CHINESE LEADERS, THAT OF ZHOU Enlai has been the hardest to crack. The Chinese Communist Party tore down most of its former heroes in internal purges—Jiang Qing and those lumped with her as the Gang of Four, Lin Biao and his generals, the secret police chief Kang Sheng, and Mao's ghostwriter Chen Boda. The great oak of Mao was one of the last to fall, hollowed out by memoirs from his Cultural Revolution victims and their families and then by revelations from his private physician. Few Chinese were surprised: they had whispered about his personal cruelties and sexual indulgences for years.

But Zhou remained immaculate. While most Chinese have long known that his official image was too good to be true, they had no details: he was too skilled at hiding his tracks. The facts about Zhou's strange personality and its tragic consequences for China have now come out thanks to the personal odyssey of Gao Wenqian, a one-time researcher-writer at the secretive Chinese Communist Party Central Research Office for Documentation (*Zhonggong zhongyang wenxian yanjiushi*).

Like many dictatorial regimes, the Chinese Communist Party obsessively collects its own documents and with equal obsessiveness keeps them secret. National-level Party and state civilian archives reaching back to the early history of the Communist movement and up to the recent past are kept by the Central Archives (*Zhongyang dang'anguan*), located in a large walled and guarded compound more than twenty miles to the northwest of Beijing. Local government archives, military archives, and archives of the pre-1949 Nationalist regime are held elsewhere. Drafts and originals of official telegrams, reports, decisions, meeting minutes, and the like are sent to the archives by leaders' offices, Central Committee departments, and government ministries after having been kept in their original units for a number of years. The archives also collect photographs, tape recordings, interview transcripts, and other documentation.

In the past the archives were off limits except, in rare cases, to high-ranking Party officials. Today, the materials are used by official compilers, who can see documents relevant to their assigned projects strictly on a need-to-know basis, by appointment at the archives complex, with access to sensitive materials graded by the compiler's rank. Their job is to write and rewrite history to fit the changing official line. Mr. Gao's unit in the Central Archives was tasked with compiling the chronologies, biographies, and collected works of Mao Zedong, one-time head of state, Mao rival Liu Shaoqi, Mao aide and post-Mao leader Deng Xiaoping, economic decision-maker and Party elder Chen Yun, and, of course, Premier Zhou Enlai.

It was on the Zhou projects that Gao chiefly worked for fourteen years. He focused on the period from the start of the Cultural Revolution in 1966 to Zhou's death in 1976. He also participated in work on Zhou's youth and career in the Party up to 1949, and in research on Mao's role in the Cultural Revolution, a role which, of course, was central to the high politics of that period. In this way, he came to know more about Zhou's life and character than perhaps anyone who had not worked directly with the premier, and more about the high-level politics of the Cultural Revolution than any but a few participants and Party researchers.

Gao Wenqian's research in the secret Party archives allows for the first fully human portrait of China's premier. Rather than the Zhou

Enlai of legend, Gao portrays a complicated man, whose skill at adapting to Mao Zedong's mercurial moods enabled him to survive the Cultural Revolution relatively unscathed and to break ground in relations with the Western world. At the same time, his even-handed treatment reveals Zhou's culpability in serving Mao Zedong's destructive whims during the Cultural Revolution.

Gao shows insight into all the main actors of the Cultural Revolution—the suspicious Mao, the trusting Liu Shaoqi, the raucous Jiang Qing, the stubborn Deng Xiaoping. The rolling power struggles of that period, it turns out, were the result less of competing ambitions among leading politicians than of Mao's machinations, fostered by his constant suspicions of those he had himself promoted. Gao shows how Mao launched the Cultural Revolution out of unfounded jealousy of Liu Shaoqi, how he pushed an unambitious Lin Biao into power and then manipulated him into fleeing the country, how he created and secretly sustained the group he himself eventually labeled the Gang of Four while keeping a public distance from them, and how Mao brought Deng Xiaoping back to power from internal exile not to assist Zhou Enlai but to counterbalance him.

But Gao's most important revelations concern Zhou and his relationship with Mao. In order to bring Zhou to life, Gao masterfully interprets his opaque, evasive language, a style that Zhou cultivated in order to avoid triggering Mao's anger. He shows Zhou straining to interpret Mao's wishes, to support Mao's changing line, and to absorb Mao's unpredictable attacks. He portrays Mao's cruelty to Zhou in his last years—his denial of medical treatment for bladder cancer and the exhausting, humiliating political inquisition he forced on Zhou in the last months of the premier's life, an inquisition based on fake evidence and aimed at destroying any legacy the dying premier would leave for those who might try to reverse Mao's line after his own death.

The mystery is less Mao's sadism, which has been exposed by numerous writers, but Zhou's submission. When Mao denied him an operation he complied, when Mao subjected him to unjust criticism he hastened to criticize himself. Gao shows that Zhou had made a decision relatively early in his career as a revolutionary, which he stuck to until the end of his life: not to challenge Mao. This was the tragic rigidity in the character of this most flexible of men.

Although Party historians have attacked Gao for desanctifying Zhou, it would be more accurate to say that he shows sympathy for Zhou's own regret for his role in the Cultural Revolution. Gao gives Zhou credit for softening the impact of Mao's policies, for protecting a number of people, for keeping the country going, for trying to restart the economy, and for achievements in foreign affairs. Yet he also makes clear that without Zhou's support Mao could not have kept the disaster going as long as he did. Mao needed Zhou. Although Zhou may not have had the power to overthrow Mao, he could have withdrawn his support (paying, to be sure, the ultimate personal price) and Mao would have been unable to go on as long as he did. By working to mitigate the effects of Mao's rampages rather than to oppose them, he became Mao's enabler. Even on Zhou's deathbed, when he suffered over the memory of the things he had done against his own convictions, he devoted his small remaining energy to self-denunciations aimed at preventing Mao from purging him.

Why? Not because he believed in what Mao was doing: Gao makes clear that Zhou was under no illusion that Mao's maneuvers were good for the country or needed for the revolution. It was because of a deep-seated need to affiliate, an inability to take existential risks, a psychological need to be another leader's number two. Gao traces this attribute to Zhou's childhood as the beloved child of two mothers (one biological and one adoptive) who lacked an active father, and who was thoroughly trained in the Confucian arts of yielding, tolerance, and compromise. On Gao's analysis, it was during a series of intra-Party struggles in the early 1930s and in the 1940s during the Yan'an purges that Zhou's servant mentality found its master. In a series of fierce conflicts Zhou found himself demoted from a top position in the Party to the status of Mao's indispensable yet despised assistant.

Although gifted like other revolutionary leaders with intelligence and physical endurance, Zhou was unique among them in his capacity to endure abasement in pursuit of long-term goals. What was tragic for his country was that he found no higher goal than fealty to Mao. The two were mutually dependent, yet unequal, with Zhou intermittently subjected to the blistering force of Mao's anger and fused in a permanent posture of servitude. As a result, his great skills went to abet his master's doing of huge damage. Much as Zhou yearned for order and development, his country could not set out toward these goals as long as Mao imposed his nightmare upon the nation. Sadly, Zhou must go down in history as the man who let it happen.

In 1989, Gao Wenqian's life took a new turn. He witnessed the June 4 crackdown on student and citizen demonstrators in and around Tiananmen Square and decided to break with the Party. It took some time, but he eventually came to Harvard University on a fellowship to write a truthful, independent book on China's premier. He prepared for this task by moving his note cards out of China in small parcels. (Even the Party's official scribes never keep copies of documents; for security reasons they must work from laboriously transcribed note cards.) Using the method, as the old Chinese adage goes, of "the ant who moved Mount Tai," Gao sent small packets of cards to the West with a few trusted friends over the course of two years after he left China. The cards formed the raw material for Gao's best seller in Chinese, *Wannian Zhou Enlai* (*Zhou Enlai's Later Years*), published in 2003. That book has been adapted here for Western readers by adding the story of Zhou's earlier years and by elaborating the political context of the Cultural Revolution and the behavior of other actors.

For thirty years after his death Zhou continued to serve the Party perfectly, this time as a graven image of its wisdom and rectitude. Now at last we are privileged to know him as a man. A major contribution to our understanding both of China's iconic administrator and of the inside story of the Cultural Revolution, *Zhou Enlai: The Last Perfect Revolutionary* is a richly rewarding work. By the end of his life, Zhou Enlai had traded his humanity for complete dedication to the regime that destroyed him. To better understand him is to gain insight into a tragic chapter in China's history, and to question, once again, the ability of dictatorship to provide good rule.

THE KISS OF DEATH

Zhou Enlai, the seventy-three-year-old premier of the People's Republic of China, stood in a chill, winter wind on the tarmac of the Beijing airport, surrounded by Chinese Communist Party representatives, leading government officials, and army officers. It was not quite noon, February 21, 1972.

They were scanning the horizon for some sign of the aircraft that carried Richard Milhous Nixon, the first president of the United States to visit the People's Republic.

The occasion was restrained. No red carpet, furled or unfurled, awaited the arrival of the president and his entourage; no military band stood on hand to blast the welcome notes of the national anthems of the countries; no members of the Beijing diplomatic corps had come to swell the ranks of the greeting Party. No cannons were poised to honor the arriving Americans with the customary twenty-one gun salute accorded to heads of state.

It was a bleak winter scene. The two countries had not yet established diplomatic relations. The very spirit of the occasion seemed to have an edge of apprehension. Only the two lone flags of the

People's Republic and the United States half-heartedly flapping atop the terminal building provided the day with any signal that some immense diplomatic moment was at hand.

With a low rumble, "The Spirit of '76," the presidential jet, appeared in the sky. The form of the plane took shape like some great calm prehistoric bird as it slowly descended to the tarmac and with a roar touched down on the North China plain. Lumbering across the field, the plane finally came to a stop before the group that had assembled to greet the president and his party. Workers rolled a gangway up to the jet entrance in double time.

The entire world was watching.

When the hatchway opened, Nixon stepped forth. A man of tremendous pent-up energy, he bounded down the steps, hand outstretched, so eager was he to grasp the hand of his host.

Zhou Enlai did not raise his hand in greeting until the president was advancing at him on hard ground. Then, and only then, did he offer his own hand, and he raised it to the level of his elbow only, because a war wound that had maimed his forearm many years earlier prevented him from lifting it any higher.

In his memoir, Nixon fondly reflected on the epochal welcome he received from the premier of China who noted "'Your handshake came over the vastest ocean in the world,'" said Zhou Enlai in the car on their drive from the airport. "'Twenty-five years of no communication.'" [Richard M. Nixon, *RN: The Memoir of Richard Nixon* (New York: Grosset & Dunlap, 1978), p. 560]

Yet Zhou Enlai was far from exuberant. He was too aware of the political risks he was taking as he welcomed the "number-one imperialist" in the world. The reconciliation was the personal decision of the Communist Party leader Mao Zedong and, indeed, as premier, Zhou Enlai was acting on the Chairman's decision. But it was also something for which others would have to pay a high price if things went wrong. Mao was infamous for changing his mind and punishing those who had failed to follow his mercurial reasoning. Zhou Enlai, the man who had facilitated the meeting with President

Nixon, was the ideal scapegoat if this rapprochement struck the wrong nerve.

Zhou Enlai made sure that the photograph released to the press the following day was one his personal photographer had taken, one that showed Nixon, hand outstretched, stepping off the gangway toward Zhou Enlai, who stood with a fixed smile on his lips, hand at his side.

At the welcoming banquet on the night of Nixon's arrival in Beijing, when he walked over to toast the American president, Zhou waited until the rim of his glass was on a level with Nixon's glass before he clinked it in a welcome toast. This may seem like a negligible detail, but in such details resides the well-evolved language of Chinese diplomacy. Zhou, whenever he hosted other visiting dignitaries, always lowered the rim of his glass to clink it against the middle of his guest's glass, to show hostly respect for his honored visitor. Zhou had choreographed his restrained posturing well before the American president arrived. He would be "neither servile nor arrogant, neither warm nor cold," a spirit he hoped to subtly convey not to the international audience glued to this historic spectacle, but to domestic observers lurking behind the political curtain.

Zhou Enlai's caution was not merely a manifestation of his temperament. He had his forebodings. As things turned out, he was right. But not even his caution, extreme as it was, could save Zhou Enlai from the jealous and vindictive nature of Mao Zedong.

Zhou Enlai almost never made a mistake. This was the key to his ongoing success over many decades and throughout turbulent times. As a student of acting, he knew how to master the role he was handed. For years, he had been performing the important part of the indispensable servant to perfection, much to the annoyance of Mao, his master. He was almost entirely self-effacing. He knew how to mend the broken pieces of crockery that Mao shattered from time to time. Zhou's genius for self-abnegation and the deft and artful way that he had of cleaning up a nasty mess aggravated Mao, the master, and piqued his pride. They were the odd couple, but this was no domestic comedy.

On some level, Mao hated his servant, who, he knew, was not only far too smart, but also inscrutable in his devotion, and he always kept his eyes half-open for the chance to humiliate him.

Zhou Enlai was the master tactician. It was this quality that Mao hated the most in him and the feature that of all others he relied upon in Zhou and also prized. Zhou Enlai could anticipate what Mao was thinking faster than it takes to blink an eyelid. Long before it had occurred to Mao that he might someday need to play an American card, Zhou Enlai had begun to prepare the way.

Zhou began to lay the foundation for the rapprochement with the United States at the very beginning when the Americans were preparing to kiss the Communists goodbye, before they had even come to power in China. In 1946, the truce that General George C. Marshall had tried to broker between the Communists, led by Mao, and the Nationalists under Generalissimo Chiang Kai-shek, collapsed. The door to diplomatic relations between the United States and the Communist insurgents was about to slam shut. Zhou Enlai took it upon himself to pay a visit to the American general alone, to thank him for his efforts and to bid him farewell.

In Geneva, in 1954, Zhou was famously spurned at the convention talks ending the French Indo-China War by the American secretary of state, John Foster Dulles. Yet, as he later told Mao, General Walter Bedell Smith had managed to find a way to express some comity, for although Dulles had ordered his deputy not to shake hands with Zhou either, Smith, gripping a drink in his right hand, greeted Zhou with his left, by tugging on his sleeve. And it was Zhou Enlai, who, in the early 1960s, would initiate talks in Warsaw that would lead, eventually, to an opening in U.S.-PRC relations.

All of this was the work of the perfect servant who knows how to anticipate the wishes of his master. That day came in the late 1960s when Mao decided it was time to open relations with the United States. Nixon actually raised American-Chinese relations as a possibility in a 1967 article published in *Foreign Affairs* and in his first presidential foreign policy speech following his election in 1968. Zhou Enlai had already prepared Mao for this possibility, so that when it finally suggested itself, he could imagine that he had fore-seen it all along.

Repudiated in victory by the United States in 1949, the People's Republic of China had "leaned to one side," turning for foreign as-sistance to the Soviet Union. Even so, what finally drove China into the Soviet camp was the Korean War, which broke out in the sum-mer of 1950. Up until the war began, the United States and the PRC still had some diplomatic wiggle room, even though the United States had sided with Chiang Kai-shek and the Nationalists in the civil war, and despite the sanctions that many of the Western powers imposed on the PRC after the Communists came to power in 1949. The Korean War, however, turned the United States and mainland China into deadly enemies, and doomed any hope for diplomatic re-lations between them for years to come.

Both the United States and the PRC were losers in the Korean War, which ended in an armistice in 1953. From the PRC perspec-tive, the "United States fought the wrong war in the wrong place at the wrong time." China, however, was the biggest loser in that bloody strife. Mao had wanted to prove to Stalin that he was not a radish—red on the surface, but nationalist at the core—and he plunged the nation into war before his regime had found its footing. In Korea, China suffered devastating losses on the ground. Worse still, the U.S. Seventh Fleet stationed itself in the straits of Taiwan and cut off any possibility that the PRC might have had to recover the island occupied by the Nationalists and bring a final conclusion to the long-suffering Chinese civil war.

The Soviet Union had the most to gain from the Korean War, be-cause it killed two birds with one stone: China was stuck in a quag-mire, and the United States had to maintain forces in Asia at the expense of the major Cold War front in Central Europe. In the short term, the USSR profited from the animosity between the United States and the PRC, and also from the sale to mainland China of outdated weapons left over from World War II. It's true that China also benefited from the Sino-Soviet relationship. Throughout the 1950s, Russia contributed to the massive industrialization of China, but the Sino-Soviet relationship began to go sour under Nikita Khrushchev, and by the late 1960s the Sino-Soviet split was all but official. Serious border conflicts arose between the two countries.

Zhou Enlai knew that enormous changes were underway in world politics. To prepare for the inevitable realignment he foresaw, Zhou realized that China was going to have to adjust its foreign policy. Zhou also understood that Mao was the only person in China who could engineer this kind of seismic shift. He began to feed the master information on the latest foreign policy developments. He also urged top army leaders like People's Liberation Army (PLA) marshals Chen Yi, Ye Jianying, Xu Xiangqian, and Nie Rongzhen, who were currently out of office, to conduct group discussions on international affairs and advise Mao. Zhou Enlai then discreetly removed himself while the group, which he occasionally had to prod, studied the situation between the three major powers and came to the conclusion that "the U.S.-USSR conflict outweighs the China-USSR conflict." Thus they decided that an allied war against China was unlikely, and Mao gave the nod to new U.S.-Chinese ambassadorial meetings in Warsaw, which at that point were stalled, after numerous sessions.

"China and the USSR are at war," Mao had once been heard to murmur to himself. "It is up to the United States to make the next move." He would "use the barbarians to keep down the barbarians," the ancient strategy of Chinese rulers. As the Grand Strategist, Mao, the master, would open up relations with the United States to deal with the USSR.

This was not, however, Mao's only motive. It was the late 1960s and the Cultural Revolution that Mao had inaugurated in 1966 was winding down. Mao had succeeded in destroying the pro-Soviet faction within the Chinese Communist Party. Yet he still feared his enemies. He could envision a Soviet invasion of China ending in a vindictive comeback of all those whom he had routed. He would now play the American card to neuter his enemies.

For a start, Mao put Taiwan on the back burner. "Taiwan is a minor issue," the master declared. "The world situation is a major issue. The problem of Taiwan can wait a hundred years, the world situation is the pressing issue." Zhou entirely concurred. He directed the media to back off their annual denunciation of the United States on the anniversary of its presence on Taiwan. This was in June 1969, nineteen years since the United States had intervened in the Chinese domestic conflict. In July, Zhou personally instructed the Foreign Ministry and the Public Security Bureau to treat with utmost civility two American tourists whose yacht had strayed into Chinese waters near Hong Kong, and forbade Chinese authorities to take any action until the facts were altogether clear. When the United States reciprocated by scaling down economic sanctions against the PRC and lifting a ban on tourism to China, Chinese authorities released the two Americans in custody.

The Russians, however, presented a set of problems of their own.

The Sino-Soviet border conflict had intensified. What started as an ideological dispute turned into a nationalistic border quarrel when in March 1969 Soviet and Chinese troops fought over control of the small, uninhabited Treasure (*Zhenbao*) island in the Ussuri River, which runs along the border of the two countries in China's far north. The Soviets wanted the Chinese to simmer down. Aleksei Kosygin, the Soviet premier, planned to corner Zhou at Ho Chi Minh's funeral in September 1969, and urge him to tone down the hostile rhetoric. Zhou anticipated this maneuver, and was well aware that the Soviets had planned to play a China card with the United States, which was then embroiled in the Vietnam War. A show of solidarity by the USSR and China might further weaken U.S. resolve on the ideological war front. Zhou, an old friend of Ho Chi Minh, flew in one day ahead of the state funeral to pay his respects to the late North Vietnamese leader and returned to China the same day. Kosygin, however, could not be entirely thwarted. Besides, both China and the Soviets wanted to goad the United States. Kosygin made a stopover at the Beijing airport on his way back to Moscow from Hanoi. In the VIP lounge, he and Zhou worked out a formula for easing border hostilities. After Kosygin was back in the air on his way to Moscow, Zhou reworked the language of their communiqué, deleting words like "fraternal" and "friendly" that might appear to overemphasize the rapprochement and give the United States the impression that all was well between the Chinese and the Russians. The Soviets did their part by repudiating the agreement once Kosygin was back in Moscow.

In December, the United States agreed to reopen the Warsaw talks. The U.S. ambassador to Poland, acting on the instruction of the U.S. national security advisor, Henry Kissinger, contacted China's chargé d'affaires in Warsaw on December 3. Lei Yang, China's point man in the impending negotiations, had not been expecting this particular approach. He fled in panic, but not before those in the international press corps had observed the contacts. This was the opening for which the Chinese had been waiting. Within days, the U.S. ambassador and the Chinese chargé had exchanged visits, and China released two more American tourists who had strayed into Chinese waters.

Zhou Enlai's efforts continued, both on the diplomatic front and within his own bureaucratic bailiwick of the Foreign Ministry. He hinted to the Pakistani ambassador in Beijing that the United States should take further steps to open relations with China, "although," he added with Mao-like unconcern, "if we can't get it done now, we can leave it to the next generation."

Zhou displayed no such unconcern at the ministry, where he now set out to convince the staff that this huge turnabout in Party policy was inevitable. He was going to have to invite the bureaucrats to erase the imprint of a complete mindset and reverse an attitude. To do this, Zhou invoked the prestige of the Chairman.

President Nixon showed his hand for the first time when, on February 18, 1970, in an official Foreign Policy Report to Congress, he called the Chinese "a great and vital people." He declared that the United States had no intention of making alliances to oppose either one of the two Communist giants.

At last, on February 20, Chinese representatives in Warsaw met with U.S. officials to hold their 136th meeting. Zhou had ordered one basic change in the script. Now the Chinese expressed themselves as "willing to receive" an American delegation. This was a fundamental shift from the proposed wording, which had stated that the Chinese were "willing to consider" doing so. (Zhou argued that to "receive" is cooler than to "welcome," but more concrete than to "consider" doing either.) This small shift in wording was an icebreaker. From that point on, both sides, the U.S. and the PRC, began to approach their strategic relationship from new geopolitical angles.

But all manner of obstruction blocked the road to reconciliation.

The military coup d'etat in Cambodia interrupted the progress of relations between the United States and the People's Republic for an entire year. At the same time, opponents of the U.S.-PRC rapprochement in the American State Department were stalling a meeting. The Chinese had been awaiting a formal response to their own query about the next Warsaw meeting when, in March 1970, Prince Norodom Sihanouk of Cambodia, while on a European sojourn, was overthrown. On his return to Asia, his decision to fly into Beijing, where he settled into exile, put the United States and China on opposite sides of this critical regional issue. China had begun to entertain doubts that the United States really wanted to extricate itself from either Vietnam or Southeast Asia; now it began to look to China as though the United States was getting more involved, that it had actually joined forces with the USSR to support Lon Nol, the new Cambodian leader. China played the anti-imperialist card in this round, and disclosed its staunch support for Southeast Asia and its struggle for independence. The real target of this move, though, was the USSR. "The Cambodian problem," declared Qiao Guanhua, the Chinese deputy foreign minister, "is just one aspect of the China-USSR argument."

As antiwar protests and campus unrest began to boil over in the United States, Mao took over as the world's chief spokesman for the anti-imperialists. He called a halt to the 137th Warsaw meeting and he staged a mass meeting of half a million people in Beijing. Mao's war cry, better known as the May Twentieth Declaration, invited people to "unite to fight the American imperialists and their running dogs." Zhou had no choice but to accompany Mao on this revolutionary spree. Still, he did what he could to keep the policy of U.S.-PRC reconciliation on track.

The anti-imperialist rhetoric ran its course. Mao came back down to earth, and the Chinese quietly released an American bishop who had been sentenced to twenty years in a Chinese prison for espionage.

In August, the American ex-patriate journalist Edgar Snow showed up in China. Zhou had a long talk with Snow, author of *Red Star over China,* the classic account of the 1934–1935 Long March, which had brought the news of Mao and his guerrillas to millions of American readers for the first time. Zhou wanted to use the aging Snow as an intermediary to the United States, as the Chinese Communist guerrillas had so successfully done in that earlier day, and the timing seemed propitious.

"If there is anything I want to do before I die, it is to go to China," President Nixon told a reporter from *Time* magazine. "If I don't, I want my children to." The quote appeared in early October 1970. That signal was clear enough for the Chinese. [Richard M. Nixon, *RN: The Memoirs of Richard Nixon,* p. 546]

On October 1, China's National Day, Mao appeared on the reviewing stand at Tiananmen Square with Edgar Snow and his wife. He told his staff he was sending up a trial balloon for the Americans. Zhou personally supervised the photo layout that appeared on the following day in *People's Daily,* the CCP's major newspaper outlet. He made sure that photos of Mao and Edgar Snow, Mao's American biographer, standing side-by-side reviewing the National Day parade formed the centerpiece. But the balloon did not rise high enough over the Great Wall of China. The photos did not make an impression on the Americans until they appeared the following March in *Life* magazine, when plans for Nixon's visit were already under discussion at the White House and the State Department, where officials found in them an inspiration. Suddenly, everyone remembered Edgar Snow, a long-forgotten victim of the McCarthy era in America who had lived in exile in Switzerland since the 1950s.

One thing was clear: Mao and Nixon had taken charge of the reconciliation process.

In late October at the United Nations Nixon approached Yahya Khan, the president of Pakistan, and Nicolae Ceauşescu, the Communist leader of Romania, and confided his wish to send a secret envoy to China. At a banquet in honor of Ceauşescu, Nixon, for the first time, dropped the old term "Red China" and referred to the country by its formal name, the "People's Republic of China." Mao received each message, one from Romania, one from Pakistan, and on October 18 he met with Snow at Central South Lake (*Zhongnanhai*), the leadership compound in central Beijing where he and the other top Communist Party leaders lived amid its extensive grounds in special villas, some of which dated back to the Qing Dynasty. Mao rambled on about this and that. Then he declared, "I am flirting with Nixon. All I need is a matchmaker." He also told Snow that the Foreign Ministry might decide to allow Americans from the left, right, and center to visit China. However, to resolve their relations with the United States, Mao told Snow, the Chinese would have to talk with Nixon himself. "If Nixon wants to come," Mao told Snow, "I would be happy to talk with him. If we get along, that's fine. If we don't, that's fine too. If we quarrel, that's okay. If we don't, that's okay too. He may come either as a tourist, or he may come as a president." Regrettably, nobody passed these words along until later.

On December 9, however, the message that Zhou Enlai had entrusted to Yahya Khan reached the Americans: "If President Nixon is sincere about resolving the Taiwan problem, then the Chinese government would welcome an envoy sent by the President to Beijing." Although Zhou had effectively delivered the message, it represented the wishes of Mao Zedong and Lin Biao, Mao's official successor and the chief of China's military forces. A month later, in January 1971, Zhou Enlai responded to the message the Romanians had also passed along declaring that since President Nixon had visited Communist Romania, he would be equally welcome in Beijing.

China and the United States now embarked on a public relations contest to see which one would get the credit for improving U.S.-PRC relations.

Mao thought China needed to have the upper hand. The Americans, he believed, should appear to be knocking on China's door, seeking peace. Mao knew that this was the only way that China could back away from its anti-American stand of times past and persuade people inside and outside the Communist Party to go along with this diplomatic *volta-face*.

The U.S. State Department, meanwhile, dragged its feet. In a return message, the department conveyed the vague suggestion that the two nations should meet in a third country to discuss, among other issues, Taiwan, which under the control of the Nationalists and Chiang Kai-shek though it was, China claimed as an integral part of the PRC.

Fending Off Domestic Intrusions

This game of public relations was not the only source slowing the process of a Nixon-Mao meeting. At the same time, the leaders of the PRC and the United States were preoccupied with policy campaigns of their own. The U.S. government announced a scheme to help the South Vietnamese cut off the Ho Chi Minh Trail. Mao, meanwhile, was engaged in an inner-Party campaign aimed surreptitiously at his second heir apparent, the Minister of Defense Lin Biao, through a direct critique of Chen Boda, Mao's longtime leftist ghostwriter, against whom the Chairman had now turned after Chen had thrown his support behind Lin.

Mao had been heading for a break with Lin Biao soon after the historic 1969 Ninth Chinese Communist Party Congress when Lin's succession to the CCP's top spot seemed secured. By early 1971, Mao was spreading rumors that Lin Biao opposed any rapprochement between the United States and China. Although nothing in the record suggests that this was true, Mao seized upon it to create distance between himself and Lin Biao. Lin Biao's failed coup and his subsequent death in a plane crash in September 1971 created a domestic crisis for Mao; he needed a major triumph on the world scene to deflect attention at home from this stark revelation of his own faulty judgment in appointing the treasonous Lin as his official successor. How very clever it was of Mao to have assigned to Lin Biao, well in advance, the role of enemy of diplomatic progress. Even though it seems to have been untrue, Lin was no longer around to refute the master. It was this sort of strategizing that kept Zhou Enlai on his toes, and ever watchful.

Once again, Zhou Enlai lived up to his reputation as the indispensable wizard of international diplomatic one-upmanship. In April 1971, the thirty-first World Table Tennis Championships were held in Nagoya, Japan, at which the PRC team beat the U.S. team. In the warm afterglow of the match, Zhou invited the American players to visit the People's Republic, a visit swiftly approved by the White House, where, by then, Henry Kissinger was already preparing for his first clandestine visit to Beijing.

This is the accepted version of the Ping-Pong Diplomacy, for which Zhou Enlai is always given credit. The real story is, however, somewhat more complicated.

From the very outset of Zhou's initiative, his own Foreign Ministry dragged its feet. The bureaucrats submitted, in a report, that the first Americans to visit the Chinese mainland in more than two decades should not be Ping-Pong players, especially since no American leftists had yet been issued official invitations to visit. This did not sit well with Zhou Enlai, but Zhou decided that anything this big was up to Mao to resolve. On the report, Zhou wrote: "tentatively agree and may take down contact information."

When Mao saw the report, he passed it on to others, which gave the impression that he quite agreed with this matter of precedence. If so, he must have had immediate misgivings, because, according to his nurse, the same night he passed the report along he seemed moody. She wrote: "At nightfall he took his sleeping pill, and then sat down to dinner at eleven. By the time he finished dinner, the pill had begun to take effect, and he slumped over the table in a stupor."

Then suddenly he ordered the nurse to telephone Miss Wang Hairong, his grandniece and inside agent at the Foreign Ministry, and muttered the fateful words: "invite the American team to visit." The nurse was in a quandary, because Mao had long ago announced that he was not responsible for anything that he said after he had taken his pills. She decided to wait. But Mao lifted his head off the table demanding to know why the nurse was still there, and repeated his instructions. The nurse reminded Chairman Mao that he had already taken his pills, which usually meant that what he said didn't count. But Mao waved his hand and said firmly, "Yes, it counts, every word counts. Go quickly, or it will be too late."

Mao thought that inviting a Ping-Pong team to China was a risk-free gesture that could speed the way for Nixon's visit. Mao was now in the thick of his effort, which was not going well, to undermine Lin Biao by openly criticizing his own former ghostwriter Chen Boda. If Mao decided to take down Lin, there was always the possibility that, as a last resort, supported by many in the CCP old guard who were themselves pro-Soviet, the official successor would throw his lot in with the USSR. This was Mao's greatest fear. Mao wanted urgently to clinch an agreement with the Americans to cut Lin off at the pass.

The American Ping-Pong team was met with a warm welcome in Beijing. A lavish reception was staged on April 14 in the Great Hall of the People, the giant Stalinist-style building in Tiananmen Square where China's leaders hosted their foreign guests. Zhou Enlai declared that a new era in the history of Chinese and American relations had begun. It was both a huge moment in global public relations and a victory for Zhou Enlai in the world press. On the same day, President Nixon announced that the United States was lifting sanctions on non-strategic trade between the United States and mainland China.

On the Chinese side, Zhou laid down the line to be followed in negotiations with the United States. He wrote a realistic script. Taiwan was the core to this script, as an issue between the United States and the PRC. The Chinese would never accept any proposal to create two Chinas, or one China and one Taiwan. China and Taiwan were indivisible, and Zhou Enlai's working script insisted on this fundamental principle. He did not, however, expect the United States to break off relations with Taiwan, and he made no such demand. Instead, in his script the United States would have to remove its military presence from the island gradually, and China would work toward peaceful reunification with Taiwan. Zhou's document, approved on May 29, 1971, became the basis on which the PRC opened negotiations with the United States.

Zhou sealed his success when he sent President Nixon a formal invitation to visit China. As Nixon read the message, Kissinger commented: "This is the most important communication that has come to an American President since the end of World War II." [Quoted in Margaret Macmillan, *Nixon and China: The Week that Changed the World* (New York: Random House, 2007, 183)]

Through back-channel messages conducted with the American ambassador in Islamabad, Pakistan, the PRC and the United States agreed that on July 9, 1971, Henry Kissinger would secretly visit Beijing to make advance preparations for the presidential visit.

Zhou made a study of Nixon and Kissinger, their lives, and the political philosophy of each man. He read Nixon's book, *Six Crises*. He watched *Patton*, Nixon's favorite movie, about the flamboyant World War II American general. He also put together a team, and started planning every detail of the Nixon visit, and, to prepare the nation for the great change in international policy that was about to take place, he circulated an edited version of Mao's talks with Edgar Snow.

Henry Kissinger arrived in Beijing on July 9 aboard a Pakistan International Airline Boeing 707. Zhou Enlai had sent a small group to Pakistan to escort Kissinger and his party to Beijing. There was Wang Hairong, Mao's grandniece, who had long kept an eye on things for him at the Foreign Ministry; Tang Wensheng, an interpreter, who was born in the United States and was known as Nancy Tang; plus Tang Longbin, an official from the all-important Protocol Department of the Chinese Foreign Ministry.

In Beijing, Zhou Enlai paid his first visit to Kissinger at Fishing Terrace (*Diaoyutai*) State Guest House, where the Kissinger party was housed for their two-day stay. In the small conference room where they gathered after a sumptuous lunch, Zhou, as Chinese custom dictates, invited his guest to speak first. Kissinger obliged. He indulged himself in rather ornately ceremonial opening remarks, and then cut to the chase: "No two Chinas, no independent Taiwan." This broke the ice, and Zhou and Kissinger sat down together for the next day and a half to exchange their views on most of the world's problems and some problems of their own, including how to word their joint announcement to the world that the U.S. president Richard Nixon was going to visit China.

Zhou realized that he could not quite persuade the American to accept the version he would have preferred—an announcement that Nixon had asked for the visit—so he settled for a compromise: a statement declaring that the Chinese side was "in possession of information that Nixon wished to visit China and had issued the invitation accordingly." Both sides wanted to convey that this normalizing of relations was not only about Taiwan. The Americans had long lobbied for the inclusion on the agenda of other issues, and now Zhou Enlai agreed. He suggested that in addition to normalizing relations the two sides should add, "and other issues of mutual interest," a phrase that he knew would set the Soviets on edge.

The presidential visit was set for February 1972.

Both sides announced Kissinger's secret visit simultaneously, on July 15, 1971. Either country could seize upon provender from this diplomatic bag, but the People's Republic of China may have ended up with the lion's share. Three months after the announcement, the Twenty-Sixth Session of the United Nations voted by an overwhelming majority to admit the People's Republic (including a seat on the Security Council) to membership.

SECURING DIPLOMATIC VICTORY

The visit to China by President Nixon, and the opening up of relations between the United States and mainland China, was the crowning achievement of Zhou Enlai's career. He had reached the zenith of international acclaim; he was recognized throughout the world and celebrated as a great statesman by the international media. Yet always, every living minute, Zhou Enlai was conscious of his role as Mao's servant. He severely reprimanded the New China News Agency (*Xinhua*) when it circulated the praise that the international press accorded him. Always, Zhou made it a principle to keep Mao in the limelight, especially now, at this moment of his own personal triumph, when Mao, as it happened, was in public disgrace.

Just when plans were proceeding for Nixon's visit, the "September Thirteenth Incident" exploded on the nation. Lin Biao, after an apparently botched assassination attempt on the Chairman by his overly zealous son, fled with his wife and a small entourage on board a commandeered Trident jet and crashed in Mongolia. Lin Biao's mutiny made a mockery of Mao's Cultural Revolution, which Lin had directed at Mao's behest. Zhou was now faced with how to deal with the aftermath of this calamity. He canceled the October 1 National Day parade and put Beijing on a state of alert.

The Cultural Revolution had torn the country to pieces. But the new diplomacy offered an excellent opening. Still, Zhou had to defer to Mao every inch of the way. He had to toe the line, and when Alexander Haig Jr., the then deputy assistant to the president for national security affairs, visited China in January 1972 with an entourage to finalize arrangements for the Nixon visit, Zhou took a stern line in deference to the master.

As Nixon's visit approached, Mao fell seriously ill with pneumonia that quickly developed into a pulmonary heart condition. Stress from the September Thirteenth episode and the subsequent blow to his prestige triggered this collapse. He refused treatment and eventually lapsed into a coma. This development was beyond the range of Zhou Enlai's considerable expertise. Luckily, in late January, three weeks before Nixon was due to arrive, Mao relented and agreed to accept medical treatment.

"The American president arrives on February 21," Zhou told the team of doctors called in to treat Mao. "Make sure the Chairman has recovered enough to receive him."

Mao received the president of the United States on February 21, on the very afternoon of his arrival. The president was accompanied by Henry Kissinger and Winston Lord, his aide, a future ambassador to China. The president did not invite William P. Rogers, the secretary of state, another member of his party, to attend this historic meeting. The meeting lasted just over an hour. Although speech was difficult for Mao, it was the Chairman who enunciated the themes that were fundamental to ensuing diplomatic discussions.

The result was the Shanghai Communiqué, which was agreed upon during the final days of the Nixon visit. In this document, the United States signaled its recognition of the PRC and acceptance of the one-China principle. The Shanghai Communiqué was a classic Zhou creation that allowed both sides to claim diplomatic gain. So too had Zhou overseen every aspect of public relations. He had even tried to restore some face to the American secretary of state, William Rogers, who had been shouldered out of the meeting with Mao by none other than Zhou Enlai himself, who was acutely aware that the American State Department disagreed with the White House, and especially Henry Kissinger, on the issue of Taiwan. Although Zhou had arranged for Secretary Rogers to meet with his counterpart, Ji Pengfei, China's current foreign minister, his real aim was to exclude Rogers, along with his potential defense of Taiwan, from the important deliberations with the Chairman. Zhou was well aware that Rogers had lost face in this transaction, and he hastily arranged for a special conclave for the purpose of giving the man some appearance of importance in the proceedings.

Once again, Zhou Enlai was unsurpassed in his role as servant. He deferred, always, to Mao. He labored, tirelessly it seemed, often for fourteen or fifteen hours a day, to achieve success for the master, and, in so doing, eclipsed his own brilliant star. Nixon captured a glimmer of the truth when he said that Zhou was "a great man, rarely seen in a century, yet he had to live under the shadow of Mao, always careful to let the limelight shine on Mao."

There is a profound paradox in Zhou Enlai's final huge effort at self-effacement. "Zhou Enlai Diplomacy" became a universal term among journalists and historians, who used it to explain China's diplomatic victory. Now, Zhou's star shone by itself in the international firmament. The triumph of the Shanghai Communiqué, the joint statement issued by the United States and the PRC at the end of Nixon's visit, put the final touch of brilliance to Zhou Enlai's star. It was also the kiss of death.

2

THE MAKING OF
A REVOLUTIONARY

ON MARCH 5, 1898, IN HUAI'AN, JIANGSU PROVINCE, ZHOU EN-
lai was born into a family of cultured gentility that had fallen on
hard times, and into a country that was about to undergo seismic
political changes.

In 1898, China was still under the rule of the Qing Dynasty, the last
of the major dynastic empires that had reigned over the land for more
than two thousand years. The Qing were Manchurian outlanders who
had swept into China in 1644, but, by 1898, when Zhou Enlai first saw
the light of day, this ruling clique had been violently rocked by civil
war and hostile engagements with foreign powers. In 1864, after a long
internal struggle, the Qing had put to rest the forces of the Heavenly
Kingdom in a civil war known as the Taiping Rebellion, led by one
Hong Xiuquan, the self-styled younger brother of Jesus and a failed
candidate for the imperial examinations. The ruling dynasty was victorious, but at the cost of inviting the help of foreign armies. Foreign
powers, already a troubling mercantile presence following the Opium

Wars of the late 1830s and 1840s, were granted a far greater foothold in China. The "victory" that the Qing secured also came with the loss of much central control over the country that left great areas of China in the hands of rapacious warlords. In the Sino-Japanese War of 1894–1895, the Qing suffered a terrible psychological blow when the Japanese decimated the Chinese navy and exposed for the whole world China's inability to defend itself against imperial predators. In 1900, another savage internal war erupted—the Boxer Rebellion, an uprising against Christians in China that drove the Empress Dowager Ci Xi and her court to flee the capital, Beijing, for refuge in the interior. The armies of eight foreign nations, including the hated Japanese, all with various ulterior motives, marched into the capital to rout the Boxers and plunder the Summer Palace outside the city.

Briefly, in 1898, during a time known as the One Hundred Days of Reform, Guang Xu, the young emperor, tried to bring extensive reform to China on a scale so vast and so immediate that he shook the foundations of his own political base and invited the reprisal of conservative forces led by the Empress Dowager. Perhaps, if Guang Xu's reform had taken root, China's history would have taken a different path. As it was, the Qing Dynasty was now marked for extinction.

This was the China into which Zhou Enlai was born, and which, as the revolutionary companion to Mao Zedong, it was his destiny to transform into the China we know today.

Huai'an, situated on the central plain of Jiangsu, was the site of the confluence of the Beijing-Hangzhou Grand Canal with the Huai River, one of the many waterways upon which the country depended to carry the bulk of its commercial traffic. Huai'an's history can be traced back at least 1,600 years. It was part of the fecund land of rice and fish that had, over the centuries, generated candidates for the imperial examinations who throughout the history of China had ruled the empire.

On the day Zhou Enlai was born, his grandfather lay dying. Zhou Panlong, the old man, whose given name, *panlong*, means "climbing dragon," had been a scholar, although, like many men of intellect, had failed to pass the Mandarin test that earned ambitious Chinese scholars a lifetime of government service. Panlong's first grandson was brought to the old man on his deathbed. "Benevolent light shines down, eastward the purple energy comes," the dying patriarch murmured. These eight words were the so-called *bagua*, the Eight Diagrams pronouncement that formulates a prediction of the future of a newborn child based on the time and day of its birth. When they heard the old man's divination, Zhou's parents chose the first and last Chinese characters—*en* (benevolence) and *lai* (comes)—to name their new infant son.

Zhou Yineng, Zhou Enlai's father, had married a girl from a nearby county. He was the second of four sons: Zhou Yigeng the eldest, himself, Zhou Yikui, and Zhou Yigan. At the time of Zhou's birth, his father's youngest brother, Zhou Yigan, was suffering from tuberculosis. No cure had yet been found for this disease, and the young uncle had only a few days left to live. Zhou's grandmother quickly decided that Zhou Enlai, not yet six months old, should be handed over to his dying uncle as a surrogate son. "The happiness of adopting a son can drive away misfortune" was a local adage, but beyond that, Chinese traditionally believed that if a man had failed to produce a son he had failed his ancestors in the worst way. Zhou Enlai's parents were of an understanding, good-natured disposition, and they agreed to hand their baby to Yigan so that the dying man wouldn't have to meet his ancestors in the netherworld without having produced a son. Yigan died within two months, but Zhou spent his childhood years with his adoptive mother in the house where three generations of family, including Zhou Enlai's biological parents, were all living together. Zhou's real mother was known to him as his surrogate mother. The arrangement was quite successful. Zhou's two mothers had grown up together like real sisters; their families had been good neighbors for many years.

Zhou's adoptive mother adored him. She was the daughter of a doctor who came from a family of scholars named Chen. She was the most attractive and also the most intelligent of three sisters. She had learned the arts of writing poetry and painting from her father, and had mastered embroidery and needle work. When her husband died, she accepted her status as a widow, as befitted a traditional Chinese woman of the time, and although she was still relatively youthful she refused to remarry. Zhou Enlai was her only companion in life and a source of great spiritual comfort. She devoted herself heart and soul to his upbringing; doting on and pampering him, she also hired a wet nurse to feed him.

Zhou's adoptive mother rarely left the house. Instead, she spent her entire life instilling him with her love and providing him with an education. (She began to teach Zhou how to read when he was three.) Zhou proved his intelligence early on. The large Zhou family, appropriately for a part of China populated by so many learned clans, was distinguished by its erudition and scholarship. All the children who attended the schoolroom in the courtyard of the Zhou residence were taught from an early age how to read and write poetry. Zhou earned a reputation for his insatiable curiosity.

Later in life Zhou recalled that one of the first books he ever read was *Journey to the West*, the famous sixteenth-century novel that chronicles the adventures of Sun Wukong, the monkey king who learns the art of warfare and the secrets of immortality in the quest to bring the Buddhist sutras back from India. As a boy, Zhou was also impressed by the story of Han Xin, a capable military commander in the service of Liu Bang, the founder of the great and long-lasting Chinese Dynasty of the Han (206 B.C.–221 A.D.). Han Xin was considered one of the greatest generals in Chinese history with a strategic mind second to none. Han Xin had a destitute childhood following the early death of his father, which taught him the supreme values of restraint and self-control. According to legend, while he was playing alone on the street, Han Xin was confronted by a couple of hoodlums who decided to humiliate Han by forcing him to crawl between their legs. Han Xin realized that if he tried to fight this pair he'd be at a great disadvantage, so he followed their instruction. People on the street burst into laughter when they saw Han Xin crawl between the legs of the two thugs. Instead of allowing himself to become a victim of his misfortunes, Han used the event as a stepping stone to achieve his ambitions. Within a few years of the episode on the street, Han Xin had mastered the art of war. "You must practice restraint as a child," he said. "To deny restraint will cause your downfall." Once, in early childhood, when he was very hungry, an old lady gave Han Xin a meal. He promised the old lady that he would repay her graciousness in years to come, after he became a powerful man, but she just laughed at this suggestion. Years later, when Han Xin was ennobled as the king of the state of Chu soon after the collapse of the great Qin empire in 207 B.C., he showed kindness to those who had offended him in his childhood. He made one of the hoodlums who had humiliated him that day on the street the chief of police of the city of Huai'an in Jiangsu where Zhou Enlai was born. Zhou Enlai was deeply influenced by Han Xin's example—as a man who had been able to swallow insults and move on.

In 1907, when Zhou Enlai was nine years old, his biological mother died of esophageal cancer and his adoptive mother died soon thereafter of tuberculosis. The loss of his adoptive mother came as a terrible blow to Zhou. During his student days in Japan, Zhou burned incense to mark the tenth anniversary of his adoptive mother's death and tearfully recited her poems. He often noted the longing he felt for her in his diary. "I do miss my mother," he writes on one occasion, "I'm unable to sleep," and, on another, "The ink of her poems is still so fresh; her voice and image will remain with me forever. How sad."

Circumstances forced Zhou Enlai to grow up fast. Zhou's biological mother had kept the entire family afloat after the death of old Panlong, Zhou's grandfather, by taking over the family's commercial affairs and feeding and clothing the many members of the Zhou family, including Zhou's two younger brothers. Zhou's father, Zhou Yineng, had no business of his own. He was too poor to afford a rosewood coffin for his wife, and after her death he was forced to pawn a number of family heirlooms, including three highly prized ancestral houses, to cover the cost of the funeral. The funeral of Zhou's adoptive mother swiftly followed, and now the family faced a mountain of debt. Zhou's father went far from home to live and work in Hubei Province, where he soon managed to lose his job and ended up living off a relative, unable to support himself, let alone his family. Zhou Enlai, on his own, took his two younger brothers under his wing and returned with them to his mother's hometown, where he took care of his siblings and other family members, making ends meet and repaying debts by pawning valuables. When creditors showed up at the house to demand payment, Zhou Enlai would deal with them diplomatically before returning to the pawn shop to secure more loans. Throughout his childhood, Zhou learned to carefully observe his surroundings and the subtleties of human nature as he figured out how to prevent anyone from sneaking up on him from behind.

Zhou Yigeng, the elder brother of Zhou Enlai's father, had become head of the Zhou family after old Zhou Panlong, the grandfather, died the night when Zhou Enlai was born. For years, Zhou Yigeng worked outside his hometown, saved money, and sent money home to support the family. Zhou Yigeng did not have children of his own. Of all his nephews, he considered Zhou Enlai the most promising, and always had a plan to bring Zhou Enlai close to him to provide the best educational opportunities. While at home, Zhou Enlai always wrote to Zhou Yigeng—whom he considered his most capable uncle—to report on family affairs. Upon receiving a major promotion in Manchuria in northeast China, near the industrial city of Shenyang, Yigeng invited Zhou, now twelve years old, to move in with him. In the spring of 1910, Zhou bade farewell to his family in Jiangsu Province. Zhou's chore in the small county in the northeast was to herd local horses. He also enrolled in the best primary school in the area, and soon he was a student in the top school in Shenyang.

"There were two advantages to going to school in northeast China," Zhou later observed when he recalled those difficult times. "It forced me to do physical exercise and it changed my eating habits because I only consumed grain. I also learned to make friends with people who were very different from me. I had a heavy southern accent. My classmates referred to me as the 'lad from the south.' Every day, some of them would beat me up. This occurred over a period of two months. They used to pull my pants down to deliver their blows. I had no choice; I had to come up with my own strategies. These essentially consisted of efforts to befriend whomever I could and employ my new allies in my counterattacks. The other side eventually gave up. Those years in northeast China did me a great deal of good."

This is Zhou's earliest reference to a tactic he would employ throughout his political career when he "divided the opposition and conquered them one by one." Zhou would align himself with friends after school to take revenge against kids on the other side, but not while they were together, always one at a time. He revealed himself to be an early master at creating a united front. This was a skill that served him well in later years and may explain his capacity to survive so many hostile confrontations.

Zhou learned first-hand about imperial foreign ambitions directed against China when he lived in the northeast. This region had been a focal point of foreigners who wanted to expand their influence in the Middle Kingdom in the late nineteenth and early twentieth centuries. After they had crossed the border and come to the rescue with other foreign armies to help the weakened Qing Dynasty crush the Boxer Rebellion in 1900, Russian troops of the czar refused to leave the major cities they had occupied in Manchuria. The foreign powers demanded huge reparations in return for their intrusive support that the Chinese could not possibly pay, and to exact their pound of flesh the Russians threatened to turn the entire region into the new land of Yellow Russia. This brought out the nationalist instincts of the youthful Zhou Enlai. "Every citizen must bear the burden of determining the life and death of the nation," Zhou declared with heartfelt anguish when his teacher informed him of what the Russians were doing. These words turned out to be more than mere hollow sentiment. They were a clear indication that Zhou felt a true love of his motherland, and soon he had developed a habit of consuming the news of the nation in the burgeoning Chinese press.

Pursuing the Revolutionary Path

Zhou was introduced to a work called *The Revolutionary Army* while he was a student at the Dongguan Model School in Shenyang. The author, a firebrand named Zou Rong, attacked the increasingly corrupt and feckless Manchu emperor and called on the Chinese people to rise up and overcome their "slavish" humiliation at the hands of the Qing. Cultivating his nationalist sympathies, Zhou was greatly influenced by Zou Rong's work. Zhou never cited family or ancestors or even the desire to build a personal future for himself as so many of his classmates did when people asked them why they were attending school. He replied, instead, with Zou Rong's clear and simple declaration: "So that China can rise up."

When the October 1911 Revolution brought down the Qing Dynasty (and with it two thousand years of nearly unbroken monarchical rule), Zhou was a student at Dongguan School. The gradual process of reform that had started under the Qing with the self-strengthening campaigns of Zeng Guofan and Li Hongzhang from the 1860s now came to an abrupt halt as the nation reverted to its traditional method of regime change through internal revolt. It looked at first as though Sun Yat-sen, the Chinese revolutionary committed to Republican government, would prevail, but an internal crisis of authority overwhelmed Sun's efforts. Chinese warlords and other parasitic types got their hands on the Chinese political levers, and a military minion and favorite of the Qing Dynasty named Yuan Shih-kai soon installed himself as China's putative Republican ruler in Beijing, which set the scene for further turmoil out of which emerged the Chinese Communist Party that ultimately lured Zhou Enlai with its call to revolution.

Zhou's uncle, Yigeng, was transferred in February 1913 to the port city of Tianjin just east of Beijing. Zhou applied for admission to the American-sponsored Tsinghua School in Beijing, but the school rejected him because he had a poor command of English. Zhou attended an English prep school in Tianjin for three months to improve his performance and Nankai Middle School subsequently accepted him. Modeled after British and American private schools, Nankai was rigorous in its subject matter, all classes were taught in English, and the curriculum emphasized cultivating in students a strong sense of personal discipline. Zhou was a model student. He achieved straight A's, and became especially adept at writing compositions and performing in student-run stage plays. An attractive boy who had been raised almost exclusively at the hands of adoring women, Zhou possessed mannerisms that were somewhat effeminate. Perhaps for this reason, Zhou was often cast in female roles on stage.

Although Zhou pursued his studies diligently, he was constantly distracted by external events. The political crisis in China was spinning out of control, even though a Chinese Republic had been established in 1912. In 1915, the Japanese tried to impose on China its infamous Twenty-One Demands that called for China to virtually surrender its sovereignty to Japanese overlords. Yuan Shih-kai, the warlord Republican leader of China, was prepared to capitulate to the Japanese and sign away the national independence of China. But before he could do this he tried to make himself emperor of China in an effort that backfired, and by 1916 he was out of the picture. Thus began the warlord period of Chinese history, as Beijing became the captive, along with the Chinese government, of competing warlord armies. The Twenty-One Demands, however, left their mark on the agitated youth of China, as many, including Zhou Enlai, became increasingly aware that China was in danger of being held hostage to predatory foreign powers in league with cynical Chinese politicians. The backlash had begun.

Zhou graduated from Nankai after four years, but he had financial difficulties and no prospect of finding a job with which to support himself while he furthered his education in China. Without other prospects, he decided to head for Japan. Japan was China's great nemesis at that time, but it also provided a haven for many Chinese who sought exile outside of China. Zhang Boling, the headmaster of Nankai, did everything in his power to help Zhou Enlai, and in September 1917, a month before the Bolsheviks seized power in Russia, Zhou boarded a boat bound for Japan, via north-east China and Korea.

In Japan, Zhou Enlai enrolled in a Japanese-language school. But he had trouble performing well enough on the exam necessary to yield a Chinese scholarship. He learned from afar that his father's other younger brother, Zhou Yikui, who had remained at home to help support the Zhou family, had died. The news hit him hard, and he failed at his first attempt to enter Tokyo Normal University. He now had to resign himself to informal courses offered at Waseda University. Zhou tried to improve his chances for academic success by dedicating himself to his studies. But it became increasingly difficult for him to steer clear of political activities involving the fate of China.

When the Bolsheviks seized power in Russia, their revolution sent tremors through the world that went to the very heart of the Chinese who were studying in Japan. The economic and political philosophy of socialism became the hottest topic of the day among Chinese students, who were outraged when the Japanese government joined forces with the United States, Great Britain, France, and Czechoslovakia in an international brigade (formed under the rubric of the Joint Proclamation of Emergency Government and Neutrality) to land troops in Siberia to undermine the Bolshevik Revolution. They were even more exercised when they found out that the decision contained secret provisions that would further restrict China's national sovereignty. The call went out to all Chinese students in Japan to return in protest to China. Zhou Enlai with his long-standing Nationalist inclinations was immediately drawn into the campaign. He failed a second time to pass the Japanese-language exam in early July. This hit him hard. Zhou was embarrassed and depressed. In China he had always been a straight-A student. To make matters worse, his fellow students from Nankai had all managed to pass the exam and won entry into good Japanese universities. Zhou now felt that he had disappointed all those who had maintained great expectations for him: his family, relatives, former schoolteachers, and classmates. He returned to China for a brief stay. He was listless and had lost face. Possessed of no credential other than a secondary school diploma, he could expect nothing in the way of professional opportunity. When he returned to Japan in October 1918, Zhou moved into a student dormitory where residents joined in doing common chores such as cleaning, cooking, and shopping. His companions noted that academic work was not on Zhou's mind. When they looked at his monthly expenditures, they decided that Zhou was depressed. He seemed concerned only with going out about town seeking pleasures. Yet like many of his compatriots in Japan at the time, he was ever more attracted to the study of Marxism.

In December, Zhang Boling stopped off in Japan to meet with his former students. He was returning to China from a research trip to the United States. He informed his former students that Nankai had decided to establish its own university. Zhou immediately made plans to return home.

Zhou Enlai returned to China in April 1919, poor and disillusioned. His experience in Japan had exposed him to failure and emotional despair. The Japan years provided a crucible of pain and failure, however, that gave Zhou a certain maturity, and when he returned to China, he returned not as a youth, but as a young man.

Zhou's timing was impeccable. He arrived in China in the spring of 1919 on the eve of a revolutionary tide that swept into China with the May Fourth Movement. His arrival at this seminal moment was one of destiny and opportunity for Zhou Enlai, who became an important figure in modern Chinese Nationalist politics at the very beginning of this fresh revolutionary phase and never looked back.

The May Fourth Movement—the opening shot across the bow of Western imperialism in China—was the most important event in modern Chinese history. Triggered in 1919, at the Paris Peace Conference following the First World War armistice, where representatives of the Chinese government had expected to secure the return of territories occupied by the Germans in Shandong Province, the sacred birthplace of Confucius, the Great Powers all but ignored the Chinese delegates and decided instead to transfer the former German concessions to Japan, which at that time was an ally of the West.

By doing so, the Powers struck a blow at China's national pride and aroused the intelligentsia and students who took to the streets in Beijing and moved to organize popular resistance. The maneuver instantly transformed the domestic political chemistry in China, which had inclined toward Western-style democracy and scientific enlightenment. Educated Chinese turned abruptly against the United States and Britain, powers they felt had lured them with democracy and freedom only to betray them at the Paris Peace Conference. Young Chinese as disparate in background as Zhou and Mao Zedong jettisoned their Western values and turned toward the Socialist ideas of the brand-new Soviet state and its Russian leaders. This was the ground upon which the Chinese Communist Party was laid two years later, in 1921.

Zhou, who desperately wanted to save his country from foreign predators, fell immediately in step with the patriotic movement. He decided that his personal failure in Japan was of little significance now that such huge tasks lay before him, and every day he showed up at Nankai School to participate in activities of popular protest and agitation that had been activated by the May Fourth outbreak. Zhou quickly emerged as a central figure at the institution.

Most people were convinced after two months had passed that the student campaign of demonstrations and demands had achieved its goal to force the Chinese warlord government to disavow the Treaty of Versailles. Pro-Japanese cabinet ministers in the government had resigned along with the ineffective prime minister after intense student protests, some of which had led to violence. Ultimately, Chinese diplomats refused to sign the peace treaty with Germany in Paris. Most of the schools that had been at the center of the agitation decided to close early and send students home. Zhou Enlai, however, was among those activists who believed that the movement had just begun. Zhou and his cohort initiated a more intense campaign to arouse popular support and bring about a fundamental political and cultural transformation of China along the lines suggested by the New Culture Movement that had preceded the May Fourth Movement.

Throughout the summer of 1919, Zhou devoted his energies to founding a new publication, *Nankai Student Union Alliance News* (*Nankai xuesheng lianhehui bao*). It was a tough undertaking. New publications played a very important role in rousing public support during the May Fourth Movement, and altogether more than four hundred newspapers had broken into print, but Zhou Enlai had a hard time finding financial assistance to publish, and there were other difficult obstacles to overcome, not the least of which was the requirement that newspapers register with the police bureau to publish in Tianjin. Zhou put on plays to raise money and used his negotiating skills to win the support of workers at the local printing plant. Zhou was a one-man band. On the editorial side, he wrote articles and organized submissions, and on the production end, he did the typesetting, layout, plate design, proofing, printing, and even oversaw the distribution. The inaugural issue contained a reprint of Abraham Lincoln's Gettysburg Address, along with a motto on the front page that read: "Democracy: of the people, for the people, and by the people." Zhou wrote the first editorial, "The Heart and Soul of the New Revolution." In it, he proposed the basic reforms needed in Chinese society, including a major change in the dominant mode of thinking. *Nankai Student Union Alliance News* swiftly became an outlet for Zhou Enlai's exclusive personal expression on current affairs. He used it to report on patriotic events, including the organized boycott of Japanese goods that had quickly sprung up all over the country in the wake of student demonstrations. The paper, which circulated in major cities, was selling twenty thousand copies a day within five weeks of its initial publication. Almost overnight, Zhou Enlai became famous as a leading figure in the Tianjin student movement.

In September 1919, important players in the Tianjin student movement met secretly to form an underground group, the Awakening Society, and called on Zhou to draft its manifesto. Endorsing the concept of gender equality, the society recruited ten male and ten female members. Zhang Ruoming, Zhou Enlai's first real love, was among the new female members. So was Deng Yingchao, who ultimately became Zhou Enlai's lifelong wife and companion. The Awakening Society organized with a system of committees that ensured the participation of all its members and adopted the characteristics of an underground organization, assigning each member a nom de guerre to be used for all internal communication and published articles. Throughout the years of underground struggle in the CCP, Zhou Enlai would use his Awakening Society pen name, Fifth Warrior (*Wu Hao*). Later in life this nom de guerre figured prominently in a major political battle among top Communist Party leaders in the heat of the Great Proletarian Cultural Revolution.

Nankai University was formed in the fall of 1919 and offered a college-level curriculum. Zhou Enlai was given a waiver on the required entrance examination and entered with the first class of undergraduates. Zhou, however, was far too inflamed by student activism and his own effectiveness as a radical leader to devote his talents to academic endeavors. He used the university as a staging ground for his renewed efforts to lead the student movement, especially after he was elected executive director of the Tianjin Student Union. Zhou now occupied a high-profile position. He represented the student union in negotiations with the local Tianjin Trade Association to organize a boycott of Japanese goods, a now nationwide effort. Under Zhou's leadership students were organized to check the merchandise in every shop in the city and confiscate all Japanese goods, which they put on display at the Nankai campus. Students then organized a mass rally on the student playing field. More than ten thousand demonstrators gathered as ten truckloads of Japanese goods were burned on site. This was followed by a parade through the city.

The Japanese government immediately issued a statement protesting its "serious opposition" to such actions. Japanese political and economic interests had continued to escalate in China despite the May Fourth Movement, and because it did not want to create a dispute with the Japanese, the Chinese government ordered the Tianjin Student Union to disperse. Students openly defied the order. The Awakening Society appointed Zhou as its general commander for a large-scale action against the government order, and on January

29, 1920, Zhou led anywhere from five to six thousand students from a number of Tianjin schools on a march to the local governor's office. The government decided to teach the students a lesson in obedience and dispatched a large contingent of police to the governor's office, where they lay in wait for the demonstrators and forcibly broke up the march. More than fifty students suffered severe injuries during the police encounter. Zhou Enlai and three other student leaders were arrested.

Zhou Enlai spent the next six months in jail. It was the only time in his long career of revolutionary activism that he would spend behind bars. He was detained at first at the Tianjin Police Station, but after he embarked on a hunger strike he was transferred to the detention center of the Tianjin Local Inspection Bureau. Conditions there were considerably better. Zhou joined other jailed students, among them two women, and he had limited freedom to move about, read books and newspapers, and receive outside visitors. Most of those held in the detention center were students and teachers. To pass the time, they initiated a sort of prison university of their own. Anarchism was the prevailing Socialist idea with the greatest popularity at the time in China. The theories of Karl Marx were generally unfamiliar to most Chinese. Zhou Enlai took it upon himself to deliver five lectures on Marxism at the so-called prison university.

In prison, Zhou Enlai was transformed from a burning young student radical to a serious revolutionary. Prison was considered the ultimate taboo in Chinese society, and no one from Zhou Enlai's family had gone to jail. In the first days of his incarceration, Zhou's fellow prisoners were death row inmates, and conditions in the prison were deplorable. Zhou witnessed a dark and ugly underbelly of Chinese life that few people in Chinese society ever saw, and it made a lasting impression on him. Zhou noted in later years that his most basic thoughts were shaken in prison, and that his revolutionary conscience was born there. In prison, Zhou realized that he was a true revolutionary, someone who had taken upon himself the awesome task of overthrowing the old society to replace it with a more humane social order.

Prison also offered Zhou the opportunity to engage in his first romantic interlude. Women considered Zhou a prince on a white horse. He possessed good looks and a graceful manner, and many radical young women set their sights on him, among them Zhang Ruoming, who had been jailed at the same time as Zhou. Chinese tradition frowned severely on open expressions of affection between men and women, but after the May Fourth Movement this pillar of the ancient order had come under assault as students from single-sex schools began to meet to discuss current events and jointly take revolutionary action. The Awakening Society prohibited social contact among its members, but Zhou Enlai and Zhang Ruoming shared political ideals. Beautiful and talented, Zhang Ruoming came from a well-to-do family. Zhou, as a student at Nankai, had made it known that he was a confirmed bachelor—one who worshipped platonic, or spiritual love—although he also made it clear that he was not opposed to the new discovery of free love between male and female youth. He often discussed this subject when he was living in Japan. "Love," he said, "comes from sexual desires. In one's life, love is one thing and marriage is something else." In prison, Zhou and Zhang's suffering brought them closer.

Deng Yingchao entered Zhou Enlai's life at the same moment. She was only fifteen at the time, but she was already so clearly capable and decisive that she had emerged as a leader in the Tianjin student movement. When Zhou was arrested during the student demonstration, Deng Yingchao personally organized a rescue plan. After, when she visited Zhou, she volunteered to act as his stand-in in prison.

Zhou and other student leaders belonged to an elite company in a society that revered educated people, and when their case came to court after six months of incarceration, they received considerable support. When the newspapers added their defense of the students for taking patriotic action, the government moved quickly to close the cases and the students were released. Shortly after his release from jail, Zhou was expelled from Nankai University. But Zhou was no longer interested in academia, and he went back to work full time for the Awakening Society. He proposed a major unification of all organizations committed to reform—large and small—in a common effort to save the Chinese people from further suffering.

It was while he was attending a meeting convened in Beijing to bring together diverse groups in a common political effort that Zhou Enlai was introduced to Li Dazhao, a professor at Peking University, who was probably the most liberal intellectual in China at the time. Li relayed the importance of the Russian October Revolution to China when his work "My Marxist Views" appeared in the liberal publication *New Youth* in 1919. Li Dazhao was evidently favorably impressed by Zhou Enlai. He encouraged Zhou to travel to Russia for study, and even made the effort to arrange a meeting for Zhou with a Russian professor who was a resident at that time at Peking University. Zhou, however, had already formed a plan during his stay in prison. He wanted to travel to France to continue his studies in the most liberal and sophisticated of all the countries of Europe and one of the geographical homes of Communism. France had become familiar to many Chinese who had traveled there in great numbers during World War I as conscripts to work as laborers on the battlefields. Now, nearly two thousand Chinese students were living in France. They were ambitious to enrich their minds and find a way to rescue the future of the Chinese nation.

Zhou faced one dilemma: He didn't have the money to realize this ambitious plan. As fortune would have it, much-needed support came to Zhou from Yan Xiu, the founder of Nankai University, who had recognized and valued Zhou's talents. Yan had singled Zhou out among his student colleagues as the one who possessed "a talent to one day become prime minister." Yan set aside seven thousand Chinese dollars to establish a scholarship fund for Zhou Enlai and another student named Li Fujing. To this fund, Liu Chongyou, the defense lawyer in Zhou's trial, added another five hundred dollars. Zhou also made a deal with the *Beneficial News* (*Yishi bao*), a local Tianjin newspaper, which agreed to pay Zhou's living expenses abroad if he served as its European correspondent.

3

A YOUNG
COMMUNIST
IN EUROPE

ZHOU ENLAI WAVED A FOND FAREWELL TO FAMILY AND FRIENDS AND
sailed out of Tianjin on the maritime mail ship *Porthos* bound for
Marseilles. Zhang Ruoming was among Zhou's fellow passengers.

The *Porthos* arrived in Marseilles in mid-December. Zhou was
sick on arrival, after thirty-six days spent eating bad food in steer-
age class with two hundred other young students. He went to
Paris, and soon after he sailed to England, which was the plan he
had agreed upon with his benefactor. In London, however, Zhou
soon discovered that the money Yan Xiu had provided was grossly
insufficient, barely enough to pay for his living expenses, with
nothing left over to cover his tuition. Zhou then decided to apply
for admission to the University of Edinburgh, in Scotland, where
living costs were lower and the only examination the university
required was in English. But the English test was not scheduled

until September. Zhou decided to spend the intervening time improving his English and writing articles for the *Beneficial News*, but was forced to return to Paris. Scotland was rapidly draining away his finances.

Many of the two thousand Chinese students who lived in France had been radicalized by the May Fourth Movement and, like Zhou Enlai, would later become top figures in the Chinese Communist Party. They were on work-study programs in France. France had been thrown into a deep recession by the aftermath of World War I. Factories had closed down, unemployment was high. Chinese students had to settle for jobs performing hard labor in construction, rubber refining, coal mines, and ports, at pay that amounted to half of what French workers earned. The French working class resented the young Chinese visitors. Ultimately, many Chinese students lived off small odd jobs such as cleaning houses, collecting garbage, selling newspapers, and polishing shoes. These newly radicalized students felt what it was like to live like pariahs in France, an experience that only radicalized them further toward revolution. Supported as he was by Yan Xiu, Zhou was financially better off, relatively speaking, than most of the Chinese students, but what he witnessed in France struck him as utterly contrary to how he had envisioned a European haven for Chinese intellectuals.

Zhou found the freedom in Paris to explore various schools of thought and ideologies that could provide a way out for China. He did not immediately embrace the Russian model of revolution and progressive politics involving revolutionary change. Such a path, he thought, would certainly lead to suffering for the Chinese people. He did not find the British model of gradual political reform all that enticing either, although, as a natural mediator, Zhou in typical Confucian fashion searched for some middle way that would combine these two diametrically opposed models of revolutionary change.

Shortly after he had returned to Paris, Zhou met with Zhang Shenfu and Liu Qingyang. Liu had made a name for herself during the May Fourth Movement as the director of the Tianjin Women's

Patriotic Comrades Association and the first female member recruited by the Awakening Society. Zhou and Liu had come to know
each other quite well in China. Liu's husband, Zhang Shenfu, was a
well-known professor at Peking University, where he had earned a
very favorable reputation in the academic world. (A close associate
of Li Dazhao, Zhang had once met with Zhou when Zhou was
meeting in Beijing with other youth groups.) It was exhilarating for
Zhou to meet old comrades in a foreign land, and it was a source of
excitement to discuss the merits of various political ideologies late
into the night with them.

Zhou was unaware, however, that Zhang was actively and
covertly involved in the organizational activity that led to the formation of the Chinese Communist Party. Zhang was the secret
messenger between Li Dazhao and Chen Duxiu, another Peking
University professor and major CCP leader. Together, these three
men had set up the Beijing branch of a Communist cell in October 1920, which preceded the CCP that was formally established in
July 1921. Ostensibly at the University of Lyon Faculty of Humanities and Law to lecture on philosophical logic, Zhang was also
there on a mission to develop overseas branches of the infant CCP.
(In Paris he was the head of the Communists' branch.) One of
Zhang's first recruits to the CCP was his wife, Liu Qingyang. Together, in March 1921, they brought the talented Zhou Enlai into
the organization.

Just how Zhang and Liu persuaded Zhou to end his internal tug-
of-war between competing approaches to China's future is still a
mystery, but Zhou, in later years, was very explicit that these two
people had guided him onto the revolutionary path. The procedure
for actually inducting Zhou was very simple since the Chinese Communist Party apparatus was not, as yet, fully formed, and he did not
have to undergo the swearing-in ceremony that subsequently became standard procedure for new recruits. They simply sent a report
of his admission back to China to Chen Duxiu, who immediately
approved the decision.

Joining the Communist Cause

The Paris branch was one of eight cells that formed the original CCP in its infancy. In March 1922, Zhou Enlai moved with Zhang and Liu to Germany, where the cost of living was half of what it was in France. There, the trio worked together to organize a German branch of the CCP, and Zhou frequently traveled back and forth between Berlin and Paris as a pivotal figure in the organization of the European branch of the Communist Youth League.

In June 1922, the European branch of the Communist Youth League was formally established at a meeting attended by Chinese students and intellectuals in Paris. The three-day gathering took place in a forested area of the Bois de Boulogne, in a quiet glade. The participants rented eighteen metal folding chairs from an old woman who ran an open-air café. To passersby, they must have looked like a group of attractive young people who had assembled for a picnic. As one participant recalled, Zhou Enlai, who wore a yellow jacket, was "neatly dressed, not like someone working in a factory." Zhou moved gracefully into the role of leader as he delivered a draft of the organization, and over the course of three days participants elected a three-man executive committee. They put Zhou in charge of propaganda. As the secretary, they chose Zhao Shiyan, who later became a labor organizer whom Chiang Kai-shek would execute in the April 1927 crackdown on Communists in Shanghai. Li Weihan, an early associate of Mao Zedong in Hunan Province, was put in charge of organizational matters. Soon afterward, Li Weihan was dispatched to China to report on the work of the new European operation and, while he was gone, Zhou took over the mundane, but critical, task of building a functioning organization.

Zhou was now a professional career revolutionary, who wore a Western-style business suit paid for by the Comintern, the international Communist organization. The First National Conference of the CCP had convened in Shanghai, in July 1921, and at the outset the leadership, faced with a financial problem, immediately decided to join the Comintern, which effectively converted the CCP into the "China branch" of the Communist International. This provided the CCP in its infancy with necessary financial support courtesy of the Soviet Russian government, but it obligated that its China branch follow orders from Moscow.

At the time of the CCP's birth, Zhou was involved in a torrid love affair with Zhang Ruoming, who lived outside of Paris, but with whom he maintained a loyal correspondence. Zhang joined the European branch of the Communist Youth League in 1922, and she translated many of the works of Karl Marx into Chinese that Zhou later took back with him to China. Zhang was a hard worker, who cultivated her French and soon outranked most of her fellow Chinese students. But although she was a revolutionary sympathizer, she had no real commitment to Zhou's political cause. She had joined the Youth League to be near Zhou Enlai. She was temperamentally arrogant, not an easy person with whom to have a relationship, and this was partly because she was also vulnerable, emotionally, when she had to face personal problems. Zhou Enlai was twenty-four in 1922, and he was looking for a wife who was also prepared to live the life of a professional revolutionary. He decided to end the affair with Zhang. "I had become a firm believer in Marxism," he recalled in later years, "and thus my need was for a lifelong companion who would share this devotion with me, a comrade-in-arms who would bear the hard times with me and survive to see a better day. So I initiated the talk with Zhang Ruoming to clarify my stand and began to exchange letters with Deng Yingchao whom I soon decided to issue a proposal of marriage."

When he first met Deng Yingchao during the May Fourth Movement back in Tianjin she had impressed Zhou as something of a little girl. She was full of enthusiasm and was also warm, decisive, and very likable, but she was six or seven years younger than Zhou Enlai, and not, at the time, someone he thought of even glancingly as a romantic possibility. She only made a lasting impression on Zhou

Enlai sometime later, according to her own account, when she stood up at a gathering to give a speech and wooed him with her "very attractive eyes." Deng was fifteen years old. She had fallen secretly in love with Zhou. Before his departure for Europe, she had knitted a sweater for Zhou. Inside the collar she had embroidered the message, "Offering you warmth—Little Yingchao." Zhou got the message. Once he had broken up with Zhang Ruoming, Zhou wrote a flurry of postcards to Deng Yingchao. One postcard he sent her in 1923, Deng recalled years later, depicted an oil painting of three young girls dancing toward a gushing spring, and on the flip side of this Zhou had written: "Jaunting toward the springtime of freedom! Breaking all boundaries! Bravely go forward, forward!"

On another postcard, which featured a portrait of Robespierre, Zhou wrote: "Some day we too will meet together to confront the guillotine arm-in-arm."

Deng Yingchao understood the implied message. It was Zhou Enlai's way of proposing to her. Deng's mother, who had had an unfortunate marriage, and had raised Deng by herself, wanted her daughter to wait until Zhou returned from France before she made up her mind. In spite of her mother's reservations, Deng accepted Zhou's advances and agreed to marry him upon his return to China.

Zhang Ruoming, as it happened, became a tragic victim of the Chinese Communist regime that Zhou Enlai ultimately came to represent. After her relationship with Zhou, she had a stormy career among the Chinese Communist exiles in France. Early in 1924, when, as a representative of the CCP, she attended a memorial service for Lenin in Lyon organized by the French Communist Party, French police seized Zhang and interrogated her, threatening to deport her from the country because of suspected subversive activities. She became embroiled in constant quarrels with the branch leader of the Communist Youth League, who engaged in a campaign aimed at persecuting Zhang, until, unhappy with the way things were going, she left the Youth League, abandoned politics altogether, and devoted herself to studying French literature. She became the first woman to obtain a doctorate in literature in France.

Zhang returned to China in the 1930s with her husband, Yang Kun, and taught French literature at several universities. She became a victim in the countless rounds of persecution that occurred after the Communists came to power. When Mao Zedong invited intellectuals in 1958 to "open up your heart to the Party," that is, to confess political crimes, Zhang took him at his word and turned over to CCP authorities letters of complaint that her son had composed. The authorities immediately labeled Zhang's son a "rightist" (*youpai*) and sent him off to a labor camp in the far reaches of the country. Zhang they accused of being a traitor, rounded her up, and denounced her at a series of struggle meetings that went on for months. It was too much for Zhang to bear. At the age of fifty-six, she plunged to her death into a river.

Zhou committed himself to a firm, if unexamined, belief in Communism during the four years he spent in Europe. Zhou met and worked with people in Europe who became important contacts in the years of revolution to follow. In France, he came to know Deng Xiaoping, and, in Germany, Zhu De, a student who was later celebrated as the father of the Red Army. He became acquainted with Nie Rongzhen, later known as the founder of the Chinese nuclear and space programs, and Cai Hesen, one of the most prominent intellectuals among the early Communists. Others who moved in the same orbit were: Zhao Shiyan; Li Lisan, who briefly led the CCP in the early 1930s and with his overly aggressive policies almost destroyed the Communists; Li Weihan; Wang Ruofei, who was to die tragically in a plane crash; and Li Fuchun, who, after 1949, became a major figure in the realm of economic planning in the Chinese policy-making apparatus. Zhou also met and worked with Hu Zhiming, whose Vietnamese name was Ho Chi Minh, and who later served as Chairman of the Vietnam Communist Party. The relationships that he had cultivated in Europe were indispensable to Zhou Enlai—they allowed him to become a key member of the CCP, the military, and a familiar figure in the international arena. Equipped with these contacts, and with his talents and skills, Zhou rose to prominence during the pivotal time of collaboration, beginning in 1924, between the Nationalists and Communists.

Zhou Enlai married Deng Yingchao in the broiling heat of Guangzhou (Canton) in the summer of 1925. They had exchanged love letters during Zhou's sojourn in Europe, and Deng had joined the Chinese Communist organization in Tianjin, but when Zhou Enlai returned to China to take up work in Guangzhou, he and Deng Yingchao had not actually set eyes on one another since the heady days that had followed May 4, 1919. Members of the CCP had to obtain permission from superiors in the Party if they wanted to marry. Zhou had reached an age when marriage was deemed not only acceptable, but necessary: he needed a wife to take care of his everyday routine, and he obtained speedy approval to marry Deng Yingchao. Deng was transferred from Tianjin to Guangzhou, where she became a member of the Guangzhou City Party Committee and director of its Women's Movement.

Zhou's bride-to-be arrived in Guangzhou in the middle of the summer. She might have expected her future husband to greet her at the boat, but a workaholic even at that early age, Zhou sent a security officer named Chen Geng with Deng's photograph to fetch his betrothed. Chen Geng was an extraordinarily capable person, but on that particular day, when he went to meet Deng on the crowded dock, he managed to miss her. Deng went off to search for Zhou at his mailing address. Later, when Chen finally ran into Deng Yingchao, he escorted her to the headquarters of the Guangdong General Worker's Union, where Zhou was conducting a meeting with a host of people. When he saw Deng enter the room, Zhou gave her a quick smile, but he continued his intense discussions, and, when the meeting ended, he got up and hustled out of the headquarters building without bothering to greet his bride-to-be. So began Deng Yingchao's long career as the wife of a prominent revolutionary devoted to the cause.

Zhou Enlai and Deng Yingchao had originally planned not to celebrate their marriage with a ceremony and wedding banquet because Zhou believed that revolution transcended all such personal needs, and, in a way, this kind of disciplined approach was one aspect that helped the Chinese Communists in their struggle. Even so, Zhou Enlai was a charming, popular, attractive man surrounded by many friends both in the CCP and among the Nationalists, and he couldn't quite get away with a simple wedding. When news of his planned marriage began to spread, friends and associates of the couple pressured them into having a celebration, to which Zhou agreed as a way of offering consolation for his less-than-warm greeting when Deng arrived in Guangzhou. The couple celebrated their wedding on August 8, 1925. Zhang Shenfu, the intellectual who had persuaded Zhou Enlai to join the Party in France, was the host of a banquet at a Western-style restaurant in Guangzhou attended by future luminaries. Many guests wanted to know how the couple had met, and Deng Yingchao, who had a rich background in propaganda during the May Fourth Movement, did not hesitate to rise to the occasion. Standing up on a chair she described before the crowded room her fondest memories and recited, without skipping a beat, the words Zhou Enlai had written on the back of the postcard from France: "Jaunting toward the springtime of freedom! Breaking all boundaries! Bravely go forward, forward!" This won a round of applause from the assembled guests.

For his part, Zhou Enlai consumed three bottles of brandy. It was the only time in his life that her husband was drunk in front of other people, and Deng Yingchao didn't let him forget it. From that time on, Deng never failed to remind her husband not to drink too much. Zhou always loved to drink at dinner parties and banquets, and this was a source of frequent quarrels with Deng, who disapproved of the fondness he displayed, when he drank, for personal gallantry.

Soon after the marriage, Deng Yingchao got pregnant. A high-profile leader at the time among women's circles in Guangzhou, she was serving as director of the Women's Movement in the city and was also playing a role in women's activities organized by the Nationalists under the rubric of the First United Front (1924–1927). Like many female revolutionaries of the time, she had no desire to stay at home and play the role of wife and mother. She realized that if she gave birth, her revolutionary career would be over. She was also envious of the decision that her husband had made to give top priority to his revolutionary work. Because she considered it to be her personal decision, Deng chose to sacrifice her child for the revolution.

Without informing her husband, Deng acquired the necessary drugs from a street vendor and aborted the fetus. She lost huge quantities of blood after taking the medicine, and she had to be rushed to the hospital for emergency treatment. Zhou was off on the so-called Eastern Expedition military campaign at the time to vanquish the powerful local warlord Chen Qiongming, who ultimately fell to defeat at the hands of a force of three thousand men whom Zhou Enlai had helped to lead. When he was informed of what his wife had done, Zhou lost his temper. Tragically, although Deng conceived another child the following year, the infant died after a grueling three-day labor. Deng was almost immediately forced to go on the run when, in April 1927, the Nationalists split from the Communists, and began to arrest Communists wherever they found them. Deng Yingchao's womb never recovered properly, making any future pregnancy virtually out of the question.

4

BUILDING
THE INFRASTRUCTURE
OF REVOLUTION

When the Nationalists turned on the Communists in April 1927, they ended a three-year alliance between the two parties. It was an association that had begun when their Comintern masters pressured the Communists to form a united front with the Nationalists in Guangzhou, where Sun Yat-sen had finally managed to establish a revolutionary base with the help of Soviet Russia. Once the Communists had agreed to work with the Nationalists, a revolutionary force was forged to challenge the northern warlords who had been running China since the collapse of the Qing Dynasty, but the Comintern, not the Nationalist Party, was the organization that controlled this situation in the south.

Zhou Enlai made his way to Guangzhou soon after this tenuous alliance was formed. Once he had returned to China from Europe, both sides, the Nationalists and the Communists, sought him out as one of the few people with the organizational skill to galvanize the United Front. In Guangzhou, the CCP and the Comintern appointed Zhou to head the municipal Party committee, and he also became the director of the politically essential propaganda department.

For their part, the Nationalists also wooed Zhou. They appointed him director of the political department of the newly established Whampoa (*Huangpu*) Military Academy that Sun Yat-sen had founded in 1924, with Soviet help, for the purpose of training an officer corps that could lead a Chinese Nationalist army northward and defeat the warlords. Sun Yat-sen assumed the titular leadership of the academy as premier; his protégé, Chiang Kai-shek, who had trained briefly in the Soviet Union, became the principal of Whampoa; and Liao Zhongkai, a major Nationalist figure who was later assassinated because he was a political liberal, served as the representative of the Nationalist Party.

Zhou's experience as a political instructor at Whampoa was an essential building block in his political career. At Whampoa, where Soviet military heroes like Marshal Valery Blyukher provided instruction, Zhou laid the foundation for the critical role he played in both the CCP and the KMT. Zhou became the director of the political department during a time that became known as the golden era of the Chinese revolution, when the major revolutionary forces of the KMT and the CCP were joined in the common effort arranged by the Comintern, which footed the bill for the Whampoa enterprise. Some in the CCP had balked at this enforced United Front, particularly Chen Duxiu, one of the original founders of the CCP, who later became the head of the Trotskyist movement in China. As a "branch" of the Comintern, however, the CCP was in no position to refuse to join the United Front. Guangdong Province was the center of revolutionary hope in China, and anyone who wanted to effect change in China in the 1920s went there. At Whampoa, the two parties shared a common cause. But it was not the perfect relationship that people who were there recalled many years later. Inevitably friction arose between the Communists and the Nationalists, but Zhou Enlai was in his element, working with both sides to transform the Chinese nation.

Zhou, in truth, was responsible for maintaining a smooth rapport between the disparate elements at Whampoa. This is because Chiang Kai-shek recognized Zhou's talents and gave him the latitude he needed to handle the political training so that Chiang, the future generalissimo, could focus on military matters. Chiang readily agreed to most of Zhou's ideas and suggestions. When the cadets met every week to listen to Chiang Kai-shek deliver a speech, Zhou Enlai delivered a report of his own on political developments at home and abroad. Zhou's speeches, consistently inspiring and always well received, left a deep impression on cadets and instructional staff alike.

Zhou had an affiliation with the Nationalists and Chiang Kai-shek, but he used his key position at Whampoa to advance the interests of the CCP whenever he could. He hired Party members to act as political instructors at the academy, and he used every opportunity to promote Communist ideology. Zhou secretly went about the task of recruiting Whampoa cadets to the CCP and the Youth League and even set up a special Whampoa branch of the CCP. Party members used their notable ability to organize and their devotion to the cause and took advantage of the popularity of Communist ideology among hot-blooded youth to expand their ranks with young cadets, often at the expense of the Nationalists. In one year alone eighty cadets were enrolled in the CCP organization, which ensured that the Party would have a core of talented military leaders who over the years would come to regard Zhou Enlai as their mentor and form the vanguard of the Chinese Communist march to power. Zhou had no formal military training of his own, but he claimed an intimate bond with the CCP military confederacy as a political tutor and Whampoa colleague.

The top leadership organization at Whampoa Academy was the Special Party Bureau, which consisted of two committees: the executive and the inspectorate. The bureau was elected by the entire staff of instructors and cadets. This included the position of academy premier, since virtually no executive position was exempted from the election process. In the first election, in which five new members of the executive committee were elected to the Special Party Bureau, Chiang Kai-shek was the only Nationalist elected. The other four were members of the CCP. In the second election, Chiang Kai-shek actually failed to win the necessary votes. Of the seven members elected, six were from the CCP, which was an indication of the superior organizational skills of the Communists. Chiang suffered a loss of face and refused even to show up at the academy. He left it to Liao Zhongkai, his nemesis, to repair the damage. Liao, a member of the executive committee of the Nationalist Party, used his power to appoint Chiang as a member of the academy's inspectorate. Chiang now had first-hand experience of the Communist organizational ability. He quickly set out to counter CCP influence by recruiting cadets to the KMT. By the time that Chiang had awakened to the reality on the ground, however, the CCP was already in a position to make the host and the guest exchange roles at Whampoa. This situation posed a great danger to Chiang's overall strategy, which was to gain political dominance through military means over the evolving Chinese revolution.

The First United Front swiftly deteriorated after the death in 1925 of Dr. Sun Yat-sen, the man who is often called the father of modern China. Many conservative old-time Republicans in the KMT, Sun's Nationalist organization, had disliked the way Dr. Sun had yoked his fortunes to the support of the Comintern and the Chinese Communist Party. After Sun's death, Chiang Kai-shek became the champion of these reactionary Chinese, many of whom were still allied with local capitalists and saw the Communists as a threat to the economic future of China. In 1926, Michael Borodin, the Comintern agent whom Stalin had sent to China to oversee the evolving Nationalist movement, gained the upper hand after the second KMT Congress, and appeared to have cemented his power in Guangzhou. Chiang Kai-shek, however, controlled the army and was using his power as the head of Whampoa to consolidate his position as the conservative gatekeeper against Communist intrusion. Chiang declared martial law in Guangzhou in March 1926 when the acting commander of the Republican navy received a forged order to sail to Whampoa in an apparent direct threat to Chiang. This—the *Zhongshan* gunboat incident—handed the future generalissimo a spurious excuse to assert that the Communists were planning to stage a coup at Whampoa with the help of Soviet agents. Basically, Chiang himself had staged a coup. He threw all the alleged conspirators in jail and surrounded the Soviet consulate with soldiers. He ordered all Chinese Communist Party members at Whampoa to leave the academy and resign their positions in the First Army of the National Revolutionary Army that was being prepared for the Northern Expedition against the warlord forces that controlled North China. The message that Chiang Kai-shek was sending out was clear: The right wing of the Nationalist Party was now in charge.

Zhou Enlai held the highest post of any member of the CCP in the Nationalist military forces. He was deputy Party representative and director of the political department of the First Army. Zhou had just returned to Guangzhou from the port city of Shantou (then known as Swatow) on the eastern edge of Guangdong Province on the eve of the *Zhongshan* incident, in which his own naval commander had been duped. Zhou had instinctively smelled danger in the air, and he immediately alerted his Russian allies at the Soviet consulate. They generally dismissed his warnings. Soon afterward, the Russians were thrown in jail along with their Chinese allies, and Zhou Enlai rushed to the local currency printing plant, where some of the Communists had been detained, and immediately tried to negotiate with his Nationalist allies, who put him under house arrest for a day.

This inauspicious occasion turned out to have momentous implications, for it provided the opportunity for Zhou Enlai to establish, for the first time, a working relationship with Mao Zedong. As it happened, Mao was also in Guangzhou at the time, working out of the Peasant Training Institute, where he was delivering lectures on how to organize a revolution based on the peasantry. Mao was staying at the residence of Li Fuchun, a fellow revolutionary from Hunan Province, who lived next door to Zhou Enlai. Zhou took the opportunity to meet with Mao and discuss national affairs. So began the political alliance that would endure for more than half a century. After Chiang Kai-shek's coup, the two future leaders of China displayed the kind of bravado that would ultimately bring them to power when they called for an immediate counterattack. Their ever-cautious Russian advisors, however, poured cold water on their proposals, and they were forced to accept defeat at the hands of the Nationalists. All known Communist Party members had to resign from Whampoa and the First Army. Although Chiang reinstated him briefly in the run-up to the Northern Expedition that the Nationalists launched against the northern warlords in July 1926, Zhou, too, was stripped of all his military positions within the Nationalist Army, even as his efforts to reconcile the two sides revealed for the first time his genius at handling difficult and seemingly impossible situations.

The *Zhongshan* gunboat incident may have forced Zhou Enlai and his Communist cadets to disengage with the Nationalist forces, but Zhou had acquired military experience while he served with the First Army, especially in the successful Eastern Expedition campaign against Chen Qiongming, which provided him with the highest standing within the fledgling CCP. Driven from the KMT, Zhou now assumed command of the military committee of the CCP's Guangdong Regional Bureau.

Zhou was dispatched to Shanghai once Chiang Kai-shek had launched his successful Northern Expedition up into the Yangtze River Valley of the central Chinese interior. This is where he began to plant the seeds of his great future influence within the growing CCP organizational structure. As a major figure in the crucial organization department of the CCP, Zhou now commanded cadre recruitment and promotion. He was also a member of the CCP's military committee. Chen Duxiu, the general secretary and top leader of the CCP, also served as the director of the organization department and, as such, was Zhou's superior. Chen, however, was a scholar. He was largely uninterested in matters of daily routine, and he left these to Zhou to administer in his name. It was a key to Zhou's later success when he served Mao Zedong, who, like Chen, showed little interest in quotidian organizational detail.

In the fall of 1926, the armies of the Northern Expedition, led by Chiang Kai-shek, turned unexpectedly and began to move downriver, in the direction of Shanghai, on the east coast of China. The plan, as the local CCP organization understood it, was that, as the Nationalist armies approached the city, workers, armed by the CCP, would rise up and seize the city and all the factories in it. Although the workers were armed with no more than one hundred and fifty old guns and little ammunition, and although they faced a Shanghai police force five thousand strong, Zhou made the best of things. He oversaw military training lessons, battle planning, personnel and weapon distribution, target checks, communication methods, and propaganda aimed at enemy forces. He also supervised the final battle strategy. On March 21, 1927, in the early morning hours when factory whistles blew, eight hundred thousand workers in Shanghai went on strike, and armed worker brigades took over police headquarters in the city, along with the post office, the arsenal, and the railway station. Workers also seized the key areas of Pudong and Wusong. Zhou was not one to remain at headquarters, issuing orders. He moved around the city and visited the areas under attack, especially the Zhabei district, where some of the heaviest fighting was taking place. Zhou went to the front lines of key battles, including those at the North Railway Station, the East Library, and the office of the Commercial Press. The workers' brigades fought for thirty hours. Finally, they prevailed. They took firm control and awaited the arrival of their Nationalist allies who under Chiang Kai-shek were moving toward the city.

It was a miracle. Forces under the command of the CCP had taken the great commercial city of Shanghai with relative ease in an alliance they had made with left-wing elements of the KMT. On April 12, 1927, Nationalist forces under Chiang Kai-shek entered the city. As they arrived, the Soviet dictator, Joseph Stalin, in alliance with Chiang, sent orders to leaders of the CCP to disarm the workers, who naïvely believed that the Nationalist forces would assume protection of the insurrection and guard the city. This set the scene for one of the greatest betrayals in modern history. Chiang had also entered into an alliance with local secret societies and underground gangs, many of which were under the command of the Shanghai Chinese police. Together, these forces turned on the workers and began a city-wide massacre in which more than five hundred Communists were brutally killed. The reprisal transformed Chiang Kai-shek from the general commander of a victorious army into a murderer of Communists.

Chiang was in league with capitalist Chinese forces in Shanghai that wanted to rid the country of colonial domination and assume control of China's economic future. Western foreigners represented an intolerable intrusion into the ambitions of these bankers, real estate moguls, and industrialist entrepreneurs. So did the Communists, with their plans for urban revolution and worker solidarity. Chiang Kai-shek was determined to unify China under his own Nationalist rule, as the heir he believed himself to be of the late Sun Yat-sen. He wanted to eliminate the threat of all foreign intervention from China. His goals dovetailed with those of the Shanghai money men, who pledged to bankroll Chiang's cause if he liberated the city from his former Communist sidekicks, as Chiang proved to them he was more than willing to do. He tricked the workers into believing that he was on their side when, on April 12, he made a show of faith by ordering his troops to tie up gangsters outside the Shanghai Union headquarters of the insurrectionists, who opened their gates to troops who moved in and began to slaughter the pickets. Thus began the so-called April Twelfth incident as soldiers opened fire throughout the city on the shocked and outraged workers who began yet another strike to protest the bloodbath.

Zhou, general commander of the Shanghai Workers Armed Brigades, had already experienced betrayal at the hands of Chiang Kai-shek in Guangzhou. He had entertained forebodings before the April 12 massacre, but he chose to believe that he could continue to work with the Nationalist Army. He was always looking for ways to mediate between contending forces, and, as tension began to rise in Shanghai, he was willing to allow himself to be lured to Nationalist Army headquarters to discuss a possible deal. The Nationalists then detained him, which robbed the insurrectionists of their commander at a critical moment. Unquestionably, it gave the Shanghai Union members the illusion that the Nationalists were friendly, and duped them into opening the gates of their headquarters to the enemy without a fight.

Chiang Kai-shek had launched a wave of terror. Nationalist soldiers scoured the city for suspected Communists. Zhou Enlai was at the top of their most-wanted list. The Nationalists put eighty thousand dollars on his head. He had managed to slip out of the Nationalist headquarters before April 12 and had gone into hiding in the attic of a worker's house just outside the city. In the rapidly shifting circumstances, Zhou did whatever he could to attend secret meetings of the remaining Shanghai CCP leaders to discuss strategy. Zhou at this time drafted a proposal to the Party Central to bring down Chiang as soon as possible. "Surveying the overall situation," Zhou wrote, "no further delay can be afforded in our political strategy, nor can any compromises be accepted. We committed major mistakes when we took over Shanghai successfully with armed worker brigades. If we don't regain the initiative, we'll be forced to retreat and our side will undergo constant changes because political leadership at the national level will be increasingly dominated by Rightists. This," Zhou concluded, "will not only lead to a loss of faith on the part of our allies on the left, but will also place the entire future of the Chinese revolution in doubt."

On this occasion, however, Zhou's usually persuasive powers failed him. He was up against Stalin and the Comintern, who had thrown in their lot with Chiang Kai-shek. The CCP leaders were not prepared to follow Zhou's aggressive line. They continued to hope that they could broker deals with other important non-Communist elements such as the left-wing Nationalist leader Wang Jingwei and the relatively liberal warlord, the Christian general Feng Yuxiang, who remained in control of Wuhan, the central Chinese city. Once they had accomplished these alliances, the Chinese Communists, they argued, would isolate Chiang Kai-shek. There was an argument to be made in their favor. The insurrection had been carried out by Shanghai workers. Most of these armed guerrillas had been disarmed if not murdered. The Communists had no army, as such, with which to fight Chiang's Nationalists. They had to depend on warlord forces like those of Feng Yuxiang. In late April at the Fifth National CCP Congress in Wuhan where radical revolutionaries were still in control, Zhou was elected secretary general, a post ranking him second in the Party hierarchy. Despite his reservations about the top leadership of Chen Duxiu, who would be quickly cashiered in July, and the dreamy poet Qu Qiubai, who would later die under the broad swords of the Nationalists, Zhou was also elected to the Politburo and soon after was appointed the military director of the Party. He was now the top military official in the Communist movement. He personally missed the Congress, however. He got off to a late start and was delayed on his upriver trip as he dodged Nationalist efforts to find him. He failed to arrive in time to lay the necessary groundwork for a new military strategy.

The Shanghai massacre of April 12 and its aftermath had a profound impact on China. Many hot-blooded students, radicalized by the May Fourth Movement, had thrown themselves into the revolutionary cause, heart and soul, because they believed that they were part of a worldwide revolutionary movement led by the Bolsheviks. They wanted to make fundamental changes in China's ancient social identity. They were also devoted followers of the great Chinese Nationalist leader Sun Yat-sen, founder of the KMT, and they had worked alongside the Nationalists in common cause. Chiang Kai-shek's betrayal of these revolutionary true believers changed the rules of the game. They were out for revenge, and they were ready to play for keeps. Their new revolutionary slogan was written with the blood of those who had died in the Shanghai bloodbath: "To lose one's head in the name of truth is of no consequence." It was a phrase that captured CCP members recited when they faced execution. It signified that the new revolutionary in China was prepared to die for fallen comrades. Out of this crucible a new leadership emerged. Gone were Li Dazhao and Chen Duxiu. The former died in Beijing, a victim of the garrotte; the latter, a May Fourth activist, a founder of the CCP in 1921, and, like Li, a Peking University professor, was soon forced out of the leadership. Others who had survived the Nationalist onslaught, including Mao Zedong and Zhou Enlai, moved into the leadership vacuum.

Zhou Enlai was now charged with the task of overseeing the fledgling military arm of the CCP, which probably numbered no more than ten thousand men. He was intimately familiar with the Nationalist army, and he had successfully engineered the worker insurrection in Shanghai. He was the man, therefore, to assume a critical position in the Front Committee newly organized to set up shop in Nanchang, the provincial capital of Jiangxi Province, south of the Yangtze River, where Nationalist strength was limited. Here he decided to stake the fortunes of the CCP on a military uprising.

Zhou's new military position was ripe with danger, but he believed it was the last chance the Communists had to save the situation and improve the position of the CCP. It was a huge mission, and Zhou did not underestimate the gravity of his undertaking. Communist forces were pitted against a Nationalist army that was increasing in force every day. Zhou possessed one strong card. Disaffected Nationalist military figures like those who headed such units as the Twenty-Fifth Division of the Eleventh Nationalist Army, commanded by Ye Ting, turned out to be Zhou's ace in the hole. Ye Ting was friendly toward the Communists. Opposed to the right-leaning Chiang, Ye brought his forces to areas around Nanchang and the city of Jiujiang.

Zhou Enlai left Wuhan on July 26, 1927, and traveled southeast to Nanchang, incognito, where he booked a room at the Jiangxi Hotel, which would serve as his headquarters for the planned uprising. Many of the best people the Communists could muster came to the Jiangxi Hotel to contribute their skills to the venture, including He Long, another disaffected Nationalist commander, and Chen Yi, Ye Jianying, Nie Rongzhen, Zhu De, Liu Bocheng, and a low-level officer named Lin Biao, who would with nine other generals be promoted to the top military rank of marshal in the People's Liberation Army following the Communist victory in 1949. Zhou, the core leader, expected He Long's Twentieth Nationalist Army to play a key role in the uprising because it possessed the greatest firepower, and Zhou appointed He Long general commander of all forces involved in the uprising. Ye Ting assumed the position of general commander of the Front Committee headquarters.

On August 1, 1927, twenty thousand troops who had participated in the Northern Expedition, but who now had pledged their loyalty and their lives to the CCP, opened fire on forces loyal to the KMT. On this day the Chinese People's Liberation Army was officially born during the Nanchang Uprising. Over one evening, the pro-CCP forces fought with uncommon bravery. They effectively destroyed the enemy, and the provincial capital city of Nanchang fell to Communist control.

The Communists, however, had forgotten one all-important matter: They were still under orders from Moscow and the Comintern, which had failed to support the CCP in Shanghai and now failed to support them in Nanchang, after one Nationalist commander, newly converted to the Communist cause, got cold feet and betrayed a key military unit to the opposition. Moscow ordered the Communists to leave Nanchang after three days. One contingent, led by Zhou Enlai, headed for Guangdong Province. Other units, under Zhu De, Chen Yi, and Lin Biao, headed to the southwest to join the guerrilla forces of Mao Zedong, who had decided to conduct his own warfare from the remote Chinese countryside. Zhou continued to act on Comintern orders. He did not forsake the concept of urban insurrection, as Mao had done. He moved toward the port city of Shantou, where he had been told to expect the delivery of a shipload of weapons from the Soviet Union to use in yet another uprising.

Chiang Kai-shek realized that Guangdong had remained the center of the revolutionary movement and that the CCP still retained a grip on parts of the population. If the tiger returned to the hill, the next Communist attack would pack a bigger punch. Chiang therefore sent troops to harass units under Zhou Enlai's command as they made their way back to Guangdong and moved toward Shantou. Zhou's plan was to occupy the city of Haikou in Guangdong. From that base, he intended to launch a second expedition northward, like the Northern Expedition that Chiang Kai-shek had led against the northern warlords. When they arrived in late September, Zhou and his cohort soon learned that the Soviet ship had remained at sea, before returning to home port, afraid of a clash with Western powers and the Nationalists. Suffering from fatigue, and with few soldiers and weapons, Zhou's forces lost hope. At the city of Chaoshan, they suffered an overwhelming defeat at the hands of Nationalist troops.

Before this defeat, the CCP had ordered Zhou Enlai to stay with the remnant of his military forces, while the rest of his commanders withdrew to Shanghai and Hong Kong. Zhou was now suffering from a severe case of malaria. He continued to work with a high fever for days on end. In this situation, Zhou revealed the kind of personal tenacity that he would display in years to come. He called a meeting at Chaoshan, where he laid out plans for further land reform and armed revolution in the local area. Nationalist troops suddenly surrounded the conclave. The participants terminated the discussion. They fled with Zhou Enlai, whom they carried on a stretcher, in an escape that proved to be nearly fatal. When his bearers deserted him, Zhou continued by foot with the help of a few comrades. As he ran, burning with fever and almost unconscious, Zhou shouted out, "Charge! Charge!" When they came upon a small boat, Zhou and his bedraggled group escaped out to sea and sailed for two days before reaching the safety of Hong Kong.

The failure of the Nanchang Uprising and subsequent attempts at armed insurrection badly hurt the Communists. They had lost the opportunity to reverse the losses that they had suffered at the hands of Chiang Kai-shek in Shanghai in April, and they had lost almost all of their military assets, except for units under Mao Zedong that had made it into the remote interior of Jiangxi Province. From the vantage point of history, however, the events of late 1927, in which

Zhou Enlai had played such a pivotal role, may clearly be seen as the first steps the Communists took down the road to ultimate victory and power in China. Zhou Enlai began his career as an agitator and organizer, but, from the Nanchang Uprising on, he committed himself to the military cause of the Communist revolution. All that remained for him was to meet up with another survivor of the 1927 debacle, a man who had steadfastly resisted the direction of the Comintern and whose views on the revolution had been consistently militant. That man was Mao Zedong.

5

BIRDS OF
A DIFFERENT FEATHER

MAO ZEDONG ROSE TO POWER IN 1949 AND RULED OVER THE world's most populous state for a quarter of a century as legendary Chairman Mao of the Chinese Communist Party. His minister, Zhou Enlai, lived those years in the shadow of Chairman Mao, performing tirelessly, like a compliant, docile daughter-in-law, the tasks that his master assigned to him. This is the relationship as the rest of the world perceived it. But the story is more interesting, the history more complex. It is the story of two men who needed each other, and enabled each other, to survive from the early years of the Communist struggle in China. There was a time, one that lasted many years, when Zhou Enlai held the whip over Mao Zedong. It may be said that Mao owed his early salvation to Zhou Enlai, a bitter truth that Mao tasted all his life and never learned to like.

The entire history of the Chinese Communist Party from the early 1920s into the 1970s might be told as the history of the working relationship between these two men. In the years that followed the collapse of the Qing Dynasty in 1911 and the formation in 1912 of the Republic of China, Mao and Zhou both emerged, from disparate backgrounds, as progressive young men "without a penny to their names, but genuinely concerned with matters of the world." They were both emboldened by political ideals to reform China under the banner of the newly formed Communist Party that followed immediately upon the great wave of the 1919 May Fourth Movement. They were both men of South China, too, as was almost every Party member in that first revolutionary generation that created the Red world of modern China: Zhou was a child of the fecund land of rice and fish near the Grand Canal in Jiangsu Province, Mao the son of rural Hunan Province.

Mao was born in Xiangtan, a remote and rustic village in the hinterland of Hunan Province. Here he spent his youth, the peasant son of a simple-minded family tyrant with a dictatorial personality whom Mao grew to detest. The importance of this relationship cannot be underestimated. Mao fought his father relentlessly from his earliest years. In boyhood he hated authority, and applied all his resources to the practice of undermining first the dictates of his father and, as time went on, all forms of provincial authority. In his resistance to any and all authority, Mao formed a militant character and a combative unruliness, an antiestablishment attitude that found its expression in perpetual struggle. Mao had immense energy and was the first person to take on any task, or challenge, on behalf of local political change. "Boundless happiness in fighting heaven, the earth, and men." That was how Mao liked to put it.

Nurtured by the love of an adoptive mother, Zhou grew up without a father to emulate or to challenge. His manner reflected a tolerant nature, an aptitude for forgiveness. He possessed a certain adaptive genius that enabled him to deal with all varieties of personality. With a strict Confucian upbringing, he personified modesty. "Mild mannered, honest, somewhat emotional and always friendly, trying his best to help his friends." This was written in the yearbook when Zhou graduated from Nankai School. Zhou believed in the middle way—the ultimate Confucian ideal. If Mao was by nature a disruptive, provocative personality, Zhou was the diplomat, supremely poised, smooth, charming.

Mao and Zhou did not meet each other until 1926, in the southern city of Guangzhou during the impending crisis with the Nationalists spawned by the *Zhongshan* gunboat incident. But their careers as revolutionaries with absolute devotion to the cause of transforming China had taken similar paths. In Hunan Province, Mao reorganized the New People's Study Society, one of many progressive student associations formed in China in the May Fourth aftermath. He edited and published the *Xiang River Review*, a weekly newspaper, in which the future Chairman of the CCP set forth his grand vision for "a great union of the popular masses," which established his credentials as a revolutionary thinker of great repute. Zhou Enlai, in Tianjin, long before his meeting with Mao, helped form the Awakening Society and oversaw its publication, *Awakening (Juewu)*, a vernacular magazine that attracted not only many young readers, but also the interest of local police, who soon banned the publication as heretical. Mao participated in the First Congress of the Chinese Communist Party in July 1921, in Shanghai, in the company of eleven other Chinese delegates and a Comintern representative. He was, therefore, one of the official founders of the Party while Zhou was off in Paris establishing the European branch of the Chinese Communist Youth League. Following the Shanghai convocation, which was nearly broken up by the local police, Mao returned to Hunan Province. There, his efforts among workers and peasants in his village quickly caught the eye of Chen Duxiu, the official leader of the CCP, who was impressed by Mao's leadership skills. In 1923, at the Third Party Congress, Chen awarded Mao with his first position in the CCP. Chen made Mao secretary of the Central Bureau, an executive organization of five members that evolved into what later became the Politburo. As his assistant, Mao was responsible for overseeing day-to-day Party affairs for Chen, the general secretary.

Real power in the CCP, then and in years to come, did not belong to the Chinese founders, but to the Comintern, the International Communist directorate, based in Moscow. Following the Bolshevik

Revolution in October 1917, the new Russian rulers had sent emissaries to China who influenced both Chen Duxiu and Li Dazhao, two prominent Peking University professors who were the major force behind the establishment of the Chinese Communist Party in 1921. They organized the first start-up cells for Communist indoctrination that captured the revolutionary fervor following May Fourth of intellectuals and progressives, like Zhou and Mao, who became the ground troops behind the emergent Communist movement. These early revolutionaries, working with the emissaries who had filtered across the border into China from the Soviet Union, established a base for Communism in China. In the early 1920s, the top Comintern agent in China was Hendrikus Sneevliet, a Dutchman who used the nom de guerre Mekka. It was a time when the Comintern was trying to fashion a partnership between the CCP and the Nationalist Party of Sun Yat-sen, the Republican revolutionary. Mekka promoted Mao as a revolutionary insider, and talked him up in conversation, which undermined the favorable position in which Mao had started out as Chen's fair-haired boy. Mao was also inclined to throw his weight around, and this was something other leaders in the CCP and KMT disliked. He was not a company sort of man. The Comintern ultimately cashiered Sneevliet and, by 1924, had replaced him with Gregory Voitinsky, a more diplomatic agent. Mao drifted away from the central circle of Communist Party leaders. He took sick leave, which became a chronic feature of Mao's political life whenever he had to confront awkward political realities. It took the form of depression, which people used to call neurasthenia, a condition that plagued Mao off and on until he died. Mao liked to make light of his uneven start in Communist Party politics. "I joined at the First Congress," he jested late in life, "but missed the second. I made it to the Third Congress, where they elected me to the Central Bureau, but then, at the Fourth Congress, I withdrew my membership. I guess I'm an odd year kind of guy."

Mao got off to a good early start in Party politics and then careened to near disaster. Zhou's entry came later, but once launched, his career moved along on a much smoother trajectory from his decisive first act, joining the Paris branch of the Chinese Communist Party, to his subsequent role as director of the political department of the Whampoa Military Academy. His Whampoa experience made Zhou the first CCP leader among the Party leadership with real military credentials. It also gave him a base of support on which he could always depend for survival. It was capital of a kind that Mao Zedong would never possess.

Following the near destruction of the CCP's urban apparatus at the hands of Chiang Kai-shek in Shanghai in April 1927, an act of brutal betrayal known as the Shanghai coup, Zhou and Mao both managed to escape the butchery and ensuing manhunt and fled, each to pursue separate paths with one purpose in mind: to somehow revive the shattered revolution.

Mao took to the interior to organize a peasant revolution deep in the Chinese countryside. He favored a revolutionary approach that was, strategically speaking, unorthodox, if not actually heretical, in the eyes of the Comintern sponsors and CCP leaders, who continued to cling to the belief that the revolution in China would erupt in the cities. Mao had a profound admiration for those Chinese revolutionaries who in ages past had led peasant rebellions that had shifted the entire course of Chinese history. Yet despite such audacious visions, Mao's first attempt at organizing rebellion in Hunan Province in September 1927, called the Autumn Harvest Uprising, ended in disaster. Party leaders unceremoniously accused the reluctant Mao of "having no faith in the revolutionary strength of the masses" and of having engaged in "military adventurism." Escaping capture and sure execution by local militiamen, Mao retreated with the remnants of his forces, less than 1,500 men, to Well Ridge Mountain (*Jinggangshan*), a nearly impregnable redoubt in Jiangxi Province on the border with his home province of Hunan. Here he established the first revolutionary base area, near the small market town of Ciping. In his own words, he had become a "revolutionary King of the Mountain."

Mao came from a peasant background. He understood the countryside. He knew, by instinct, how the vast population of Chinese peasants responded to the circumstances in which they now lived, and he was convinced that his approach to revolution, which was based on the belief that the peasant, not the urban worker, would form the revolutionary force behind social change, was correct. Mao dared to challenge the Russian revolutionaries and their Chinese followers who continued to concentrate on winning power in the cities. Mao had decided that the Chinese revolution would be won from the countryside when forces from the hinterland encircled the cities, and that the Communist Party would ride to power on the backs of peasants, not at the side of the urban proletariat.

The quick run of military defeats that Zhou's forces suffered in Nanchang and elsewhere might have wrecked his standing with the CCP. One defeat had done so to Mao, who now operated like a rogue elephant out in the remote regions of Jiangxi Province. In contrast, everyone in the CCP leadership recognized Zhou Enlai's organizational skills and his talent for interpersonal relations. At an expanded meeting of the Politburo in Shanghai in November 1927 the new CCP leadership with its pro-Soviet bent let Zhou Enlai off lightly for the failures of Nanchang and Haikou. They gave him a warning. Furthermore, they let him keep his seat on the Politburo and then put him in charge of military and secret service affairs. The leaders punished Mao. They accused him of serious errors and stripped him of his Politburo membership. They issued a stinging denunciation of his independent streak. From that time on, for the next seven or eight years, Zhou served as Mao's superior in the Party hierarchy. That was the price that Mao paid for disagreeing with the Comintern approach to seizing revolutionary power in China. Zhou was a Party man. He was a stickler for internal Party discipline who believed in the principle that the Chinese revolutionaries should obey the dictates of international Communism that issued out of the Kremlin. Inevitably, this put Zhou Enlai in conflict with Mao Zedong, who insisted on going his own way. Zhou did not relish heated confrontation, least of all with Mao Zedong, but on occasion he felt compelled to impose higher orders on Mao.

Twice in the early stages when he was establishing the Red Fourth Army in Jiangxi Province, Mao came up against Party leaders who disagreed with how he was waging war. Both instances drove Mao Zedong into fits of rage against Zhou Enlai. He never let himself forget these wounds to his ego, and later in life when he was sore at Zhou he would revisit these events. They provided a source of vitriol when he wanted to snipe at his premier.

Joseph Stalin had put Nicolai Bukharin in charge of the CCP's Sixth Party Congress, which was held in Moscow in May 1928, at a safe distance from China. Bukharin had not the remotest understanding of conditions prevailing at that time in the Chinese countryside, but in his ignorance he decided, not unreasonably, that troops, when concentrated in great number in one place, made an easy target for the enemy. He also concluded that it would be hard to keep forces in such numbers adequately supplied with food and other necessities without creating a local crisis wherever they happened to be encamped, one in which "the last hen would be eaten in the village." Bukharin personally delivered a dressing down on the subject to Zhou Enlai, who had managed to attend the Moscow conference. He told him that the Red Army units in China should disperse. Zhou returned to CCP headquarters in Shanghai and in February 1929 sent letters to Mao Zedong and Zhu De, Mao's top military companion who had fled toward Mao's Jiangxi redoubt following the defeat of the Nanchang Uprising. In his letter, Zhou repeated everything that Bukharin had proposed. On orders from the Party Central, the Fourth Army, as Bukharin had decreed, dispersed throughout the countryside.

This new strategy was a disaster. Top leaders in the Party targeted Mao and what they called his patriarchal leadership style and excessive centralization of power. They ripped into Mao's ability as a leader, denouncing him as an autocrat. Mao had founded the Red Fourth Army. The Party now delivered a body blow to Mao's political vanity. In July 1929, at a full-scale Fourth Army Congress, Mao failed to be elected as secretary of the Front Committee, the CCP body that oversaw military affairs and strategy at the battlefront and also ensured that in the Chinese revolution "the Party commands the gun." This was the end point of policy dictated by the Comintern out of Moscow and set forth by Zhou Enlai in his February letter. Stripped of his operational command over the Fourth Army and his control of the Front Committee that was now ceded to Chen Yi, with whom he would later engage in political combat, Mao once again requested sick leave, and retreated into depression. For several months, as conditions worsened, the military leadership implored Mao to assume his former posts, but he refused to budge. This was the first of two confrontations between Mao and Zhou.

The only person who could break the deadlock with Mao was Zhou Enlai. Zhou called on Mao and Zhu De to put aside the differences that had arisen over military strategy and asked them to resume their control of the Fourth Army. Zhou, realizing that dispersing troops had only led to one disaster after another, criticized the strategy he'd proposed in the February letter. In a spirit of fairness, Zhou split his criticisms of Mao and Zhu fifty-fifty. He also, however, instructed Mao to stop sulking in his tent. He criticized Mao's tendency to retreat into depression when things weren't working out the way he wanted and told him to stop maligning revolutionary prospects. The Central Committee now drafted a second letter, the September letter, to Mao, which reflected Zhou's new approach. They restored Mao to his position as secretary of the Front Committee and announced their decision to shelve the controversy over Mao's strategy.

Thus did Zhou, using the September letter, manage to assuage Mao, even as he criticized him. He supported Mao's leadership and gave him a face-saving way to reverse his decision to resign from the Fourth Army. In doing so, Zhou now prepared the foundation for his future position in the Party. The first incident that pitted Zhou against Mao had ended amiably and caused no real harm to their relationship.

The second incident, the one that rankled Mao and left him seething with vengeance toward Zhou Enlai, flared up in October 1932, after a conference held in Ningdu, a town in central Jiangxi

Province. In December 1931, the Central Committee, which still operated at great danger out of Shanghai, had decided to send Zhou Enlai to Jiangxi. As the Party emissary, he was assigned to keep an eye on Mao's rural military campaign. Zhou kept a respectable distance from Mao. The two men did not exactly hit it off. Mao behaved like his self-described "revolutionary King of the Mountain" out in Jiangxi. Mao knew how to roil the waters of authority wherever he found it, and Zhou disliked the way Mao, by doing things his own way, tried to sabotage the basic Leninist principle of iron discipline that guided the CCP. Zhou expressed his reservations about Mao's independent streak the moment he joined the Central Committee, which was the inner sanctum of the CCP leadership. He'd always insisted that if the time ever came when Mao's troops were inspected and regrouped and Mao tried to take it out on the central leadership with a nasty attitude, the "King of the Mountain" would have to be replaced.

Zhou was the Central Committee's man on the scene replacing Mao as secretary of the Central Bureau, and he liked to play the military leader. But Mao was the real military commander, and Zhou knew it. The Politburo wanted Zhou Enlai to take direct command and serve concurrently as political commissar of the First Front Army, but Zhou resisted. He needed Mao's military expertise. Ever the diplomat, Zhou Enlai tried to relieve Politburo doubts about Mao's political attitudes that were so radically opposed to those Zhou shared with the committee. He did this because he knew that he had to hang on to Mao as a military advisor, but at the same time keep him from exercising any real independent power. Zhou thought he could somehow control Mao this way. As the old Chinese adage goes: "Easy it is to invite the fairy in, but to see him out the door is quite another matter." Zhou Enlai learned the truth of this particular ancient wisdom after the 1932 Ningdu Conference.

The CCP Central Committee called a conference in the town of Ningdu in October 1932, because the Nationalist armies under Chiang Kai-shek had begun a major campaign to isolate the guerrillas in their Jiangxi stronghold and wipe them out. The Nationalist troops had encircled guerrilla territory, and the ad interim Central Committee, acting, still, on directives from Moscow, wanted to actively attack these forces. Chinese historians have long insisted that the Ningdu Conference exposed the conflict in the early history of the Red Army between the leaders at the battlefront and those at the rear echelon over how to fight the revolutionary war. Mao and Zhu De, who, since 1931, had headed the newly created Military Affairs Committee of the CCP, disagreed with the conventional theory of frontal assault—the "forward offensive line"—favored by Moscow and the Central Committee. They wanted to avoid direct assault. They believed that to wage an effective war the guerrillas should concentrate their forces and pounce on the enemy by surprise—"When the enemy advances, we withdraw; when the enemy withdraws, we pursue." They understood the terrain. They realized that in the rural hinterland no clear lines of battle existed. The armies were like ink blots spattered over a vast and uneven terrain, one suited to the unorthodox tactics favored by Mao that confused and misled the enemy.

Zhou Enlai, the formal chairman of the conference, wanted to broker some sort of compromise between the CCP leadership, now established in the rear areas of the Chinese Soviet Republic created in 1931 out of territory secured by the Red Army, and delegates from the battlefront, not far from Ningdu. In a telegram to the leadership, Zhou urged them to expand the conference so that, once and for all, Politburo members could resolve their differences. He never mentioned Mao by name. Even so, he voiced his frustration with the wayward warrior. On virtually every occasion, when matters were brought up for discussion, Zhou noted that Mao "launches into his abstract, metaphysical speculations while the real concrete problems confronting us are left unattended, as if there is no answer to any problem, major or minor."

Zhou was a man of compromise, not a pathfinder. But at the expanded Ningdu Conference he was caught in the cross fire between the Central Committee representatives and the proponents of guerrilla warfare. Politburo members, led by Ren Bishi, who hailed from Mao's home province of Hunan, opened fire on Mao, criticizing him for his tactic of waiting for the enemy to strike first. Zhou Enlai, however, wanted to keep Mao at the front. He wanted to hang on to Mao's military expertise, even while someone other than Mao actually directed the war. Ren Bishi and other members of the Politburo would have none of it. They wanted Mao's hand removed from their military strategy. In their opinion, Mao would better serve off the battlefield where he could concentrate on government work. The Politburo, instead, wanted Zhou Enlai to take over the battlefront. Zhou was appointed general political commissar, which put him in control of the entire First Front Army, the crack Communist force in Jiangxi, while Mao was unceremoniously cashiered from the Military Affairs Committee overseeing operations in the Soviet base areas.

Zhou made a last-ditch effort at a two-part compromise: He would take over the battlefront and Mao would serve as his assistant, and, second, Mao would carry out the operational direction of the fighting while Zhou would oversee the execution of military policies. The Politburo might have gone along with Zhou's compromise to make Mao his assistant, but they refused absolutely to consider the second proposal. They did not trust Mao. He was a loose cannon. They trusted the disciplined Zhou.

Mao, moreover, was not at all interested in Zhou's proposed arrangement. He turned down Zhou's offer to be his assistant at the front before retreating with "diplomatic disorders" to an army hospital, a converted Taoist temple, for several months. Mao didn't actually break with the Party. Mao understood that the Shanghai Politburo boys, directed out of Moscow by the Comintern, hated him. Still, he didn't want to burn his bridges. From his retreat, he sent forth word that "the front can recall me at any time." He knew how to deal with the Central Committee. Mao was a master at this kind of gamesmanship. It was a turning point in this power play with Zhou, too. Zhou wasn't tough enough to be a leader and he wouldn't have the guts to confront the Shanghai boys. Zhou couldn't see the big picture and act accordingly. This Mao understood.

For two years the Party brass left Mao alone, abandoning him in political isolation. He called himself "a stone at the bottom of a rural outhouse." He said that not even a ghost gave him the time of day. As for Zhou Enlai, his mantra of discipline to central orders led him to join in blocking Mao's return to military power.

It was the second time that Mao and Zhou were pitted against each other. Zhou, despite his temporary elevation to a key military and political role, came to believe that this incident was the biggest blunder in his life, the root of every future major conflict that erupted between him and Mao.

6

A RISING STAR

Under Mao's leadership, the Red Army had defeated three attempts led by Chiang Kai-shek to encircle the Communist redoubt in Jiangxi and strangle the Communist revolution. After the Ningdu Conference, just when the Politburo cashiered Mao and denied him any role in military policy, Chiang Kai-shek launched yet another, far more ambitious encirclement campaign (the Fourth Encirclement) against the Central Soviet areas. Chiang had learned from his first three failures and this time decided on a much-improved strategy. The relatively inexperienced Zhou Enlai assumed command over Red troops who were staring at almost half a million Nationalist soldiers. It was a dire time. Zhou and Liu Bocheng, his chief of staff and ally from the days of the Nanchang Uprising, pledged themselves to forge ahead.

Fortitude was in short supply back in the rear echelons of the Central Soviet, where support for Zhou Enlai suddenly wavered after the Politburo members returned from the Ningdu Conference. The Politburo started to express their doubts about Zhou to Wang Ming, Stalin's new man in China, who was now the key leader in the ad interim Central Committee back in Shanghai. They put it bluntly. "Not firm in political struggle—his weakest point," they wrote. Zhou immediately agreed. "I admit," he said, "that I was lukewarm about criticizing Mao, but I disagree with the notion that I was unclear about the political line in the struggle." Zhou also once again tried to explain why he wanted to keep Mao involved in military policy. "He has years of experience at the front lines," Zhou argued. "His interest is in commanding battles. If he's sent to the rear, he'll languish, and that will dull his intellect." Zhou finally won the confidence of the Shanghai leadership, which sent a telegram stating their change of heart and offering support. "The standpoint taken by Enlai at the Ningdu Conference is correct," the message declared. "Any claim that Zhou is the leader of the so-called 'compromise faction' is false."

Zhou won the battle with the Central Committee over his position at Ningdu. The pressure was on him now to show his stuff and defeat Chiang Kai-shek's intensified effort to annihilate the Central Soviet and eradicate this alternative Communist administration in the heart of Republican China. Zhou Enlai set about constructing a workable campaign to stifle this threat. His attention to detail and his method of execution paid off. Jiangxi was the single card the CCP held. Zhou saved it, with the help of Zhu De and Lin Biao, his student at the Whampoa Academy, who had also participated in the Nanchang Uprising. But Zhou and his lieutenants did it on Mao's terms, not those of the central leadership of the CCP. Zhou violated the Central Committee policy of a forward offensive line. Instead, the Red Army, under Zhou Enlai's command, attacked the flanks of Chiang's troops while large-scale military formations went after KMT support units. The Red Army won two major victories, at Huangpu and Caotaigang, that halted the Fourth Encirclement and temporarily ended the threat posed by KMT troops to the Central Soviet base areas.

Zhou's reputation in the Red Army soared. The CCP awarded him the Order of the Red Star military medal. Zhou's victory over the Nationalists seemed to end any hope that Mao might have entertained of returning to a leadership role in what everyone knew was the power base of the Chinese Communist Party: the Red Army. Mao's compatriots shunned him even more. He was out in the cold. He was bitter, especially now that Zhou Enlai's attitude toward him seemed to shift. Before his new military acclaim, Zhou had kept a respectable distance from Mao. Now he made a point of avoiding him altogether. He gave Mao the cold shoulder, and turned his allegiance to Wang Ming and his Comintern minions. For this, Mao never forgave Zhou. For his part, Zhou Enlai regretted his actions toward the man who later became the chairman of the Party that ruled all of China.

Within a year, Chiang Kai-shek threw yet another encirclement campaign around the Communist forces in Jiangxi Province. It was his Fifth Campaign, and this time he surrounded Red areas with cement-block houses, constructed to corral enemy forces and squeeze them into ever-tighter formations in which they were increasingly easy to slaughter. This procedure was the brainchild of General Hans Von Seeckt, the German officer who in 1934–1935 was Chiang Kai-shek's main military advisor. Nationalist forces built these concrete structures, and the effort began to pay off. So ended Zhou Enlai's stature as the Red Army "genius." Chiang Kai-shek was annihilating Communist forces. The Red Army took a savage beating near the village of Guangchang, sidelining Zhou Enlai, who now joined Mao Zedong in disfavor. The head of the CCP Politburo, Qin Bangxian, also known as Bo Gu, one of the so-called Twenty-Eight Bolsheviks (also known as the Russian Returned Students) who had trained in Moscow and returned as Stalin's men in China, got the nod from the Comintern. He took over as political commissar and effectively became commander in chief of the Red Army. Almost immediately, as Nationalist forces moved in for the kill, Bo Gu adopted Mao's original plan to break out of the Central Soviet areas to engage in Mao's kind of mobile warfare—"when the enemy rests, we harass, when the enemy tires, we attack"—moving west and north to evade the Nationalist blockade encirclement. By October 1934, the historic Long March had begun. It was a strategic retreat that would last a year and take Communist forces from their Jiangxi redoubt through western and then northern China. When it was all over, the Communist Chinese forces would look back on an epic journey of eight thousand miles that took them, finally, to the remote town of Yan'an, in Shaanxi Province.

The Red Army had its own German military advisor: Otto Braun, a member of the Comintern, who used the Chinese nom de guerre Li De. Everything he and Bo Gu thought up to stop Chiang's blockhouse strategy from grinding in on the Red Army ended in defeat. Braun, the German, and Bo Gu had shoved Zhou Enlai aside and now the top military commander and his aide presided over a string of horrific blunders as the Red Army fled the Jiangxi Soviet, first at the battle of the Xiang River crossing in December 1934 and then, when, thanks to these "tactical geniuses" and their botched plans, Nationalist troops mauled Red Army soldiers and their civilian porters as they passed through Hunan and Guangxi provinces. The range of their incompetence was staggering. By the time the main military units of the Red Army finally reached the small town of Zunyi in Guizhou Province, in January 1935, the Red Army had lost fifty thousand soldiers.

The new leaders now commanded a force that had shrunk from eighty thousand to thirty thousand in a few short months. The troops that made it to Zunyi let Bo Gu know what they thought of this rout. Their outcry drove him to the brink of suicide. Zhou Enlai, also deeply depressed by the catastrophe, intervened personally to talk Bo Gu out of taking his life.

When the Red Army reached Zunyi and achieved a short-term pause in the Long March, the top leaders called a conference to discuss the military debacle and reorganize the Red Army top brass for the struggle to come. The time had come to consider the terrible toll of the past year. Here it was that Mao began his ascent as a formidable figure in the CCP. Here he engaged in the first stages of his devious endgame to win control of the levers of CCP power. He did not arise, fully formed, from the depths of the earth, even though myth later made it appear this way. His rise to power might not have happened at all without the ingenuity of Zhou Enlai, who, pushed aside by the pro-Soviet leadership, would now clear the way for Mao. From this moment on, Zhou would be indispensable to Mao, an ever-present necessity and yet a chronic irritation, a virus in Mao's ambitions to occupy, alone, the summit of Chinese political power.

At Zunyi, at an expanded Politburo conference that brought in both high-level political and military figures, the leadership scrutinized the planning that had ended in military disaster during Chiang Kai-shek's Fifth Encirclement Campaign and the mistakes that had tripped up the Red Army during its flight out of Jiangxi, and had devastated its fighting force. Bo Gu ascribed its failure to "objective forces." This was not how Zhou Enlai characterized it. He took an independent position that set him distinctly apart from Bo Gu and Li De. The Politburo began its considerations on the understanding that the men who so far had been commanding the Red Army—Zhou Enlai, Bo Gu, and Li De—had to go. Zhou Enlai volunteered to resign. Yet again, however, he put distance between himself and the other two members of the so-called Troika Gang who, up to that moment, had been making all the important CCP policies. When he offered to resign, Zhou made apparent his position: He was someone who put the revolution above his own interests. The top leadership gave him a vote of confidence. Bo Gu and Li De were removed as military leaders.

Until Mao's death in September 1976, the story of the relationship between Mao and Zhou Enlai, as it evolved at the Zunyi Conference, remained a state secret, along with the events of this critical conference, locked away in a document called the "Outline Report of the Enlarged Meeting of the Politburo at the Zunyi Conference." Prepared by Chen Yun, who in later years became China's economics czar, the document listed the major changes that the CCP instituted at Zunyi. First and foremost, Mao was elected to the Standing Committee of the Politburo, the top decision-making body of the CCP. Second in priority was the decision to entrust to Zhang Wentian, a member of the Twenty-Eight Bolsheviks who used the nom de guerre Luo Fu, the important task of drafting the official resolution of the conference that, once it was examined by members of the Standing Committee, would be released for consideration to Party branches. Along with one Wang Jiaxiang, another of the Twenty-Eight Bolsheviks, Zhang Wentian was the only Chinese leader trained in the Soviet Union to break with the Comintern. Mao Zedong had affixed himself to Zhang for political purposes. In his outline document, Chen Yun noted that third on its list of important decisions at the Zunyi Conference, the Politburo resolved to distribute work assignments among members of the Standing Committee in an appropriate way. The Politburo also terminated the Troika Gang that had run the Party. That was number four on Chen Yun's list of items. At the same time, the Party authorized Zhou Enlai, along with Zhu De, who had often clashed with Mao over military strategy, to remain at the highest level of the leadership structure. Chen Yun's document reveals the falsehood behind the assertion that Mao promoted, once he came to power in 1949, that the Zunyi Conference was a personal triumph that elevated him to the highest position in the CCP. It did no such thing. The Politburo stripped Bo Gu of military command, but he remained, disgraced though he may have been, top Party boss, replaced only subsequently by Mao's close collaborator, Zhang Wentian. Zhou Enlai, not Mao, now replaced Otto Braun, also known as Li De, as top military leader. The Politburo elected Mao Zedong to the Standing Committee, but he was a lowly member, assigned to assist the new military guru, as Zhou Enlai addressed himself, to the problems of military strategy and tactics that faced the fledgling Red Army.

Zhou Enlai had set it up this way. It was the very arrangement that he'd tried to get the leadership to grant him at the Ningdu Conference, when he'd lobbied to retain Mao as a military advisor while retaining final authority as political commissar. He understood, as everyone in the Party now agreed, that Mao was the only commander in the Red Army who could boast success. They needed Mao's military wisdom. But no one in the top leadership wanted to give Mao much political power, least of all Zhou Enlai. Zhou also knew that if he had actually allied himself with Bo Gu and Otto

Braun, Mao might have managed to split the Party in half. With the help of Zhang Wentian, Mao had been preparing to ruin the Troika Gang, an act that would have driven a crowbar through the heart of the Politburo. Zhou's keen political insight had saved the CCP. He knew what Mao was doing, and assumed the blame for the failed policies during the Fifth Encirclement Campaign, once again saving face for the Party. But Zhou also got what he wanted: the military assistance of Mao Zedong.

The ravaged remains of the Red Army were facing sure annihilation by land, by air, and as a result of punishing weather and increasingly rough terrain, as they moved into some of China's most remote and hostile mountain areas heavily populated by non-Han minorities. Nothing in Zhou's limited military experience had prepared him to deal with this particular situation. Vanity was one thing, reality another, as Zhou had discovered when the new leadership sent him out to Jiangxi to run the war. He knew the stink of military failure, and what it was like once the big boys back in the rear echelon gave you a vote of no confidence. Zhou did not want to have to go through anything like that again. He was not like Mao. He did not have the intestinal fortitude for the battlefront that Mao relished. This time, after Zunyi, Zhou left his right-hand man in charge of the field and beat a safe retreat to Party headquarters. He turned the war over to the natural authority of Mao Zedong. It was as though Zhou, as the host of a large gambling party, had turned his establishment over to an honored guest and walked away, leaving his guest in charge of the game.

Once he was holding the military reins, Mao immediately began to demonstrate his enormous political cunning. He swiftly made it clear for all to see that no one in the CCP could hold a candle to him when it came to military strategy. Classic guerrilla warfare was in his DNA. He and his small band of warriors took on one hundred thousand Nationalist Chinese troops. He feinted to the east before attacking them on the west. He skillfully maneuvered his troops across the River of Golden Sand in the rugged upper reaches of the Yangtze and shook off pursuing KMT forces, which freed the

Communists to make their way to the redoubt they would occupy in Yan'an, in Shaanxi Province, for twelve years.

Mao then showed the Party a card trick. He exploited the decision the Politburo had made at the Zunyi Conference to force a division of labor among the leaders and remove Bo Gu as top leader of the CCP. Zhang Wentian, the Russian Returned Student, had broken with the Comintern and affiliated himself with Mao. Nevertheless, he was a man with his own international connections among those who still called some shots in the CCP. With Mao's endorsement, Zhang replaced Bo Gu as the Party leader. Since Zhang was Mao's surrogate, this development hugely and instantly inflated Mao's reputation in the Party. He had now moved so close to the supreme leadership that he could almost taste it. He was no longer the guest, even though he had not yet formally occupied the place of the host. To assume that position, he'd have to win the house. To do that, he'd have to stack the deck against Zhou Enlai and play a few more rounds.

Mao Zedong understood that the key to power in the Communist revolution in China in the years to come would belong to whoever held the highest position over military affairs within, and outside, the Party structure. Mao's chief rival for supreme command of the Red Army was Zhang Guotao, one of the original founders of the CCP in 1921, who had emerged as one of the most powerful military men in the Communist movement leading the Fourth Army, which had evaded Chiang Kai-shek's assaults on the Soviet enclave along the Hubei, Henan, and Anhui provincial borders (the *Eyuwan* Soviet) and later in Sichuan Province. With an army that at one time numbered eighty thousand men, Zhang wanted to use his new military power as a stepping stone to ultimately command the entire Red Army. Mao, the ever-prescient political card shark, anticipated Zhang's ambitions. By suggesting Zhang for the role of general political commissar, he was proposing to sabotage his military command. In his new position, Zhang would replace Zhou Enlai. The very suggestion was enough to becalm Zhang's efforts to win battlefield command. It also called into question the influence of Zhou Enlai, who remained an obstacle to Mao's own ambition to assume complete control over the military structure, even as he helped Mao's return to power.

In the midst of this restructuring of power, Zhou Enlai was incapacitated for an entire month because of an abscess on his liver. In her memoir, Deng Yingchao recalled how Zhou Enlai lay in bed for days with a high fever while doctors worked night and day to bring his temperature down by applying ice to the area around his liver. Zhou slipped into unconsciousness. Meanwhile, the medical staff urgently tried to find ways to purge Zhou's system. When he did revive, Zhou expelled large quantities of viscous green and yellow fluid, and his fever began to subside. But in Zhou's convenient absence, Mao reversed the decision the Politburo had committed to paper at the Zunyi Conference and seized the top military post assigned to Zhou. In less than six months, Mao thus managed to gain control of the Red Army. Now he owned the very title that he had dangled before the eyes of the ambitious Zhang Guotao. Zhou Enlai was in no position to stand in Mao's way. To put the finishing touch on this coup, Mao, in his new capacity of chief military leader, split Red Army forces once again, and in the first half of September 1935, he dispatched Zhang Guotao and his Fourth Army to the south and headed north in command of the First Front Army. Zhou Enlai, still disabled, was unable to stop him.

During the latter stages of the Long March in northern Sichuan Province at the small town of Ejie, the enlarged Politburo held another meeting. There, in late September 1935, members of the Politburo made the decision to amalgamate existing military forces into the Shaanxi-Gansu Branch of the CCP Workers' and Peasants' Revolutionary Army. Peng Dehuai, a rough-hewn man from very humble beginnings who had once served as a Nationalist officer and had joined Mao's forces years earlier on Well Ridge Mountain, now became the official commander of this army, and Mao Zedong became its political commissar. The Politburo also gave its stamp of approval to a new five-member group formed to oversee military affairs comprised of Peng, Lin Biao, Mao, Wang Jiaxiang, and Zhou. Mao organized this new arrangement through Zhang Wentian, his puppet, who had replaced Bo Gu as leader of the Politburo. Mao, with Zhang's help, had now severely weakened Zhou Enlai, and all but completely closed him out of any role in the process of military decision-making. Almost, but not quite. Mao wanted to administer the ultimate coup de grace when the Red Army arrived in northern Shaanxi Province. Once the Long March had ended in October 1935, Zhang Wentian proposed a few changes on the military committee. Zhu De, chairman of the Military Affairs Committee of the Revolutionary Committee of the Communist Party, had been attached to Zhang Guotao's Fourth Army units that were heading south where they would confront military disaster. Now that Zhu was out of the picture, Zhang Wentian wanted Mao to serve as the chairman. In this shuffle, Zhou would now oversee Party affairs.

This time Mao had overreached. His blatant grab for power invited the opposition of Wang Jiaxiang and other former supporters and collaborators of Mao. Wang argued that Zhou, who had years of experience in military matters, should retain a role in the Red Army. Mao realized that Zhang Wentian could not muster enough votes in the Politburo to pull off this leadership sleight of hand. He made a deft about-face, proposing that Zhou should occupy the top role in military affairs while he, Mao, would serve as Zhou's assistant.

During the Politburo session when the military leadership was being considered, Zhou had nominated Mao to be chairman. But he had no desire to be eliminated altogether from playing a role in military policy. It worked out well for him that others in the leadership opposed Mao's ambition. Even so, Zhou was ever the diplomat. He resisted the opportunity to fight it out with Mao Zedong. Instead, he considered Mao's offer, and then proposed that Mao should continue as the top military leader, and serve as chairman of the military committee, while he, Zhou, continued to play a subordinate military role. Mao, a master political tactician, knew when to make a move and when to disengage from a power struggle. Zhou had his supporters and Mao understood his value. Thus it was that Mao became the chairman of the Chinese Soviet Northwest Revolutionary Military Affairs Committee. He now possessed the keys to the house. He held the highest position over military affairs within and outside the formal Communist Party structure. Zhou was now his guest. He would serve as vice-chairman of the committee.

Despite these gains, Mao was not through. No sooner had the leadership arrived in north Shaanxi Province than Mao made further moves to consolidate his power within the inner political circle of the CCP. With Zhou acquiescing to Mao's takeover of military policy, Mao turned his attention to Wang Ming, the Russian Returned Student, who, after spending several years in the Soviet Union in the early 1930s, returned to China in 1937 with the charge to carry out Stalin's war plan that called for the CCP to once again work with the Nationalists in a joint effort to oppose Japanese advances in China that could threaten the Soviet Union's eastern flank. Wang put his fealty to Stalin on immediate display when at a crucial December 1937 Politburo meeting, he argued for a strategy of directing Communist forces against the Japanese, a view that won support from a majority of the Chinese leadership, including Zhou Enlai. While Mao wanted to conserve Red Army forces for the inevitable battle with the Nationalists, Zhou criticized Mao's plan and called for putting the interests of the nation above that of the Party by engaging the Japanese. Not only was Zhou aware that Wang was backed by Stalin, he also believed that the Communists should set a good example for the entire Chinese nation by directly confronting the Japanese threat.

Mao was no fool. As the old Chinese adage goes: "Two tigers cannot occupy the same mountain." Mao knew the real intention of Wang Ming's strategy was to win ultimate power in the CCP. Given his considerable support with CCP ranks, Zhou Enlai, Mao understood, was the key to determining the outcome of this struggle. Where Zhou, an old ally of Wang, stood on this issue would determine which side, Wang Ming or Mao Zedong, would win.

Mao's first move was to separate Zhou from Wang. Following the establishment of the Second United Front between the Communists and Nationalists in a deal brokered by Zhou in 1936 during the famous Xi'an Incident, Zhou was sent to Wuhan to represent CCP interests. Then in what turned out to be a godsend for Mao, Nazi Germany attacked the Soviet Union in June 1941, which cut the legs out from under Wang as his Russian masters lost all interest in foreign Communist movements as they fought to stave off the Nazi juggernaut. Now Mao went in for the kill, launching the Yan'an Rectification Movement under the rubric of "summarizing the historical lessons of the Party," the real purpose of which was to purge Wang Ming and his followers. During an expanded meeting of the Politburo in September of 1941, Mao jumped all over the "errors" and "mistakes" Wang and his Russian Returned Students had made during their period of ascendancy from 1931 to 1935, claiming it represented a fundamental "struggle between two lines in the Party"— the ultimate sin in the Communist liturgy. Within two years, Mao managed to isolate the Wang faction by performing major surgery on the all-important Central CCP Secretariat, pushing out not just Wang and his fellow Russian Returned Students—Bo Gu, Zhang Wentian, and Wang Jiaxiang—but also Zhou Enlai. In its place, a three-man power group made up of Mao, Liu Shaoqi, and Ren Bishi was established with Mao anointed as the Chairman (*Zhuxi*) of the Politburo and Secretariat with "final decision-making authority." Mao's dream of gaining absolute power had finally been realized while Liu Shaoqi—Mao's major supporter in the Rectification project—was single-handedly promoted by Mao to second in command. In a flash, Mao—the Chairman—assumed a new iconic image in the arena of Communist politics, which would have a lasting impact on the history of the CCP and modern China.

Mao may have won out in his struggle with Wang Ming whose position had been further weakened by the formal dissolution of the Comintern in July 1943. But Zhou Enlai still presented a problem, in no small part because of his extensive support among key leaders such as Zhu De, Peng Dehuai, and Chen Yi, all of whom had close ties to the wily Zhou. Bolstered by his own strong support from Liu Shaoqi, the secret police chief Kang Sheng, Peng Zhen, Gao Gang, Lin Biao, and Deng Xiaoping, Mao was fully aware that outmaneuvering Wang Ming had secured him supreme power, but to maintain it he would have to conquer Zhou's support base as well.

Mao cabled Zhou Enlai ordering him to return to Yan'an from Chongqinq—the Nationalist wartime capital—where since 1940 Zhou had maintained liaison with the Nationalists. Right away Zhou realized that the political climate in Yan'an had undergone a profound change and that support for Mao's supreme authority was now virtually unstoppable. Unless he played his cards right, Zhou sensed that he would become the next target for Mao while the newly appointed Chairman finished off Wang Ming. Just as he had shown fealty to all previous leaders of the CCP—from Chen Duxiu to Li Lisan to Wang Ming—Zhou fell into line and at a meeting welcoming him back to Yan'an, displayed his undying support for the Chairman. "Anyone who in the past had opposed or expressed doubts about Comrade Mao Zedong's leadership or opinions has been proven completely wrong. The direction and leadership of Mao Zedong," Zhou declared, "is the direction of the Chinese Communist Party!"

Mao, of course, was delighted. But one speech by a man who had wronged him at the 1932 Ningdu Conference and allied with Wang Ming was not going to be let off the hook so easily. In a series of Politburo meetings from September to November 1943, Zhou was targeted as the leader of a faction that had sided with the now disgraced Wang Ming. Writing thirty thousand words of study notes and self-criticism and at one point spending five days delivering a series of speeches the tone of which was set by Mao, Zhou admitted to a series of political crimes and labeled himself as a "political swindler" who suffered from enormous personal vanity, selfishness, and a lack of principles. Citing his roots in a "run-down, feudal aristocratic family" and blaming the doting, pampered upbringing he received from his mother for making him overly obedient and too willing to compromise, Zhou further admitted to a fear of offending people, along with an over consideration of weighing gains and losses as, he now confessed, had driven his actions at the Ningdu

Conference. "I developed the habit of neglecting the true nature of a matter and concentrating only on the surface, which led me to act without direction and to violate discipline. While I play along with situations outside the Party, I am overcautious about important inner-Party matters, always very obedient." After delivering the longest self-criticism that he would ever make in his entire political career, this decision to cave in marked a crucial point in the historical relationship between Zhou and Mao. The Chairman had now become, Zhou believed, the symbol of truth and power in the CCP, replacing forever the Comintern and any other potential competitor. Mao was the ultimate leader of the Chinese Communist Party, while Zhou Enlai would forever serve as the faithful assistant.

But Zhou was also a smooth operator who knew how to handle people; he also had a knack for organization and a good eye for detail. Mao was a man of immense talent, but he could not run the entire show all by himself. He needed Zhou Enlai. Throughout the decades to come, Mao was plagued by this paradoxical relationship. He had to keep Zhou at bay to prevent him from ever again gaining the upper hand; at the same time, to stay ahead of the game and keep his eye on the big picture, Mao grew even more dependent on Zhou Enlai. He had to draw Zhou close even as he raised the whip, and sometimes lashed the man he could not live without. This paradox is like a code. To understand the code is to understand the curious relationship between the men who ruled what, on October 1, 1949, became the People's Republic of China—a relationship that remained locked in place as long as they both lived.

7

TRAPPING
THE "CHINESE KHRUSHCHEV"

OCTOBER 1, 1949. MAO ZEDONG STOOD ATOP THE GATE OF
Heavenly Peace (*Tiananmen*) in central Beijing and announced the
formal establishment of the People's Republic of China and his position as the new head of state. Initially, at enormous disadvantage to
their Nationalist antagonists who outnumbered their Communist
counterparts and possessed new American equipment, Mao and
Zhou had fought side-by-side from 1946 to early 1949. But with deft
military moves the Communists had gradually gained the upper
hand as Nationalist units became increasingly demoralized. With
the Nationalist government suing for peace in January 1949, the
Communists were on a winning streak and, by March, Mao and
Zhou, who together had endured more than two years of tough
fighting and illness, entered Beijing. From there, they directed their
forces to continue the offensive across the Yangtze River, defeating
Chiang's once superior military power and forcing the Nationalist
leader to flee the mainland for Taiwan. The new Communist power

on the block, the PRC, now dramatically altered the world geopolitical landscape. But ideologically and militarily, the Chinese had to play second fiddle to the Soviets, who, under Stalin, still ran the international Communist world.

The Communist world changed in March 1953, when Joseph Stalin died. Mao had been forced to play supplicant to the Soviet leader, visiting Moscow as one of his first official acts as China's head of state in December 1949. Mao, the newest leader of international Communism, was left virtually unattended for two weeks before Stalin acquiesced to Chinese demands and agreed to sign the Treaty of Friendship, Alliance, and Mutual Assistance between the two Communist giants. Once Stalin had made his exit from the stage, Mao decided that he had become the tiger on the mountain and intended to dominate the international Socialist scene. To accomplish this personal task Mao thrust China into a political and ideological contest with the USSR. His ultimate goal was to assume in perpetuity an immortal niche in the pantheon of great Socialist leaders to which Stalin, it seemed, had already ascended.

When, in 1956, Nikita Khrushchev denounced Stalin during the famous secret speech, in which he deplored the "crimes of the Stalin era," he struck fear in the heart of Mao Zedong, who realized that this could also be his fate after death. Khrushchev also changed the menu of Soviet Communism from one of ideological rectitude to Goulash Communism—one with a decidedly economic flavor— which Mao detested. Starting in the late 1950s, fear began to gnaw away at Mao that some "Chinese Khrushchev" would rise up in the CCP and throw Mao, much as Khrushchev had thrown Stalin, into the trash pit of history and turn Communism in China into nothing more than a formula for economic growth and prosperity. This was Mao's particular obsession in the spring and summer of 1966, as the huge tidal wave known as the Great Proletarian Cultural Revolution swept China, viciously uprooting the country. No one had predicted that this chaos would last for a whole decade, least of all Zhou Enlai, who celebrated his sixty-eighth birthday on the eve of the Cultural Revolution and spent the last years of his life trying to contain it.

Mao's justification for the Cultural Revolution? To preserve the purity of Chinese Socialism. But that was just window dressing. The Cultural Revolution was really the product of his paranoia, triggered by de-Stalinization in the Soviet Union and his dread of how that might foreshadow the fate of his own legacy and prefigure the future of China. The Cultural Revolution was a result of Chinese totalitarianism, a bureaucratic and organizational system, one that subjected nearly a billion people to the will of a single man: Mao Zedong. It was also a system that nurtured deeply suppressed defects and internecine divisions in every segment of society. When Mao decided to destroy Liu Shaoqi, his heir apparent, and attacked him as China's Khrushchev, widespread rancor exploded into a series of ongoing conflicts and attacks that spread to the highest levels of the Chinese Communist leadership.

Starting in the late 1950s, Mao presided over a series of utterly impracticable efforts to transform Chinese society that resulted in an enormous human catastrophe, one that brought death by starvation to an estimated twenty million Chinese peasants. To this folly may be traced the origins of the Cultural Revolution.

Mao had launched his program of reform in the late 1950s under the title Three Red Banners. The first of these initiatives called for "going all out, aiming high, and achieving greater, faster, better and more economical results in Socialism." The second, the Great Leap Forward, launched in 1958, involved the CCP in a massive and rapid agricultural and economic expansion. The goal of this enterprise was in fifteen years to overtake, through the construction in the countryside of so-called backyard steel furnaces and huge water conservancy projects, the output of Great Britain. People's Communes, the third Red Banner, an essential component of the Great Leap Forward, called for a radical reorganization of agricultural production. These campaigns inspired deep antagonism within the CCP. They also provoked complaints outside the PRC from China's Soviet Big Brothers. Khrushchev himself tried to steer Mao away from such grandiose policies. He ventured to suggest that Mao was "living in a universe of his own." These and other efforts to dissuade Mao only convinced him that numerous "Khrushchevs living at home and abroad" had all joined forces to thwart him.

China's real Khrushchev, Mao came to believe, was none other than his first heir apparent, Liu Shaoqi, who had been head of state (also known as state chairman) of China since 1959, when Mao, in the midst of the generally negative reaction to the Great Leap, had relinquished the post. Liu was Mao's intimate political crony. Liu Shaoqi had provided key political support to Mao during the crucial Yan'an Rectification campaign against Stalin's agents in the 1940s. He assumed a prominent role as a leader in 1959, when it became clear that the Great Leap Forward and the People's Communes had visited disaster on the Chinese people. Marshal Peng Dehuai, at the famous Mt. Lu (*Lushan*) Conference in July–August 1959, had inveighed against these programs that Mao had initiated, and the power of his scorn had forced Mao to retreat from his role as a leader in the formulation of policy. Mao divided the Party Central between two leadership fronts, and that's when Liu Shaoqi assumed command of the first front, with the critical task of managing the routine daily affairs of the CCP while Mao moved to the so-called second front disengaging the Chairman from direct involvement in major policy decisions with hints he might soon retire.

To Mao's great surprise and dismay, Liu seized this opportunity, intended only to rectify the errors of the Leap, and created for himself a preeminent political position. He formed a second major headquarters in the Party Central leadership that would counteract the Party chairman's authority and effectively negate the Three Red Banners. Liu had proclaimed that he was the "one and only state chairman during an extraordinary era." He had announced that China faced a "dire situation," that the national economy was on "the verge of collapse." These pronunciamentos had driven Mao into the sanctuary of the Party's rear echelons. Liu seemed to be aiming his efforts at upsetting the very leadership of the CCP, such was the provocative vigor with which he acted. He was a threat to the supremacy of Mao, who decided that when the right moment presented itself he would have to destroy this Chinese Khrushchev.

Zhou Enlai immediately sensed the tension between Mao and Liu. He could tell, for instance, that when Liu relaxed state control over the agricultural sector throughout the early 1960s, the new state chairman was hatching policies utterly at odds with Mao's utopian Socialist vision. Zhou was unwilling to get directly involved in the conflict, but he tried his best to regulate the tension as it boiled up between the Party and state chairman. Refusing to align himself with either of these political titans, Zhou employed his fabled Confucian strategy and tried to find a middle way. Zhou agreed with the economic readjustment policy that Liu promoted to give farmers more influence over how basic decisions were made about agricultural production. Zhou went along with this plan that radically reduced the role of People's Communes because he was well aware of the terrible famine that the Great Leap had unleashed throughout the countryside in areas like Henan Province. Zhou also keenly understood that Mao would never admit that he had committed any major blunders. He also knew that Mao was already looking for a way to get even with Liu for behaving like such a brazen upstart, threatening to upset the delicate political balance of the central leadership that, ever since his appointment as Chairman of the CCP Politburo in 1943, had maintained Mao at the pinnacle.

STAVING OFF ATTACKS

From 1960 to 1962, Zhou Enlai devoted himself to solving the food crisis in China. He was given the job of overseeing the collection and distribution of grain to provide famine relief to peasants in dire need of food. This called for classic Chinese statecraft, and it was an assignment that Zhou held until 1966. At the height of the emergency, as China confronted the greatest disaster of the modern era, Zhou engaged in constant consultations with officials from the Food Ministry, and purposely kept his distance from Liu Shaoqi and other political luminaries involved in the rapidly gathering political whirlpool that would soon suck the entire Chinese state into its turbulent gyre. Even so, Zhou never forgot his relationship with Mao, and did everything he possibly could to shield his status as the unassailable Chairman of the Chinese Communist Party. He wanted to show Mao exactly where he stood on the leadership issue. The National Economic Plan was issued in 1961, during the "three bitter years" of famine and drought that afflicted the Chinese nation, and Zhou wracked his brain day and night to find just the right way to address the crisis, but in a way that did not offend Mao. He replaced the word "rectify" (*zhengfeng*), so suggestively censorious to the Chinese ear, with the kinder, gentler word "adjustment" (*tiaozheng*). Zhou also introduced an equally kind term: "filling out" (*chongshi*). This was an inspired phrase. Ultimately, it was folded into what became known as the "eight character policy" of "adjustment, consolidation, improvement, and filling out" that marked a dramatic attempt to force the economy back into balance even as Mao was still committed to the massive increases in domestic steel production that had been the centerpiece of the Great Leap.

At the Seven Thousand Cadres Conference in January–February 1962, Zhou displayed his characteristic diplomacy in addressing a precarious political situation when the growing animosity between Mao Zedong and Liu Shaoqi broke out in the open. Most official Chinese convocations, choreographed well in advance, leave nothing to chance. The Seven Thousand Cadres Conference, held in Beijing, which came on the heels of the disastrous Great Leap Forward, was much more spontaneous and, at times, even confrontational. Three very different voices, reflecting the disagreements that Mao's policies had provoked at the top, spoke out.

Liu Shaoqi, first of all, issued the official Government Report, in which the state chairman admitted to the large gathering of assembled cadres, who had actually borne the burden of carrying out central policies, that the national economy did, indeed, confront a dire situation. Liu did not directly challenge Mao. That would have been unthinkable in Chinese politics at that time. Even Mao's best-known and biggest critics tossed him bouquets of praise. Instead, Liu made it a point not to use the expression "nine fingers to one," Mao's favorite phrase when he wanted to emphasize achievements over setbacks in any overall assessment. Liu argued that this formula glossed over mistakes because it diminished the severity of the situation that the country was facing. Liu invoked the words of peasants in Hunan whom he had visited the previous year when he asserted, instead, that the difficulties that the nation confronted were more on the order of "seven fingers to three," and he added that "seven to three" was a ratio not of achievements to setbacks, but one of man-made to natural disasters, both of which had brought lasting suffering to the Chinese people. Liu nevertheless refused to criticize the Maoist idea of the Three Banners. He argued that an overall summary of the situation could wait, along with final judgments, which would be rendered over the long term, perhaps in five or ten years' time. Thus did Liu strive to save Mao's face.

Other leaders were not so kind. Peng Zhen, who, as mayor of Beijing, was Liu's top general, mentioned Mao by name when the Government Report was in the drafting stages soon after the official convocation of the conference. Peng held Mao personally responsible for "blowing the Communist wind" in 1958 and promoting the rural canteens that, by allowing peasants to eat freely, had proved so calamitous to the grain situation. Unless Mao admitted, at least in part, to his real mistakes, "we cannot clear this situation up with the Party," which Peng argued would suffer accordingly.

Next came Lin Biao, who in a speech to the conference praised the Chairman with unembarrassed effusiveness in a song of adulation that completely bypassed the dire aspects of the economy. "Whenever in the past our work was done well, it was precisely when Mao's thought received no interference," sang the upstart Lin. "Every time that Chairman Mao's thought was not respected or suffered interference, there has been trouble. That," Lin added, "is essentially the history of the last few decades." This was an encomium that Mao could really appreciate. He called it a "wonderful and heavy piece of oratory," one that deserved to be distributed among cadres at the meeting for study. Lin hastened to do just that.

In Zhou Enlai's address, the premier mentioned the current difficulties Liu Shaoqi had addressed, but he restricted his commentary to economic matters. He spoke not a word that might have suggested political differences. He spoke on behalf of the State Council, the top government body that was charged with implementing economic policy, and he made it clear that he shared responsibility for the current state of affairs with the Chairman, and assumed much of the blame in the self-criticism that followed. "This is my mistake," he declared. "I must confess." This mea culpa awakened even in Mao a remnant of pity. "Fine," the Chairman blurted out. "You've confessed. Once is enough." Aware of the enormous gap that had opened up between the Chairman and Liu Shaoqi, Zhou ended his speech with a call for Party unity, which he called "our most important goal." He cited the famous exhortation to "seek truth from facts," one Mao Zedong liked to quote, as he called for everyone always to tell and seek the truth and to formulate policies to confront the economic realities in China. It was quintessential Zhou Enlai. He managed to express his deeply held conviction about how the Party should move ahead and, at the same time, he tried to build a bridge across the new divide that had opened up within the once-united leadership.

In this effort, Zhou was destined to fail. In those three discordant voices expressed in early 1962 can be heard the origins of the Cultural Revolution that soon ripped apart the very fabric of Chinese society, a catastrophe far beyond anything even Zhou, brilliant strategist that he was, could prevent.

When the Seven Thousand Cadres Conference was over, Mao Zedong left Beijing to make the round of ancient Chinese historical sites. This was one of the political tricks he had put to good use over the years. His real reason for absenting himself was to observe from afar how Liu Shaoqi planned to play his cards while he was gone. It didn't take long to find out that Liu was determined to make a dramatic course correction when, at Western Hall (*Xilou*), on the grounds of the Central South Lake leadership compound, Liu immediately convened a gathering of senior economic officials in an enlarged meeting of the Politburo to take a closer look at the extent of the economic crisis. Liu had the most important role in routine Party matters, and he put it to good use. Mao took the position that the economic crisis had passed. This wasn't how Liu saw it. He thought that the only way to proceed was to make a complete assessment of the Great Leap Forward and its impact on Chinese society. Liu proposed various recovery strategies, prominent among them the idea of adopting an "agricultural responsibility system" that would, in effect, return production decisions in the countryside to individual households. On his tour of ancient China, Mao saw what Liu was doing in Beijing. He didn't like it, and he let Liu Shaoqi know this when he got home. Liu Yuan, Liu Shaoqi's son, makes this crystal clear in an article entitled "Why Mao Attacked Liu Shaoqi." Liu writes:

On a pleasant, sunny summer afternoon in July 1962 Liu briskly approached the Chairman while Mao was floating around in his Central South Lake pool and greeted him warmly from the poolside. "What the hell is all the big hurry about?" The Chairman wanted to know. This took Liu by surprise. He went over and sat down next to the changing room and kept his thoughts to himself. Mao finally climbed out of the pool and that's when Liu told Mao that two of the biggest critics of the Great Leap Forward, Chen Yun, the economics czar, and Tian Jiaying, one of Mao's many secretaries, wanted to meet with Mao. "They've expressed their opposition within the Party confines the way they're supposed to, according to CCP organizational principles, and now they want to present their views to you," Liu told the Chairman. "This shouldn't pose any particular problem." "It's got nothing to do with 'organizational principles,'" Mao shot back. "It's about the content of their opinions." "That Deng Zihui had made such a big noise at the Western Hall meeting," Mao argued, "was all nothing but darkness and intrigue. So what's the big rush?"

Deng Zihui, the minister of agriculture, had been a major critic of Mao's agricultural policies since the mid-1950s. The atmosphere grew tense between the two men. They both became heated. Mao vented his displeasure in a torrent of words, but Liu Shaoqi was not to be outdone. "So many people have died of hunger," he blurted out. "History isn't going to be kind to us. It's going to judge you and me harshly. The people need grain, and they are sending demands for relief and all kinds of petitions of protest to the Party." "The Three Red Banners have been shot down and now land is being divided up again just the way it used to be in the bad old days," Mao raged. "What have you done to resist this? What's going to happen after I'm dead?" Liu calmed himself. He didn't want to get on Mao's bad side. He patiently explained to Mao that the Three Red Banners would remain, that the high targets of the grain requisition campaign remained in force, that the rural public canteens would not be altered. Mao, too, calmed down, finally, and agreed that the economic readjustment moderating central policies should continue.

Mao was a man known to harbor bitter grudges, and he didn't like it when Liu told him that people needed grain and were submitting petitions and demands for relief. Obviously, Mao concluded, Liu planned to follow in Khrushchev's footsteps and issue a Chinese secret speech of his own and dedicate himself after Mao died to the pursuit of economic prosperity in China. Mao was convinced that Liu intended to expose and criticize him for his towering crimes while his body was still warm.

Mao was uneasy because it looked as though Liu Shaoqi now rivaled the Chairman as a popular figure among Party cadres. Mao had frequently talked about using cadres in grassroots efforts to help improve work and to gain experience, but he didn't seem to have much of an effect. Liu only uttered one sentence of warning—"No one who refuses to be sent down can ever serve as a Central Party official"—before virtually all the leading cadres had packed their bags and headed out for the four corners of the country. This sort of decisive action by Liu made Mao determined to get rid of his growing nemesis. And it was as a direct result of his desire to get rid of Liu that the idea for the Great Proletarian Cultural Revolution was born.

Mao prepared the ideological and intellectual groundwork for launching the Cultural Revolution from late 1963 to mid-1964 once the agricultural sector had recovered and the damage of the Great Leap had been brought under control. His first target was the arts. You "are toying with revisionism," Mao warned China's writers and artists, "and are coming dangerously close to becoming a Chinese version of the Hungarian Petofi club" that had provoked the 1956 revolution. Sensing the direction of Mao's political tack, Zhou immediately swung into action and joined in making the arts the center of the Party's political testing ground by becoming deeply involved in the musical production that was planned for the upcoming fifteenth anniversary of the founding of the PRC, *The East Is Red*. During his regular busy schedule, Zhou made time to check on every aspect of the production, from lyrics, to music, to costumes, and to endless rehearsals, in which Mao and his "correct leadership and extraordinary contributions to the Chinese revolution" became the central theme of the epic production. Zhou cut out any reference to the 1927 Nanchang Uprising of which he, not Mao, had been the leader, and inserted the famous merger of the First and Fourth armies during the Long March, because this was the episode that had confirmed Mao's personal domination of the Red Army. *The East Is Red* seemed to echo Lin Biao's call to study Mao's works in the PLA. It helped to set the stage for the frenzied cult of Mao that would drive the Cultural Revolution.

By the fall and winter of 1964, the political winds began to rise. People began to feel the pressure to show where they stood in regard to Liu Shaoqi. Zhou Enlai had followed the middle way at the 1962 Seven Thousand Cadres Conference, but once Mao saw the role that Zhou had undertaken—to craft the basic political message about the Chairman's personal domination of CCP history in *The East Is Red*—Mao had reason to believe he could once again count on his premier. After the 1962 Cuban Missile Crisis and other foreign and domestic crises boiled up to confront the Soviet Union, the Soviet

Politburo ousted Nikita Khrushchev. This was a godsend to Mao Zedong. He sent Zhou Enlai to Russia as the head of a Chinese delegation to the forty-seventh anniversary celebration of the Bolshevik October Revolution to take the temperature of the new Soviet leadership. General He Long accompanied Zhou as his deputy.

The whole trip blew up before the formal ceremonies even got off the ground, at the welcoming banquet. Zhou Enlai was sitting next to Rodion Malinovsky, the Soviet defense minister, who despite his personal friendship with Khrushchev had conspired with others to oust the Soviet leader. "The Soviet Union and China should be on friendly terms," Malinovsky announced to Zhou, "but that's only going to happen if evil spirits like Mao and Khrushchev aren't allowed to interfere." Zhou dispensed with his usual diplomatic savoir faire. "I don't know what you're talking about," he shot back, and then abruptly got up to leave, pursued by Malinovsky. "We Russians got rid of Khrushchev and now you should do the same thing to Mao," Malinovsky shouted after Zhou for all to hear. Zhou kept on moving as though he hadn't heard Malinovsky, and, in his rush to leave, he was joined by General He Long, who berated the Soviet defense minister as he and Zhou made their exit.

A fairly large contingent from the foreign press corps was there to witness this episode, and word swiftly went out over the wires that the Soviet Union and China had formed an agreement whereby Mao would soon step down so that Zhou Enlai could replace him as the Chairman of the Chinese Communist Party. Zhou issued a public denial and made the same point to Leonid Brezhnev, the new Soviet leader. "The whole thing is sheer nonsense," Zhou told Brezhnev, who could only agree that the very notion of trying to unseat Mao was a pipe dream. The Soviet leader also tried to make it clear that the principal disagreements between the two countries had nothing whatever to do with personality conflicts. He issued a formal apology on the part of the Soviet central government for Malinovsky's outrageous dinner-table remarks. Even so, Zhou decided that the damage had been done and that he would have to fly back to Beijing immediately. Mao was there at the airport to greet him personally when he got off the plane. It was absolutely unprecedented for Mao to make such a gesture for Zhou Enlai. Zhou had played his own hand to perfection. He had avoided the internationalist trap the Soviet Big Brothers had set for him and he'd endeared himself to the Chairman as a defender of the faith. The "minister" had served his "emperor" well.

By the end of 1964, the conflict between Liu Shaoqi and Mao was a matter of public record. Mao openly disparaged the efforts of Liu Shaoqi at a Central Work Conference held in December 1964, convened to address the issue of the Four Cleans (*Siqing*) Movement aimed at eliminating corruption among rural cadres. Mao called for direct popular involvement in the process of Party rectification in the villages. Two diametrically opposed views of how to implement policy in China were now out in the open for all to see. Liu, the consummate Leninist, thought the Party should manage all political efforts from the top down through the centrally dispatched work teams. Mao, the populist, wanted to bring the general public into mass campaigns. Mao hurled a scornful challenge at the state chairman after Liu delivered his speech on the nature of the Four Cleans.

"Shaoqi is the head, charged with overseeing the Four Cleans, the Five Antis and all economic work," an angry Mao told a small group of confidants. "I am [Party] Chairman and you Liu Shaoqi are the first vice-chairman. We all know that things can happen unexpectedly. If I drop dead all of a sudden it might turn out that you won't be able to take over after all, so I say why don't you just take over right now, become the Party chairman, the Emperor Qin Shihuang. I have my shortcomings," he went on. "I curse all the time, but it no longer amounts to a hill of beans. You are tough, you are the commander who never curses, and you've captured the premier and Deng Xiaoping in your net."

Deng Xiaoping had particularly irritated the Party Chairman before the December 1964 Work Conference actually began. As the head of the CCP Secretariat, Deng was in charge of making all the arrangements for these gatherings and making sure that everything went smoothly. He had suggested to Mao that perhaps out of consideration for his health he shouldn't try to attend the meetings every day. This put Mao in an even more defensive mood. By the time he gave his speech to the conference Mao had raised the ante in the political and ideological contest into an all-or-nothing confrontation. "The principal contradiction underlying the Four Cleans Movement is between Socialism and Capitalism," Mao bellowed. "The focus of rectification should be on those in the Party who are taking us down the capitalist road." Liu refused to back down. He even interrupted Mao's speech. "During the movement," Liu said, "various conflicts and contradictions are intertwined that make the whole thing very complicated. Our only choice," he insisted, "is to start from the reality we confront and try to solve whatever conflicts arise. Conflicts don't all have to be elevated to confrontations between the enemy and the people."

In the end, Mao and Liu could not agree. They openly engaged in a heated discussion, which made everyone at the meeting very tense. Mao was furious that Liu had dared to disagree with the Party Chairman in public. The next day, Mao strode into the meeting in an angry frame of mind, Communist Party Constitution in one hand and the state constitution in the other, and openly began to interrogate Deng Xiaoping and Liu Shaoqi in front of the entire gathering. "One tells me not to attend meetings and the other one tells me to pipe down," Mao complained. "How dare you try to deprive me of the rights guaranteed by the Party and state constitutions? Liu must apologize publicly," he declared, and signaled to the central-southern regional Party chief Tao Zhu and public security official Xie Fuzhi and others that he wanted them to "work on" Liu, and pressure him to recant.

Liu was just as stubborn as Mao, however. He refused to apologize. That left Mao alone in the cold up on stage for all to see. Zhou Enlai was the one who finally made an effort to temper the situation and end the awkward stand-off, but the gap between Mao and Liu continued to deepen, and after these public displays of disagreement, unheard of in Chinese politics, Mao was determined to get rid of Liu. He knew he could count on the support of Zhou Enlai. He knew that no one in the CCP would dare to oppose him when he went about disposing of Liu Shaoqi. Mao regained his tranquility, but he also began to make plans to unleash the Cultural Revolution that would eradicate Liu and the "revisionist" branch of the CCP.

To prepare for his battle with Liu Shaoqi and the substantial segment of the Communist Party that supported Liu's policies, Mao worked out strategies on the theoretical, organizational, and military fronts. Mao did whatever he could to give Liu the impression that he would soon "meet with God," to lower Liu's defenses, but below the radar he went about digging up old articles and documentary material from the revolutionary days when criticism had been directed at Wang Ming, the Soviet agent in China during the 1940s. At the same time, he dusted off nine key polemical articles from the Yan'an Rectification of the same era, including some that had praised Liu Shaoqi and criticized Zhou Enlai, and by distributing these seemingly harmless historical works, he succeeded in confusing his opponents. Meanwhile, Mao continued to raise the subject of "maintaining vigilance against revisionism at the Party Central." This way, he kept alive the tension in Party ranks that the December 1964 Work Conference had created.

Mao also decided to put his wife, Jiang Qing, into the game as part of his political offensive. This was something he'd promised the central leadership he would never do when, back in the Yan'an days, he had made the Shanghai actress his third wife. But Mao's historical legacy was on the line, an epic battle was about to begin in the CCP, and the Chairman needed a big cannon he could aim at his enemies. Jiang Qing fired her first salvos at a rather innocuous play, entitled *Hai Rui Dismissed from Office*, by a man named Wu Han, who happened to be the vice-mayor of Beijing and a member of the political network of Peng Zhen. The play was criticized in secret sessions in Shanghai, where many of Jiang Qing's supporters in the field of art and literature resided. Wu Han's play told the story of a Ming Dynasty (1368–1628 A.D.) official who was summarily dismissed after he "upbraided the emperor" for neglecting peasant welfare in the midst of a famine. Many believed that this was an allegory for Mao's abrupt assault in 1959 on Peng Dehuai, who had raised similar issues at the Mt. Lu Conference in the middle of the disastrous Great Leap Forward. Wu Han, however, was but a pawn. Jiang Qing's real target was Peng Zhen, the mayor of Beijing, who had launched some of the most intense personal criticism of Mao at the 1962 Seven Thousand Cadres Conference and whose own mentor was none other than Liu Shaoqi.

8

"PREPARING
TO TAKE THE TEST"

The manner in which the Cultural Revolution began was so devious and so nefarious that perhaps the only person who could understand its inception was Mao Zedong. Mao's method resembled the military feints he employed during the mid-1930s in the early stages of the Long March to avoid destruction by the Nationalist armies. Now, to wage war on a variety of forces in the Party that did not align with him, the Chairman adopted a circuitous strategy of "uniting with Lin Biao, grabbing on to Zhou Enlai, rectifying Deng Xiaoping, and attacking Liu Shaoqi." This way, Mao set out to confuse Liu Shaoqi, while leaving potential allies like Zhou Enlai in political stalemate.

By the mid-1960s, Mao had spent almost all his political capital in the Party. He had very little power left and he knew it. The only force he could count on was the People's Liberation Army, which, since the purge of Peng Dehuai in 1959, had been under the command of Lin Biao, who had shown his "eternal allegiance" to the

Chairman in that fawning speech he'd made at the 1962 Seven Thousand Cadres Conference. Mao was no fool. He could see that Liu Shaoqi, who realized how important it was in Chinese politics to "command the gun," was making moves of his own to create support for himself in the military. Putting the squeeze on Lin Biao to give up his position as minister of defense, Liu also worked at luring to his side He Long and Luo Ruiqing, two important generals. To this end, he made a public declaration that Luo, one of the earliest members of the Red Army in the 1930s and the minister of public security in the 1950s, would soon take over as minister of defense. Before he authorized an attack on Luo, Mao decided to confuse the unsuspecting former minister of public security by urging him to give Lin Biao a call, to encourage him to recuperate quickly so that Lin could give another speech similar to the one at the Seven Thousand Cadres Conference in which he had fawned all over the Chairman. For years, Luo had been Mao's faithful ally, but in 1962 he had openly opposed Lin Biao's fawning praise for Mao. Now in the midst of this "ultimate" struggle for control of the Chinese political system and the fate of the revolution, such loyalty was of no importance whatever to Mao, who gave Lin the green light to dispense with Luo.

As the Cultural Revolution took shape in Mao's mind, Zhou Enlai quickly emerged as a key figure with whom he would have to reckon. Mao also needed to exploit Zhou's influence for his own purposes. Isolated now as Mao was in the Party, he treated Zhou with the utmost respect in the hope that he could use Zhou's enormous popularity among Party, government, and military cadres to gain some advantage over Liu. Nevertheless, Mao's efforts to secure Zhou's allegiance were circumscribed because, although he was more than willing to talk to Zhou about how to get rid of Luo Ruiqing, the Chairman did not want to discuss with the premier other important matters that were part of his larger strategy.

As for Deng Xiaoping: Mao had decided on "rectification without resignation." The Chairman was furious with Deng because he'd fallen for Liu's policy stance on such critical issues as reducing state control of agriculture, and he wanted to rectify Deng as much as he possibly could. Even so, Mao, politically pugnacious though he was, could not forget the humiliation he'd shared with Deng when the Soviet stooges had "rectified" both of them in the 1930s during the era of the Central Soviet in Jiangxi Province. Besides, Deng possessed real political skills and charm and a strategic ingenuity Mao had always admired, qualities that had invited Mao to cultivate Deng along with Lin Biao as a possible successor. As Mao advanced in years, however, he had a growing disinclination to trust anyone, including Deng Xiaoping and Lin Biao, even though both men would become crucial players in the Chairman's efforts to challenge not only Liu Shaoqi, but, finally, the crafty Zhou Enlai, his ultimate nemesis.

Mao may have gone after Deng for his apostasy, but he didn't want to lose him, he wanted to use him. He wanted to separate him from Liu Shaoqi. The Chairman refused to yield to pressures brought by the Cultural Revolution gang of leftist polemicists composed of Yao Wenyuan, Wang Hongwen, and the Shanghai leader Zhang Chunqiao, and headed by his rabid wife, Jiang Qing. As the Cultural Revolution progressed, they would go after old cadres wherever they could find them, but Mao insisted, at least initially, that their attacks on Deng Xiaoping must cease. He wanted to deal with Liu and Deng as separate entities.

In August 1966, at the Eleventh Plenum of the Eighth Central Committee of the Chinese Communist Party, Lin Biao asserted, with Mao's apparent acquiescence, that to stay in office cadres had to adhere to Mao Zedong Thought. This raised the political stakes in China to a new level. Afterward, Mao personally talked to Deng Xiaoping and urged him to maintain positive relations with Marshal Lin Biao, who had also declared that Chairman Mao was the "ultimate headquarters of the Cultural Revolution." Deng wasn't about to brush off advice like this from the Chairman, and he hastened to have a conversation with Lin Biao, which turned into a total disaster. Lin didn't want to have anything to do with Deng. The reason for this is that Lin knew what Mao was trying to do and refused to take a soft line.

As he prepared his assault on Liu, Mao by turns concocted fake issues, and then raised real concerns in an effort to confuse people about the true goals of the impending Cultural Revolution. To keep Liu off balance, Mao even pretended that he might be willing "to relinquish power," and allow Liu to become Party chairman. Mao had no intention of doing any of this. He dangled carrots like these to isolate Liu step-by-step.

The strategy Mao used to isolate Liu Shaoqi and gradually strip him of all his allies was a classic example of what the ancient military strategist Sunzi calls "enticing the tiger to leave its mountain lair." Peng Dehuai was the ally whom Mao most of all wanted to detach from Liu. Many leaders thought that Peng should be rehabilitated, now that the Great Leap Forward had turned out to be the very catastrophe that Peng had foretold. Many in the army still supported Peng, and Mao knew this. A sustained campaign to rehabilitate the old marshal had already begun at the 1962 Seven Thousand Cadres Conference. Mao believed that Liu was contemplating an alliance with Peng: He knew that Liu had informed Peng, who was still in disgrace, that he might be reinstated as minister of defense, due to Lin Biao's ill health. For Mao, this alliance was a ghastly prospect. To prevent it, Mao dispatched the marshal to the mountains of southwest China to "oversee and reinforce work on the Third Front," the vast effort underway to build up industrial and defense facilities in the country's interior to ward off a Soviet or Western attack.

In Beijing, Mao met personally with Marshal Peng and indicated in a heart-to-heart talk that he was open to a possible reconciliation. That's how he seduced Peng into leaving town. "Maybe the truth is on your side after all," Mao confessed to Peng in an obvious allusion to the marshal's outspoken criticism of the Great Leap Forward in 1959. Mao sent General Huang Kecheng, another outspoken critic of the Great Leap, down to the southwest along with Peng to serve as the marshal's deputy. Mao also moved against Yang Shangkun, a former Russian Returned Student who, as head of Mao's personal security detail, was accused by Red Guards of placing listening devices at the behest of Liu in the special train car that Mao used when traveling across the country. Mao replaced Yang with Wang Dongxing, who would serve as Mao's faithful bodyguard for the rest of Mao's life and who became in later years a key player in Mao's future efforts to get rid of Zhou Enlai. Mao had rearranged all the organizational chairs in his favor, and now he moved to jump-start the attacks on Liu via the criticism of the seemingly innocuous play by Beijing vice-mayor Wu Han, *Hai Rui Dismissed from Office*. These shots were aimed at Peng Zhen, the mayor of Beijing who had challenged Mao personally in 1962 and, in 1965, had agreed with Deng Xiaoping that excessively dogmatic study of Mao Zedong works in which every word of the Chairman was accepted as the absolute truth should be avoided. Once he'd cut into Liu's pal Peng Zhen, who, along with Yang Shangkun and Luo Ruiqing, would be ousted in 1966, Mao could move closer to his real prey: State Chairman Liu Shaoqi.

Mao had warned Zhou Enlai that he was going to unleash a major initiative. Zhou also had an instinctive hunch in those suffocating early days building up to the Cultural Revolution that something big was in the works, even as Liu Shaoqi and Deng Xiaoping, Mao's prime targets, remained completely ignorant of the impending Götterdämmerung. Zhou didn't know exactly what this was going to be, but he'd been watching the Chairman's actions long enough to realize from experience that Mao was about to embark on a significant political campaign. There was the matter of General Luo Ruiqing, for instance. Zhou's political instincts told him that Mao and Lin had conspired to dispose of Luo, even though the general had been a longtime supporter of Mao Zedong. Zhou kept his suspicions to himself, at first. When Luo, who felt wronged, wanted to meet with Mao and Lin to clear up matters, Zhou stopped him. Then he heard that Luo, still in the dark, was planning to phone Lin. Zhou immediately grabbed the phone and called Luo and blasted the general. "You are too naïve, too naïve," he shouted over the wires, trying in vain to warn Luo before it was too late.

Mao finally sent for Zhou Enlai and described his dilemma after his opponents turned away the Chairman's first major assault. Mao launched his first attack when he authorized the publication of a political diatribe written by Yao Wenyuan, a Shanghai ideologue and ally of Jiang Qing, entitled "On the New Historical Play *Hai Rui Dismissed from Office.*" This was published in practically every outlet in China on the personal orders of Mao. Despite Mao's personal imprimatur, however, resistance sprang up in the academic community, and, in Beijing, Mayor Peng Zhen barred the local press from reprinting the article. Even *People's Liberation Army Daily*, under the aegis of Lin Biao, refused to run it. Mao was intensely annoyed and frustrated. He was more than ever convinced that Beijing had become Liu's "independent kingdom," and that his authority as Chairman of the CCP was now all but nonexistent. He departed at once for Shanghai, where he still had political capital, and that's when he summoned Zhou Enlai to come down for a visit so that he could let it all hang out. He implored Zhou to use his influence to make sure the article was reprinted in the Beijing press.

Zhou had no choice. He had to follow the Chairman's orders. That's how he got so swiftly snatched up in the political maw of the Cultural Revolution, trapped between the forces of the right and left. Zhou identified with neither of these extremes. He couldn't possibly agree with the political excesses of Yao Wenyuan. He believed that diatribes like that could only further damage the Party's relationship with Chinese intellectuals, something that Zhou had tried to protect from Yao's kind of political and ideological hyperbole ever since 1955. In his cautious way, however, Zhou was loath to confide his real thoughts to Mao. He was determined to follow Mao politically, even though it might mean moving China down the wrong road.

Caught between two titanic political forces, Zhou Enlai naturally tried to find the middle way. Back in Beijing he held a series of special discussions with Peng Zhen about Yao's editorial. He made light of its criticisms and tried to persuade Peng that if he lifted his ban, the reprinted article, at most, would probably be a tempest in the academic teapot, and would make no impact on the larger political situation. Zhou had nothing but the utmost disdain for Yao's rhetoric. The premier made this clear when he ordered *People's Daily*, the mouthpiece of the Party Central, to run the article on the paper's less-than-prestigious fifth column, which was reserved for "academic debate." Zhou made his point when he appended comments of his own to the editorial. "Our policy is to allow freedom of criticisms while also permitting the freedom to express opposing views," he wrote. "As for incorrect opinions, we also adopt the approach that employs reason, seeking truth from facts and seeking to persuade." To back up his assertion, Zhou provided extensive quotes from the famous speech Mao delivered at the March 1957 National Conference on Propaganda Work, when he laid out his relatively tolerant views about criticism and debate known as the "hundred flowers."

Mao was not exactly pleased by this approach, but he decided not to push the matter any further because Zhou had provided essential assistance and helped the Chairman solve his problems with Beijing, and Mao was happy about this victory over Peng. He decided not to expand his victory for the time being. Instead, he decided to stand once again behind the curtain and wait for his opponents to make their next move and reveal their shortcomings.

In February 1966, Peng Zhen traveled to the central Chinese city of Wuhan to present the February Outline Report that defended Beijing vice-mayor and author of *Hai Rui Dismissed from Office*, Wu Han, against leftist accusations that he had organizational links to the disgraced Peng Dehuai. Peng Zhen wanted to restrict the rapidly expanding campaign against his vice-mayor to academic circles. Mao, meanwhile, resorted to his usual cunning and revealed little of his own thinking. He appeared to be generally ambiguous about the February Outline Report, which was part of his plan to "smoke the snake out of his hole." At the same time, even as he equivocated with Peng, the Chairman sent instructions to his wife, Jiang Qing, to seek the assistance of Lin Biao by urging him to convene a "Forum on the Work in Literature and Art for the Armed Forces" that would suck the military into the whole controversy and also provide a summary document that would directly challenge the February Outline Report, thereby renewing pressure on Peng Zhen and Liu Shaoqi.

One month later, Mao launched his second attack on Liu Shaoqi. He challenged Liu's policies on China's relations with the smaller, non-ruling Communist parties in other countries. Despite the gathering conflict between the Russians and the Chinese over a host of political and ideological matters, Liu, in accord with international Communist protocol, had decided to go ahead with plans to send a Chinese delegation to the upcoming Twenty-Third Congress of the Communist Party of the Soviet Union. Liu's plan was to join up with a delegation from the Japanese Communist Party, a non-ruling CP of little status in the international hierarchy of Communist parties, to make a joint statement that without mentioning the Soviet Union by name would nevertheless allude to the growing division by criticizing modern revisionism. Mao was furious when he got wind of this proposal and directly confronted the Politburo Standing Committee, headed by Liu, which had made the decision. "Why must we attend?" Mao demanded to know. "So what if we don't show up at all? Are they going to cut off our heads?" He declared that he was "throwing down the gauntlet" in what would be the "final siege of the city." He immediately overturned the decision the Standing Committee had approved and in one fell swoop broke off all channels of dialogue between China and the Soviet Union.

But Mao did not want to stop there. Now he aimed his gun directly at Peng Zhen, Liu's pal. Mao usually gave the formal meetings a wide berth, but in March 1966, he went to the central Chinese city of Hangzhou and attended an Enlarged Standing Committee meeting of the Politburo at which he repeatedly and sharply criticized Peng Zhen. In his March 18 speech to the gathering of all major Central Party leaders, including Zhou Enlai, Mao in an acerbic tone of voice openly condemned Peng's February Outline Report. "Someone in Beijing wants to engage in open rebellion," Mao declared. This was going very far indeed. He warned that the Party Propaganda Department was in danger of turning into the very same hotbed of revisionism that had infected the Rural Work Department headed by the now-disgraced Deng Zihui that Mao had savagely attacked years earlier during the run-up to the Great Leap

Forward. By this time Mao had decided to rid himself of Peng Zhen and to destroy the "independent kingdom" that the powerful mayor had created in Beijing. By doing this, he intended to cut off the left arm and the right shoulder of Liu Shaoqi. But he lacked the requisite authority to follow through with this plan. After floating a few trial balloons with Zhou and Deng Xiaoping, and realizing that he had little support, even from Lin Biao, for such a dramatic move, Mao called off his political dogs and retreated for the time being.

Liu, after the Hangzhou meeting, began an extensive tour of Southeast Asian nations, which was fitting for a head of state to do, if not exactly wise, under the circumstances. While he was gone, security chief Kang Sheng, one of his most fervid opponents, who had until now stayed above the fray, used Liu's absence to unleash on Liu an attack of his own, which provided more fodder for future and heavier cannonades by Mao. While accompanying Mao to a meeting with foreign guests, Kang Sheng brought up the subject of Peng Zhen and the critique of Wu Han by Yao Wenyuan. Kang told Mao that Peng had asked the Propaganda Department to contact its subordinate organization in the Shanghai Municipal Government and investigate why it reprinted Yao Wenyuan's polemic attacking Wu Han and, by implication, himself, without first clearing it with Beijing. Kang was making a sharp accusation. Peng Zhen had violated Party discipline. He had done something even more reprehensible. He had dared to "rectify" Mao, who, after all, had approved distribution of the article.

Kang Sheng thus set the political stage. While Liu was still out of the country, Mao cracked open the entire case against Peng. He had concluded that Peng was engaged in a secret effort to attack the Party Chairman, that he was the major proponent of revisionism in the CCP, and that a revolutionary movement had to be mobilized against him. "If we don't carry out this Cultural Revolution," Mao declared, "then old, middle-aged and young cadres will all be 'subject to withering attack.'" From March 28 to 30, Mao held a series of talks with Kang Sheng, Jiang Qing, and Zhang Chunqiao, the Shanghai Party chief, in which the Chairman expressed his vehement disapproval of the February Outline Report for the way it confused the proper proletarian class line and failed to distinguish between right and wrong. Mao also railed against the CCP's Central Propaganda Department calling it "the kingdom of hell." He charged that the Central Propaganda Department and the Beijing Party Committee were harboring evil people, suppressing the revolutionary left, and opposing the revolution. Mao then declared that if any central organization, the highest authority in China, committed "evil deeds," then he would personally support open acts of rebellion by local authorities. After this particularly outlandish pronouncement, Mao dispatched Kang Sheng to Beijing to convey his message to Zhou Enlai, who, in the absence of Liu, retained control of the routine affairs of the Party Central.

It was up to Zhou alone to determine the direction of political developments. Mao had an inkling of how Zhou might respond, but Zhou refused to reveal his position right away. Zhou knew that Mao was unhappy with Peng Zhen, but he also realized that the Chairman's whole effort was aimed at Liu Shaoqi. Zhou had always managed in the past to tone down the Chairman's animosity toward Peng, but the situation this time was different. Zhou finally issued a report that undermined Peng's position. He had no choice in the matter. "Following the instructions issued by the Chairman ordering us to uphold the banner of the Great Proletarian Cultural Revolution," he wrote, "we must thoroughly criticize any and all counterrevolutionary activities in academic circles of history and philosophy—as nothing more than an attempt at grabbing the power of leadership over the battlefield of culture. Our duty," Zhou continued, "is to elevate the proletariat and eradicate the capitalist element in Chinese society, to organize our own troops and to crack down on counterrevolutionary academic authorities. Following this policy, a draft of a central government announcement will soon be issued and delivered to the Chairman for his personal approval." As for "the report delivered to the Chairman for approval by the five-member group headed by Peng Zhen (known as the February Outline Report author) it is now declared to be incorrect."

When Zhou issued this report, he put Peng Zhen in immediate danger. Now the judgment on Peng was collective, because it came not just from Mao, but from the Standing Committee of the Politburo, which was the ultimate decision-making authority of the Chinese Communist Party. There was only one option available to Peng once this judgment had been rendered. He would have to make a personal apology to Mao in writing and admit his "serious mistakes in this area."

In a flash, the whole political situation in China was up in the air. Chairman Mao had used his mastery of political intrigue to regain his role as the leading actor in Chinese politics. He had decisively won the first round by deposing Peng Zhen, and he was now prepared for the ultimate battle against Liu Shaoqi. Zhou had thrown his support behind Mao while Liu and Deng, who was touring the southwest, were both absent from the capital, and when they returned they had almost no room to maneuver.

Mao made it clear in his own report to Zhou Enlai that when Deng Xiaoping returned to Beijing he wanted him in his capacity as general secretary of the CCP to convene an emergency meeting at which orders would be given to implement the Chairman's instructions. Deng fell into line at the meeting and supported the Chairman's criticisms of Peng Zhen while both Kang Sheng and Chen Boda, Mao's speechwriter, tore into Peng and accused him of all kinds of mistakes on academic and other matters, along with his many so-called historical mistakes.

Zhou joined Deng and condemned Peng for his "anti-Mao line" and agreed to two decisions. The first of these was to deny, with the Central Committee of the Chinese Communist Party, the report by the five-member group headed by Peng Zhen: the February Outline Report. The second was to establish a new group headed by Chen Boda, which later became known as the Central Cultural Revolution Group, to draft a new set of Central Committee instructions on the emerging Cultural Revolution. These instructions would become the basis of the famous May Sixteenth Circular, that would launch the Cultural Revolution nationwide.

Liu Shaoqi, who was still traveling, was unaware of any of these changes, or that Peng Zhen had been pilloried. When he finally returned to Beijing from his Southeast Asian tour, immediately Liu was called to attend an expanded meeting of the Standing Committee to discuss the Peng Zhen problem. Even as he was en route to Hangzhou where the meeting was being convened, Liu was still so in the dark about the entire affair that he had prepared a gift of fresh fruits for Peng. When Liu finally realized what was happening to Peng Zhen, he put up almost no resistance to Mao's overwhelming offensive and accepted its conclusions in silence. Thus did Peng Zhen become one of the first victims of the Cultural Revolution.

Mao was now without a single important opponent. Deng and Zhou had both submitted, abjectly, to his will, and, now that Liu had caved, Mao was virtually uncontrollable. This became clear at the May 1966 enlarged meeting of the Politburo, when the "anti-Party mistakes" by Peng Zhen, General Luo Ruiqing, and former security chief Yang Shangkun were roundly condemned. The meeting also passed the provocative May Sixteenth Circular overturning previous decisions on the February Outline Report and formally established the Central Cultural Revolution Group directly under the authority of the Standing Committee that would be headed by the then-Mao-confidant Chen Boda with the ultimate strings of power manipulated by the Chairman's wife, Jiang Qing. With the birth of this new organization—the Central Cultural Revolution Group—Mao could now directly run the Cultural Revolution.

The enlarged meeting of the Politburo in May 1966 lasted for three weeks. The political temperature rose by the minute. All those who attended were thrown into a frenzy singing the praises of Mao and watching their backs, terrified that they might be next. Lin Biao set the tone of the meeting on May 18 with a fawning speech for Mao. "If Mao were to live to be ninety or one hundred," Lin effused, "he would still remain our highest leader and his thought would forever be our standard. If anyone were ever to make plots behind his back in order to give some secret speech like the one that Khrushchev made against Stalin, that bad egg would be denounced forever by the Party and the nation." Mao claimed that Peng Zhen had actually been planning a military coup. Purportedly, Lin Biao threatened to shoot Lu Dingyi, the liberal intellectual (who had been ousted along with Peng Zhen, Luo Ruiqing, and Yang Shangkun), at the Politburo meeting. Marshal Zhu De, roused from his retirement of many years, had no idea what was going on and gave a speech full of so many faux pas that he was forced to engage in a complete self-criticism.

Zhou Enlai understood the situation completely. He joined the flow. In his second speech to the committee deliberating Peng's fate, Zhou outlined three critical tasks that followed the Mao line: 1. to prevent a counterrevolutionary coup; 2. to understand the relationship between leaders and masses; 3. to learn to "age gracefully." The third point offered insight into Zhou's own inner world at this later stage in his life. Zhou joined up with Mao's crusade against reputed revisionism in the CCP that endorsed the policy of cutting off its proponents and destroying them forever. Like almost all the central leaders who managed to survive Mao's onslaught, Zhou protected himself by calling on everyone in ideological terms to "raise high the red banner of Mao Zedong Thought and unite with Mao into the eternal future." To show that, as an advocate of Mao, he was just as strong as the next man, Zhou declared, "We must follow Chairman Mao, for the Chairman is not just our leader today, but will also be our leader in a hundred years. If one fails the test of loyalty in old age, all the achievements of the past will be for naught."

The radical agenda of the May Sixteenth Circular dissolving the authority of the five-member group headed by the now purged Peng Zhen threw schools and government organs into a state of political turmoil. Mao, however, still wasn't quite ready to make his final move against Liu Shaoqi. The Chairman well understood how much ill feeling had built up within the masses toward the bureaucracies that had been established to administer Chinese Communist rule. This had become all too apparent to the Chairman during the 1957 Hundred Flowers campaign when intellectuals and commoners had railed against Communist Party authorities. Mao's new scheme was to infuriate the masses, and instigate them to direct their rage at Liu.

To carry out this task, Mao exercised his powers of remote control over Jiang Qing and her leftist allies Kang Sheng and Chen Boda. They were all too willing to serve Mao in any way that would advance their political positions. He got them to light a series of fires at the local level any way they could to attract the attention of the local press.

Mao was ever the subtle conductor of these events. He didn't force the issue, but spent leisure time outside Beijing—touring famous mountains and rivers in the south—as he waited for the right moment to deliver the final, fatal blow to State Chairman Liu Shaoqi.

Liu had no idea what Mao was up to. Faced with a firewall of political pressure, he convened an enlarged meeting of the Standing Committee of the Politburo in June 1966. Even though he wasn't quite sure what to do next, he settled on a plan to send work teams from central Party departments to Peking University and other institutes of higher learning and to Beijing area middle schools with a list of eight criteria to guide them, a sort of instruction manual for the Cultural Revolution designed to keep the situation from deteriorating further. At the same time, Liu telephoned Mao for instructions on how to proceed, and traveled in the company of all members of the Standing Committee to the city of Hangzhou, where Mao was holding court, to plead with Mao to return to Beijing and take charge of the situation. Mao, in his usual way, offered little in the way of specific opinions or instructions. His advice to Liu was to "deal with the situation accordingly." Liu thought the Chairman had bestowed on him the highest authority to proceed with his plans to send work teams to disentangle the paralysis that had struck government organs and schools and thereby bring the situation in the capital under control. He completely misinterpreted what the Chairman really had in mind. Liu believed that he was imitating Mao's own practice of dispatching work teams, which the Chairman had done in the recent past to turn the political situation around at *People's Daily* and Peking University.

On this occasion, however, the work teams that Liu sent out were caught between two opposing schools of thought that were now splitting the central government. Instead of calming the situation down, they actually made everything worse by adopting the harsh measures of the 1957 Anti-Rightist Campaign when outspoken opponents of Communist rule in the earlier Hundred Flowers were effectively silenced. These were designed to suppress every conceivable expression of political frustration that students might have wanted to use to vent their dissatisfaction. This time around, the students had been fired up by Mao Zedong, who wasn't about to insist on restraint. Following what was essentially a very conservative and bureaucratic approach, Liu walked right into Mao's trap. His strategy created an immediate confrontation between rebel students and the central government. On several occasions, fired-up students chased the work teams off the premises. This created the huge political bonfire that Mao had prepared to consume the unsuspecting Liu, who continued to wait for Mao to take control.

Zhou Enlai sidestepped the firestorm altogether. He detached himself from the issue of sending work teams onto college and middle school campuses to quell the uproar as students began to physically assault their teachers. This time, Zhou escaped the conflagration that was consuming both Deng Xiaoping and Liu Shaoqi by going away on an extended tour of Eastern Europe (Mao may have granted permission to take the trip just to make sure that his premier wasn't trapped in an impossible situation). Zhou's actual view of the situation was no different from that of Liu Shaoqi or Deng Xiaoping, for he believed that the Chinese Communist Party, operating according to specific procedures and a certain orderly process, had to control any situation of this kind. The only difference between Zhou and his cohorts now was that Mao hadn't targeted him for dismissal, and because he had a generally more moderate outlook he was in a better position to push things through.

The "big character poster" with its large, easy-to-read Chinese-language characters that the Party secretary of the Peking University philosophy department Nie Yuanzi posted as part of her assault on the Beijing municipal government and its policies in running the university provides a case in point. Zhou immediately dispatched

Zhang Yan, deputy director at that time of the Foreign Affairs Office of the State Council, to try to work things out. Zhou told Zhang that he should promote Mao's great decision on these matters in a positive light, but that he should also emphasize that posters of this sort, which began to appear on the network of walls that dominate Chinese cities, should be subject to regulation and, furthermore, that their content should promote persuasion, not coercion. Yet when Mao made his decision to broadcast the revolutionary contents of Nie's poster nationwide, Zhou held his silence. He offered not a single comment, not a word of criticism of the Chairman's actions that might raise the political temperature of the country. And when Liu proposed to send work teams to universities and middle schools in Beijing, Zhou cast an affirmative vote, but he did so sotto voce, and let Deng and Liu play center stage.

All this explains why Zhou suddenly decided to go to Romania. A quick trip to the Eastern European nation would be an excellent way to get out of Beijing and avoid the political Sturm und Drang that was beginning to consume the People's Republic. Mao was all for the idea—without Zhou around his hand would be free to employ the majority to isolate the minority. Mao had no genuine concern for Zhou. His calculations were based on decades of political infighting and concerned his own political advantage only. Mao realized that Zhou had divided the Central Committee further when basically he had sided with Deng and Liu on the need to delegate work teams to stabilize the situation in Beijing. So with Mao's approval Zhou took off for Romania.

The nonconfrontational quality that characterized Zhou Enlai's political philosophy was of great value to Mao. Zhou had made it clear to Mao when he talked about "aging gracefully" that when push came to shove the premier was not going to defy the Chairman. He was essentially loyal. Mao continued to court Zhou Enlai when he returned from his Eastern European sojourn to ensure that he remained a de facto ally. Mao dispatched Kang Sheng to brief Zhou Enlai on the evolving campaign against Liu Shaoqi, and, by doing so, offered a subtle warning: Zhou should not follow the example of Deng and Liu, whose wholehearted support of those work teams was leading them to a quick political grave. Instead, Zhou should maintain close contacts with the newly installed and radically inclined Central Cultural Revolution Group that had been assigned by the May 1966 Politburo meeting to pursue the campaign against revisionists in the CCP.

Mao even showed Zhou his personal letter to Jiang Qing written on July 8, 1966, in which he disclosed to his wife, who at the time was not even a member of the CCP Central Committee, that he was launching the Cultural Revolution "to achieve great order under heaven by creating great chaos under heaven." In sharing the letter, which he showed only to a select few, the Chairman was laying his cards on the table and providing Zhou an anatomy of his innermost thoughts. On this occasion the Chairman also let it be known to Zhou how uneasy he felt about all the flattery in Lin Biao's fawning speech of May 18, which had spread to the newspapers and other national media.

Throughout Zhou's journey to Eastern Europe the situation in China had grown increasingly tense. Between Deng and Liu, on one side, and the newly installed leftist Central Cultural Revolution Group on the other, sharp clashes had broken out over the deployment of work teams. Chen Boda and other leftists in charge of the latter had acted on what they perceived to be the core of Mao's will, which was profoundly opposed to the work teams because they impeded the mass campaign. The leftists proclaimed that the masses should be allowed to take action spontaneously, while Liu and Deng held to the classic Leninist principle that such a policy "would be equivalent to discarding the leadership of the Communist Party." Liu and Deng acted quickly to capture several of the major rebel leaders in the cause of maintaining stability, forcing members of the Central Cultural Revolution Group to beat a hasty retreat. Secretly, the leftists, however, collected documents critical of Liu and turned them over to Mao, who was watching the situation from afar while out on one of his periodic tours of the country in mid-July 1966, when he decided that Liu, who was still pushing the work teams, was approaching his final moments. He gave him a little kick. Mao made a trip to the Yangtze River Valley and took a highly symbolic swim in the steaming river, demonstrating how fit he was at the age of seventy-three. When he got back to Beijing he met with members of the Central Cultural Revolution Group, but when Liu called for his own urgent meeting with the Chairman, Mao informed him that the hour was late and he was going to bed.

Within a few days, Mao figured he had all the goods on Liu that he needed. He issued a formal statement that condemned the work teams for the destructive role they had played in obstructing the mass campaign, which made it imperative to eliminate them.

Liu and Deng now realized that soon they would have to make a full-scale retreat. Even so, they continued to lobby for the work teams at a meeting on July 23. And when Kang Sheng and the leftists, who railed against this strategy of organizational control from above as nothing other than repressing the masses, complained that Liu, who chaired the meeting, wasn't giving them enough time to speak, the whole affair ended in a stalemate. That night, Zhou decided that he had to become more directly involved in the dispute. He shot off a quick letter to Liu and Deng that he hoped would ease the conflict. "Comrades Shaoqi and Xiaoping," Zhou wrote,

> dispatching those work teams throughout Beijing was both appropriate and necessary, but with each team confronting unique conditions and specific situations in each work unit, a clear need for investigation and thorough analysis has emerged. I was at the Beijing Foreign Language Institute this morning examining the various big character posters that had been put up for display to increase my knowledge of the overall situation. I'm telling you this with all deliberate haste. Salute! Sincerely, Enlai.

The letter was dated 4:30 A.M., July 24.

Zhou had a deft talent, when he had to confront some increasingly polarized political situation, for finding some tiny crack in the wall that would allow him to appear even-keeled in his judgments. This letter managed to convey that dispatching the work teams in

Beijing was "necessary," and therefore seemingly took the side of Liu and Deng, but at the same time, by making mention of "specific situations" that required investigation and analysis as the Central Cultural Revolution Group had also proposed, it also revealed Zhou's desire to retain his options. Here is a clear indication that Zhou could set things up so that he could switch gears on a dime, which indeed is exactly what he did when Mao came out against the work teams and Zhou followed suit.

At a meeting on July 29 at Beijing's Great Hall of the People, an official announcement was made to nearly ten thousand revolutionary activists from local universities and middle schools that the work teams were being disbanded. Liu and Deng, as the two leaders who bore most of the responsibility for the policy, engaged in the appropriate self-criticisms to the throng, while the student rebels whom the work teams had victimized were now exonerated. Zhou took the usual middle way. He admitted to "mistakes in dispatching the central work teams" that Liu had authorized to calm the situation on Beijing campuses. But he also threw a bone to the leftists by exhorting "old revolutionaries to use Chairman Mao's works to become fighters and students of Mao Zedong." Liu Shaoqi, now publicly disgraced, was being burned alive by the flames that licked at him on all sides. He let out a huge sigh and proclaimed in his speech, "You people are not clear about just how we should go about promoting a Great Cultural Revolution. You ask me and I haven't the remotest idea. In fact, I don't think comrades in the Party and even in the Party Central do either."

Mao chose not to make a formal appearance at the meeting, but he entered the huge auditorium and sat hidden from view behind a curtain. He became very agitated when he heard Liu's speech, however, and he decided to deal the state chairman a lethal blow. Dr. Li Zhisui, Mao's physician, had joined the Chairman behind the curtain and described the scene this way:

> Mao did not intend to participate in the meeting. He refused to be publicly associated with the likes of Liu Shaoqi and Deng Xiaoping.

But unbeknownst to either the leaders or the students, he did go to the auditorium. Just before the proceedings began, I joined him where he sat, hidden from view behind the curtain. Listening intently, Mao said nothing until Liu Shaoqi made what he called a "self-criticism."

Liu's self-criticism was much like Mao's in 1962. Liu admitted to no wrongdoing, saying only that he and his associates were "old revolutionaries facing new problems." Inexperienced, they did not yet understand how to carry out this Great Proletarian Cultural Revolution.

When Mao heard this, he snorted. "What old revolutionaries? Old counterrevolutionaries is more like it."

My heart sank! I had been deluding myself about the Cultural Revolution, and now its purpose was clear. The ultimate targets were Liu Shaoqi and Deng Xiaoping. They were the "counterrevolutionaries" Mao insisted were hidden in the Party, the "Party people in authority taking the capitalist road." The Cultural Revolution was a campaign to destroy them.

Zhou Enlai followed Liu Shaoqi to the podium, trying to outline for the students the meaning and goals of the Cultural Revolution. Behind the curtain, Mao stood up to leave, ready to return to Room 118, his opulent suite in the Great Hall of the People, not far from the auditorium.

Then suddenly he changed his mind. "We have to support the revolutionary masses," he said.

When Zhou finished his presentation, the curtain behind the stage parted, pulled back by several attendants, and suddenly, unexpectedly, like magic, Chairman Mao stepped through the opening and onto the stage. The crowd roared. Mao waved to the cheering audience, now thundering out its approval with rhythmic chants of "Long Live Chairman Mao! Long Live Chairman Mao!" as the Chairman himself walked back and forth across the stage, slowly waving, saying nothing, his face impassive. With the chants still echoing in our ears, Mao left the stage and walked in triumph back to Room 118, with Zhou Enlai trailing like a faithful dog behind. Mao had neither looked at Liu Shaoqi and Deng Xiaoping nor acknowledged their presence, and the two men, dazed, remained onstage. Few in the audience could have missed Mao's message. He was distancing himself from Liu and Deng. [Dr. Li Zhisui, *The Private Life of Chairman Mao: The Memoirs of Mao's Personal Physician*, translated by Professor Tai Hung-chao (New York: Random House, 1994), p. 470.]

TURNING ON THE POLITICAL HEAT

Despite this triumph, Mao was worried that the situation in Beijing was "too quiet." He decided to initiate a new effort to push the Cultural Revolution. On August 1 (Army Day), 1966, the enlarged Eleventh Plenum of the Eighth Central Committee was called. Mao personally presided over the meeting, which rendered a whole host of decisions, including the decision to remove Liu Shaoqi as vice-chairman of the CCP. The Decision of the Central Committee of the Chinese Communist Party Concerning the Great Proletarian Cultural Revolution (also known as the Sixteen Points) was also passed. The atmosphere at this meeting was extremely intense. Leader after leader did his best to engage in self-criticisms. They all confessed that they had been "slow in adhering to Mao Zedong Thought," and had "committed all kinds of mistakes in their political direction." Attacks on Liu and Deng, however, were very few and far between, even though, before the meeting began, Jiang Qing and Kang Sheng did everything they could to stimulate people to unleash attacks on central leaders. Most participants revealed a complete lack of understanding when it came to what the Cultural Revolution that Mao had launched was all about.

Mao, once again, was disappointed by the evident lack of revolutionary enthusiasm and drive. Mao had fully expected that his presence at the meeting would have an electric effect on the audience, just as his appearance a few days earlier at the Great Hall of the People had ignited the enthusiasm of the young students and directed animosity against Liu Shaoqi. Mao engaged in a number of outside activities, separate from the plenary session, to drum up support, ordering the reprinting of two promotional Red Guard posters and his own letter of support to Red Guards. The materials were then distributed to more than one hundred and thirty participants at the meeting in the hope that this would light a fire under the plenum. But once again, the response was muted. Most cadres were still trying to figure out what was going on. Others expressed antagonism.

Now Mao was worried. Nobody seemed to want to assault Liu; many participants at the Party convocation continued to echo his ideas. People retained fantasies of their own about the state chairman, and they seemed reluctant to break their long habit of supporting Liu's positions. To shift the tide, Mao took the extraordinary step of convening an enlarged meeting of the Standing Committee of the Politburo in the middle of the plenary session and personally attacked Liu for having "suppressed the student movement." He claimed that Liu had engaged in activities no different from those the Nationalist leader Chiang Kai-shek had pursued during the White Terror of the 1930s, which had been designed to wipe out the Communists in China's urban centers. Liu, according to Mao, was following the "wrong political line"; he was "anti-Marxist."

At first, Liu made every effort to contain himself as he confronted Mao's blatant hostility. He accepted blame for his role in supervising the dispatch of the work teams throughout Beijing. Mao, however, in his ravening hunger, refused to halt his attacks. He even pointed his finger at Liu's nose and commented, sarcastically, "You've carried out dictatorship in Beijing! Good work!" When Mao went on to say "As far as I'm concerned, let everything collapse, that's the best thing that could happen," Liu began to lose his patience. He was on fire. He talked straight back to Mao in front of everyone assembled repeating words Mao himself had once uttered. "The worst thing would be for me to step down," he said, "and of this I am not afraid, just as I am not afraid of being downgraded to the level of a basic cadre, kicked out of the CCP altogether, divorced by my wife or even being imprisoned."

Liu's outburst only played into Mao's hands. The Chairman responded, ominously, by declaring, "Ghosts and snakes are present at this meeting." On August 5, even before the meeting had ended,

Mao fired off a big character poster of his own entitled "Bombard the Headquarters" (*Paoda silingbu*) which, without mentioning Liu's name, condemned him "for practicing white terrorism." At the same time, Mao ordered Wang Dongxing, his security chief, to travel to the northeast coastal city of Dalian, to fetch Lin Biao. Lin would replace Liu Shaoqi and be anointed as Mao's official successor.

The split between Mao and Liu was now official. It was up to Zhou Enlai to manage the routine and daily affairs of the Party Central that Liu and Deng Xiaoping had once handled. Zhou now faced quite a quandary: He knew, on the one hand, that Mao's decision to grant him such wide administrative influence was a sign of trust, a long overdue affirmation of the premier's own political performance. On the other hand, Zhou felt uneasy. He knew he was skating on very thin ice. The declaration that Mao had set forth in his August 5 poster calling on people to "bombard the headquarters" was unsettling, but what really put Zhou on edge was that, like many old cadres, he had absolutely no idea what Mao was trying to do. Moreover, Mao's ruthless handling of Liu illustrated the Chairman's capacity to turn on his own men in an instant. Zhou, as ever, could not even contemplate crossing Mao.

Zhou also felt remorse for the political catastrophe that had befallen Liu Shaoqi. For a very long time, Mao had placed great trust in Liu and used him as a counterfoil to Zhou. Although Zhou had greater experience and was more competent than Liu, he had for years been ranked below Liu in the leadership hierarchy of the CCP. On the surface, the two men were polite with one another, but in reality they were intensely competitive. For years they had maintained a respectable distance. Yet Zhou Enlai had an enormous respect for Liu, whom he took as a serious person, one of sound morals and keen mind, who pointed out problems while always paying the utmost attention to his personal cultivation. Zhou would never challenge Mao openly, as Liu had done, but he was also unwilling to let himself be used as Mao's gun in the Chairman's personal games. He again took the middle way. When he made his speech to the plenum on August 1, Zhou insisted that the work teams had been a mistake, openly accepting personal responsibility, and thereby taking some of the heat off of Liu and Deng. Unfortunately, these efforts were all in vain. After Mao had convened the extraordinary enlarged meeting of the Politburo Standing Committee in the midst of the plenum, the pressure to launch attacks on Liu became overwhelming.

Lin Biao, meanwhile, thought he knew what Mao was doing; that is, to counter his own growing power by retaining Deng. Lin therefore intensified his own attacks on Deng and asserted that, like Beijing vice-mayor Wu Han, Deng had been playing political card games. This was a conflict, Lin declared, between "the enemy and the people." This barrage forced Deng to give up his power. During these various assaults on Liu and Deng, Zhou Enlai remained silent. This was basically okay with Mao, who kept one eye open and one eye closed as, in the ever increasing frenzy of the ideologically charged attacks on Liu and Deng, Zhou assumed a low profile. Like it or not, Mao needed Zhou for the time being to operate the controls of Party machinery. That doesn't mean that he didn't test Zhou. On August 5, when Mao issued his own big character poster on the need to bombard the headquarters, and after he had made the decision to replace Liu with Lin Biao, the Chairman called on Zhou and showed him a draft of the poster. "I've watched Liu for twenty-one years and Deng for seven years and they've both let me down," he told Zhou. Then he quickly changed the subject. He began asking Zhou about possible candidates for an official successor even though Mao had already made his decision. He wanted to see how Zhou would answer.

Zhou was no fool. Of the seven current members of the Politburo Standing Committee, the highest executive organization of the CCP, Marshal Zhu De was retired and Chen Yun, the master of economic matters, had been sick for years. That left Lin Biao, Liu Shaoqi, Deng Xiaoping, and himself. Liu and Deng had now been purged, and he and Lin alone remained in contention. Secure in his own position, with no ulterior motive, Zhou once again followed the flow and suggested Lin Biao for the role of Mao's heir apparent.

The Chairman was elated; he decided to anoint Lin as his successor and gave Zhou the task of arranging Lin's return from Dalian. He also made the necessary preparations to convey the momentous decision to all Party, state, and military leaders. Zhou played an essential role as Mao continued with his effort to fundamentally reorganize the central leadership structure. On the night of August 6, he and the Chairman decided on the final sequence of the leadership rankings. The size of the Standing Committee was increased from seven to eleven members. Lin Biao was promoted from number six to second place. Lin was now the only vice-chairman of the Party, the clear successor to Mao. All the other leaders clearly occupied a lower tier.

This did not sit well with Jiang Qing. She could not understand why Deng Xiaoping, after all the errors he'd committed, was upgraded from number seven to number four. She was also concerned because she thought that Chen Boda, Mao's longtime ghostwriter, was entirely too honest and sedate and would never be able to stand up to Deng. She convinced Mao that Tao Zhu, the tough, newly-installed vice-premier, should be elevated to the number-four spot to keep Deng in line. Mao quickly altered the list that Zhou had prepared, summarily demoted Deng, and promoted Tao to number four.

Zhou helped Mao craft a new political blueprint, and he also focused his editorial eye on the important documents that had issued from the Eleventh Plenum, particularly the so-called Sixteen Points that launched the Cultural Revolution. In consultation with the newly appointed Tao Zhu, Zhou decided to cut out highly charged and politically offensive terms like "black gang" and "black line," phrases that were too vague and might have ended up affecting too many people. Zhou also tried to modify some of the more inflammatory language by calling on people to "denounce with words not violence." Zhou argued that distinctions should be made between two very different kinds of conflict: serious and not so serious. Most cadres, he insisted, should be termed good or fairly good. He also wanted to make sure that the campaign would not interfere with industrial and agricultural production and that the utmost care would be taken to protect science and technology personnel.

Clearly Zhou realized that a political storm was about to break out and that he needed to work carefully to keep it under some measure of control. He had stood back and watched up to this point and he'd even escaped abroad on occasion, but he knew now that he was going to have to play a part. Deng Yingchao, his wife, was aware of the shift in Zhou's mindset, and she resolved on a new disciplinary regime that she planned to obey: no meeting with guests, no writing of letters, and no visiting outside the house. At the same time, she called up old friends like Xu Guangping, the companion to Lu Xun, modern China's most famous writer, and Liu Qingyang, a prominent women's leader and wife of Zhang Shenfu, who had brought Zhou Enlai into the CCP in Europe in the 1920s, to warn them that the campaign was unavoidable and that everyone should be prepared to take the test.

Zhou understood the verity of the old Chinese adage that "going with the flow is easier than opposing it." It was the essence of Zhou's lifelong philosophy that "one could only learn how to swim by swimming." These were the principles that guided Zhou as he assumed his new post as the man who now ran the routine affairs of the Party Central and embarked on a political journey that would occupy the final decade of his life, with results that he never could have imagined.

9

"A MAN OF BOTH SIDES"

MAO ZEDONG EMERGED VICTORIOUS FROM THE STRUGGLE TO remove Liu Shaoqi from the top leadership and as heir apparent, but he knew that his own position in the CCP was still shaky. He feared that the state chairman could still make a comeback. Liu had managed the Communist Party apparatus for years, and his influence over key people at the central, provincial, and municipal levels was like a huge tree, so deep-rooted that it was nearly impossible to dig out. Widespread passive resistance in local Party and government bureaucracies to the very idea of the Cultural Revolution illuminated Liu's influence. Nor could the Chairman ignore the substantial influence Liu Shaoqi still exercised over the general population. When Liu visited the site of the Beijing Construction Institute during the period of the Eleventh Plenum in August 1966 to view Mao's big character posters directly attacking him, some people in the crowd shouted "Long Live Liu Shaoqi!" This sort of welcome was usually reserved for Mao. Now the Chairman had a very narrow moment of opportunity in which to destroy Liu's power base and eliminate his influence once and for all. Mao realized that if he didn't act fast, Liu would be able to exploit discontent within Party ranks and strike back.

In a high-stakes game of political survival, Mao decided to take an extraordinary, unprecedented action. He threw his entire support, unequivocally, behind the Red Guards, the groups of students and the malcontents that had only recently begun to form in Beijing. The Chairman turned these young, politically naïve adolescents into his personal attack force, and sent them to the very remotest parts of the country to build up their Red Guard ranks under the banner of promoting "great exchanges of revolutionary experiences." The Chairman used his youth brigades to shatter all resistance in local Party bureaucracies and to fan the flames of the Great Cultural Revolution. During the August 1966 Eleventh Plenum, Mao ordered units of the People's Liberation Army to take up positions outside the nation's capital. Mao seized the occasion to enjoin Lin Biao to applaud the Red Guards for their spirit, and for "daring to charge, daring to wage revolution, and daring to revolt." "Chairman Mao is our supreme commander," Lin, ever obsequious, proclaimed in his speech to the plenum, and revealed his stance to the crowd. In the letter he addressed to Red Guards on August 1, Mao expressed his "strongest support for their actions." In mid-August, the Chairman donned a military uniform for the first time since 1949 and, wearing a Red Guard armband, stood atop the Gate of Heavenly Peace to review the millions of Red Guards who, by then, had streamed into Beijing from the farthest reaches of the country.

Mao had always found inspiration in mass movements. The ecstatic reception the Red Guards gave him at his August 18 appearance atop the Gate of Heavenly Peace in Tiananmen Square provided the Chairman a vision: here was the cult of Mao. He could turn his followers' fanatical mass worship into a hammer with which to drive the last nail into the coffin of Liu Shaoqi. Mao insisted on presiding personally over a series of these mass demonstrations and greeted literally millions of Red Guards from all over the country. The Party Central was no longer willing to put up any resistance to Mao. It backed his every whim 100 percent, and to make this official it issued an order that, to facilitate the "great exchanges of revolutionary experience," Red Guards were free to travel the country, and would receive free rations and lodgings, courtesy of the government, wherever they went.

Equipped with Mao's approval and encouragement, the Red Guard movement engulfed the entire nation with extraordinary speed and ferocity. "Chairman Mao supports us; we will not fail Chairman Mao," proclaimed a Red Guard slogan. These university and middle school students were young, naïve, fanatical, and impulsive. They charged out of their classrooms with reckless abandon, passionately resolved to engage in revolution and rebellion. Lin Biao gave them their directive. "Destroy the Four Olds," he told them. These were old ideas, old cultures, old customs, and old habits. The young, ferocious Red Guards wantonly beat up elderly people, ransacked homes, cut off long hair, chopped off the high heels on women's shoes, burned books and paintings, smashed up shops, converted the traditional names of streets and lanes to ones that were revolutionary, and demolished temples.

Mao issued strict orders to the army and the Public Security Bureau absolutely not to intervene. The Red Guards staged public denunciations and attacked everything in sight. They never gave a thought to the matter of right and wrong. Their special targets were the so-called black elements in local Party and government organs, the purported followers of Liu Shaoqi. Wherever they found Liu's supporters, the Red Guards systematically dragged them out and denounced them, often violently, in public. The violent movement led by the Red Guards catalyzed local resistance, and soon, much of the fabric of normal life in China was in jeopardy.

This Red Guard situation was a source of enormous concern to Zhou Enlai. He had just taken over managing the routine affairs of the Party Central, and although he had voted to approve the decision of the Party Central to launch the Cultural Revolution, he was utterly opposed to the Red Guard's actions. Mao and the Chinese state now sanctioned disorder and chaos. These conditions were an affront to long-standing Party policy, which was designed to impose social and administrative order on the inherently fragmentary Chinese society. Zhou Enlai feared that unless he could somehow restrain the chaos China would spin completely out of control. Zhou also knew that "great chaos under heaven" was Mao's deliberate creation, and he was not about to reverse his own long-standing policy of avoiding direct confrontation with the Chairman. Zhou, the deft veteran, would figure out how to seize the opportune moment and act with great tact. He had perfected the art of walking the political tightrope.

RIDING THE TIGER
DURING THE RED GUARD TERROR

The opportunity to act presented itself to Zhou before long, when the Red Guards embarked on their campaign to destroy the Four Olds. Many of the Red Guard's first victims in this campaign were members of the non-Communist Democratic League, the largest of the so-called satellite parties that, although powerless, had been allowed to exist since 1949 as part of the CCP's united front strategy. These people had supported the Communists in the 1946–1949 civil war to defeat the Nationalists.

As it happened, around this time a prominent political thinker named Zhang Shizhao from Mao's home province of Hunan who had deep ties to the Chairman wrote to Mao to beg for help. Zhang described in detail how Red Guards from Peking University had ransacked his home and hurled denouncements at him, and he pleaded with Mao to "mediate, to the extent possible, and end the trouble." When he read about Zhang's personal plight, Mao sent out the directive, "Forward to the premier to handle as he sees fit. Should provide protection."

Now that Mao had given his personal sanction, Zhou Enlai wasted no time. He acted quickly to protect Zhang Shizhao from the Red Guards, and he also drew up a list of other senior Democratic League leaders who should be spared these attacks. These included Song Qingling, widow of Sun Yat-sen, the founder of the

Chinese Republic; General Fu Zuoyi, the leader of the Nationalist army unit that had defected to the Communist side and peacefully surrendered Beijing to the Communists in 1949; and Li Zhongren, the acting president of the Chinese Republic in 1949 who, after Chiang Kai-shek fled to Taiwan, had surrendered China to the Communists. Zhou also expanded the scope of protection to include Party and government leaders, such as members of the National People's Congress, the Chinese People's Political Consultative Conference, and the State Council, and high-level officials in various government agencies. Zhou made arrangements of all kinds to provide protection for those on his list. Some were allowed to leave their homes temporarily, others were sent to People's Liberation Army hospital 301 on "sick leave," others still were sent out of town to "recuperate," and some were provided with public security guards, who were stationed in front of their homes with orders to persuade the marauding Red Guards to spare them.

Madame Song Qingling created a special problem for Zhou Enlai. In the early years of the People's Republic she had been a non-Communist delegate to the Chinese People's Political Consultative Conference, a largely powerless but highly symbolic advisory committee to the Party leadership. She was also a vice-chairman of the PRC. Mao had dispatched Jiang Qing to visit Song at the outset of the Cultural Revolution to explain to Song why the Chairman found it necessary to launch the Cultural Revolution. Song not only snubbed Jiang; she also openly criticized the Red Guards for harming innocent people. The meeting ended badly. Mao resented Song's attitude toward the Cultural Revolution and he was also offended by Song's treatment of his wife. Jiang Qing, being a person of exalted self-esteem, was deeply insulted. She responded by directing her Red Guard stooges to stage an all-out attack on Song as a major target of their struggle. The Red Guards repeatedly raided Song's home despite Zhou Enlai's orders. They forced the elderly Song to cut off her long hair and they desecrated the graves of her parents in Shanghai and shattered their tombstones. Song was traumatized and soon became ill.

Zhou Enlai had developed a deep friendship with Song over the years and he was greatly concerned about her. He was also apprehensive about Jiang Qing, because he didn't want to directly challenge the "big female boss" in the Cultural Revolution. Zhou persuaded Song Qingling to leave her home in Shanghai and move to Beijing so that he could assign his own contingent of personal guards to protect her. Zhou invoked the authority to provide protection, and made every effort to dissuade provocateurs from plastering Song's residence with the highly inflammatory big character posters that the Red Guards pasted outside the residences of political enemies. He reminded the young revolutionaries that Song was the wife of President Sun Yat-sen, whose accomplishments had been praised by Mao himself in his famous 1949 speech, "On the People's Democratic Dictatorship."

"Song supported us through all her years of cooperation with the CCP," Zhou insisted, "and never once even remotely entertained the idea of joining Chiang Kai-shek and the Nationalists. Her cooperation with the CCP has always been steadfast," he asserted, "and so we are all obliged to respect her, and we must avoid any temptation to strike her down just because her sister, Song Meiling, happened to marry the Nationalist leader Chiang Kai-shek."

Zhou took an extra step later to give Song a little comfort when he ordered the Shanghai government to repair and immediately restore the desecrated graves of her parents and send Song photos of the finished sites. Zhou defied Jiang Qing and used the centennial of Sun Yat-sen's birth as an opportunity to make amends to Song. He instructed the People's Publishing House to reprint the *Selected Works of Sun Yat-sen*. The publisher also issued newly edited versions of the *Selected Works of Song Qingling* on which Zhou had personally inscribed the title with his own calligraphy.

The Red Guard movement swelled as officials, intellectuals, and teachers were pilloried in an orgy of public denunciations. Zhou made an intense effort to keep some control over the situation from the very moment the Party gave a green light to the Cultural Revolution at the August 1966 Eleventh Plenum. In the two months that followed, he labored tirelessly to tweak the Red Guard ideology and soften the inflammatory language encouraged by the plenum. He set forth broad directions for the movement aimed at moderating its approach. "Emphasize the dissemination of Party policy; strive to quell fanaticism and destructiveness; try to bring the situation under control," he ordered. Zhou spent sleepless days and nights attending all kinds of panel discussions and report conferences, and all the while he stayed in close contact with the Red Guards, talking to them, tirelessly urging them to "stay strictly disciplined, find common cause with the majority and denounce with words, not violence."

The Red Guards wanted to indiscriminately obey Mao's call to "bombard the headquarters." However, as he tried to modify their behavior, Zhou, in his usual tactful way, carefully sidestepped the question of Mao's original intent. "One should not take Mao's call too literally," Zhou advised the Red Guards, "and attack all Party and state organizations. It's not supposed to be an excuse to beat people up indiscriminately, or to treat all leaders as if they were 'black elements.' Party and government leaders aren't all capitalist roaders," he said as he pleaded with the Red Guards. "If you see things this way, where do you put the Party Central? And where in this scheme do you put the wise leadership of Chairman Mao?"

Now that the Cultural Revolution was in full swing, Mao kept both hands on the campaign as it developed, one through the leftist and radical Central Cultural Revolution Group headed by Chen Boda, which was actually dominated by his wife, Jiang Qing, and the other through Party Central, where Zhou Enlai was managing the routine and daily affairs of the remaining organizational apparatus. Now that the Central Cultural Revolution Group was under the direct authority of the Standing Committee of the Politburo, Mao, as Chairman, was squarely in charge of the mass movement that was unfolding.

The responsibilities of the two groups—the Central Cultural Revolution Group and the Party Central—were on a collision course. Leaders of these two groups constantly confronted each other. Jiang Qing, for instance, was furious about Zhou's efforts to assuage Song

Qingling. When she got her hands on a copy of Song's recently published *Selected Works,* with its title inscribed in Zhou's personal calligraphy, Jiang threw the book on the floor and began stamping on it with her feet, screaming, "The premier! He even inscribed it for her!"

Mao was less than pleased by reports of Zhou's moderating role in the communiqués that Jiang sent him, but he was preoccupied with controlling the overall direction of the movement. When he heard that peasants and workers in some areas were attacking rebel students, Mao was convinced that local cadres still loyal to Liu Shaoqi must have approved the attacks. He realized that although he had thrown Liu Shaoqi to the dogs, the state chairman still had substantial influence within Party and government ranks. Mao now made it his number-one priority to eliminate this major roadblock to total revolution.

Mao always turned to history for answers. This time, his model was the titanic struggle waged in the 1940s against the pro-Soviet leader Wang Ming and his Twenty-Eight Bolsheviks—the Russian Returned Students—who had challenged his leadership during the critical Yan'an period. Mao had managed to get the upper hand by accusing Wang and his supporters of pursuing a fundamentally incorrect Party line. Mao applied this strategy to the present situation and concluded that, if he directed the same accusation at Liu Shaoqi, he could undermine Liu's remaining support within the CCP apparatus by appealing to the basic ideological frame of mind of Party members who placed correct Party line before everything.

Zhou took a dim view of this strategy. As he saw it, inflating the current situation to the level of the correct Party line would only extend the attacks and accusations to a much wider range of people and drag the movement into an endless black hole. True to form, however, he made every attempt to convince cadres that they would somehow have to cope with this directive. To convince his comrades, Zhou often resorted to what can only be called rhetorical babble. "It's a source of great glory and happiness to live in such triumphal times and to participate in such a great battle," he spouted at a Central Committee Work Conference in late August

1966. Zhou then provided a convenient rationale for any errors he and his cohort might commit in the ongoing great battle. "It's no big deal if we make some mistakes," he declared. "We should all get rid of them. We should all raise the banner of Mao Zedong Thought and stride right ahead. This era in China is an even greater one than the Stalinist years of the 1930s and 1940s, for we are confronting the great issue of world revolution. Is there any aspect that we as individuals cannot eliminate?"

Zhou gave every appearance that he was caught up in the frenzy. "We have nothing to fear from attack, do we?" he said.

> We're not enemies. If wrongful attacks are committed then it's nothing more than a misunderstanding. Get to know each other through fights and learn how to bear with it, and to sustain ourselves. That's the test. In the past, we were tested by our enemies and now it's the mass movement that's testing us. When the masses struggle against you, criticize you, and have nothing good to say about you, this is very serious, and you must learn how to take it. It's the only way to emerge from this struggle as a good pupil of Mao Zedong.

If there were any doubt about where he stood on the subject of the Cultural Revolution, Zhou Enlai made himself clear at another Central Work Conference that convened in October 1966.

> Criticism by the masses is not easy to take, not as good as kind words, but overall it is good for you, a true expression of love for the leadership; as the saying goes, "Bitter medicine cures the disease." Of course what we are talking about here is not revolutionizing your entire political life. Rather, it is the "life" of the bourgeoisie that we want to launch our revolution against. The fact is that few of us had the experience of the mental preparation for this Cultural Revolution. But Chairman Mao sees everything very clearly and understands where we are going. And so if anyone is unsure about the nature or course of this movement, fear not because Chairman Mao is there for all of us to follow and none of us should falter. Only

when we follow the Chairman closely, and firmly take the correct stand, will we avoid falling behind so far we end up joining the bourgeois camp.

Actually, Zhou Enlai believed that the Cultural Revolution was utter nonsense.

"Never in my wildest dreams did I think anything like this could occur," Zhou openly admitted days later at the same October 1966 Central Work Conference. "Whenever I think about it, shivers go down my spine, and my whole body breaks into a cold sweat."

Yet even as he revealed his doubts about the entire affair, Zhou soldiered on and followed closely behind Mao Zedong.

In reality, Zhou Enlai was fully aware of the double role he was playing in the Cultural Revolution. More than once he described how during the Cultural Revolution he had "bent to do my duty until my dying day." Following Zhou's death in 1976, these words of Zhou's were frequently cited as the truest expression of his great personal integrity whereas, in fact, they reflected his true internal conflict. On the one hand, he knew Mao was dragging the country toward unprecedented chaos and disaster and yet Zhou continued to follow his personal mantra of "aging gracefully" that prevented any direct confrontation with the Chairman. On the other, his personal conscience urged him to do whatever he could to save the country. Perhaps that's why the Mao button that Zhou, like everyone in the country at this time, wore above the left pocket of his tunic, had a portrait of Mao on one side and the words "serve the people" on the other. Somehow he was trying to achieve a psychological balance between what was rapidly becoming two diametrically opposed commitments.

KEEPING THE BARBARIANS AT BAY

The low-key comments Zhou made about Liu Shaoqi provide stark evidence that he was not fully committed to the Cultural Revolution. He voiced himself on the subject of Liu in decidedly cautious terms; clearly, he did not want to be someone's hired gun. Whenever he could, Zhou emphasized that the matter of Liu Shaoqi was an internal Party matter, that the cases of both Liu and Deng Xiaoping had been solved by the Party Central. During one of Zhou's many meetings with the Red Guards in September 1966, someone suddenly shouted out, "Down With Liu Shaoqi!" Others took up the cry. Zhou turned his back to the audience as a clear indication of his disapproval without making a single comment that would allow someone to record "heretical words." He refused to rejoin the discussion until all the shouting had ceased. Then, invoking Party history that few in the room probably understood, Zhou noted that comrades who had committed mistakes in the Party line were still genuine revolutionaries and certainly could never be branded as counterrevolutionaries. Such individuals, Zhou lectured the group, were fundamentally different from people who formed true counter-revolutionary cliques, or so-called independent kingdoms. "I have my own experiences with this," Zhou confessed. "Before the Long March I made my own mistakes in Party Line, but Mao did not deprive me of an opportunity to correct them. If anyone here disagrees with me about this I'd like to sit down and talk about it and even have a debate."

Zhou's nuanced approach to the subject of Liu Shaoqi was, once again, clear when he made preparations for National Day celebrations on October 1, 1966. To Zhou, as the leader who arranged all the routine affairs of the Party Central, fell the important political task of arranging where the top leaders all stood in order of their importance atop the Gate of Heavenly Peace overlooking Tiananmen Square in central Beijing. Liu had been demoted in Party rank from number two to number eight and was no longer the heir apparent, but protocol required the state chairman to assume a prominent place on the dais. Zhou, attentive as always to every detail, decided that Mao should stand in the middle, flanked on his right side by members of the Politburo, and, on his left, in their order of importance, by members of the government, which, in Chinese political organization, is technically separate from the CCP. This placed Liu Shaoqi on Mao's immediate right, something that outraged Jiang Qing and her supporters.

The battle to seize power from Party and government authorities by rampaging Red Guards spread like wildfire across China. Persecution of officials reached an all-time high. Students turned struggle meetings into horrible displays of violence and inflicted torture and, on some occasions, death on their victims, even though Zhou Enlai had exhorted them to "denounce with words, not violence." Zhou didn't realize it, but several months later, in January and February of 1967, a number of top officials were hounded to their deaths, including Zhang Linzhi, minister of the coal and mining industry at the time, who had reportedly committed suicide. After his death, Zhang was vilified by his persecutors as a traitor to the Party. When he heard this news, and learned, also, about the death of Zhao Erlu, the vice-chairman of the State Committee for Science and Technology, Zhou Enlai was greatly shaken. In the midst of the "great chaos under heaven," however, mandated by Mao, Zhou could do very little. He ordered an investigation into the cause of the death of Zhang Linzhi, even though a cursory examination of the minister's body clearly revealed that he was the victim of a brutal beating. The premier was so powerless that he could not even arrange a proper burial for Zhang, which haunted Zhou for the rest of his days. Years later, once the chaos had subsided, Zhou personally drafted a document titled "Suggestions on Handling the Death of Zhang Linzhi" that officially classified Zhang's children as "offspring of a revolutionary cadre" to ensure that they would be entitled to state dispensation.

Immediately after he learned of Zhang Linzhi's death, Zhou Enlai moved quickly to create a comprehensive plan that would provide a measure of security for top-level Party cadres and state officials. First, he made an arrangement that allowed the heads of the more than thirty government ministries to take turns living within the relatively safe confines of the Central South Lake leadership compound in Beijing. This liberated these officials from the routine struggle meetings that took place nearly every day and threatened their health. Zhou also drew up a list of twenty or thirty high-ranking Party secretaries and provincial governors from outside the capital who were now authorized to enter Beijing for purposes of medical recovery. Once there, they took up residence at the Jingxi Guest House, where Zhou's special order afforded them personal security. Those who managed to survive were profoundly grateful to the premier and after the Cultural Revolution they likened Zhou Enlai to the "tall tree to heaven that protected Chinese heroes." One old cadre expressed what everyone felt. "God bless the premier," he declared. "The premier cannot fall, for without him we would have been children without a mother."

Zhou endeavored to protect old cadres with the utmost caution. He took Mao Zedong's political temperature at every opportunity to make sure that he had found the middle ground, taking pains not to antagonize the Chairman, Jiang Qing, or Lin Biao. Although he was sympathetic to Liu Shaoqi, Peng Dehuai, and Marshal He Long, Zhou was careful not to cross any political lines.

In one famous incident, rebel students at Beijing's prestigious Tsinghua University set a trap, in January 1967, to arrest Wang Guangmei, Liu Shaoqi's revered wife. They tricked the unsuspecting Wang to leave the safe confines of Central South Lake by telling her that her daughter had been struck by a car and was in the hospital with a broken leg. Once she was outside the compound, they arrested Wang and subjected her to humiliation. Zhou got word and dispatched his personal secretary to negotiate with the students to secure Wang's release. At midnight, when all was calm, Zhou telephoned Madame Wang. "Ah Guangmei," he told her. "You must bear this test."

Fourteen years later, when Liu Shaoqi was officially rehabilitated, and his good name as a leader of the CCP was restored, his children recalled this trauma that their mother had endured and the role played by Zhou Enlai. "At the time," they declared, in a paean to Zhou Enlai, "the trust and sympathy overwhelmed our mother. One word stirred up thousands of thoughts in her, but how could she express what she wanted to say? So her response was simple. 'Premier,' she said, 'you are so kind.'"

Zhou's ability to protect Wang Guangmei was strictly limited, just as it was to help so many highly prized targets of the Red Guards. Later, Wang was repeatedly victimized by the rebel students in humiliating ordeals during which she was dressed up as a common prostitute. Unlike her husband, she would survive the Cultural Revolution, but she was imprisoned for many years.

Sometime earlier, in December 1966, acting under instructions from Jiang Qing's Central Cultural Revolution Group, the Red Guards transferred former Marshal Peng Dehuai from the city of Chengdu in Sichuan Province, where he had been previously dispatched by Mao Zedong, back to the capital, to endure a series of struggle meetings. Zhou heard about this and immediately moved to ensure Peng's personal safety. He issued three detailed instructions by phone. "First," he said, "troops from the Chengdu Military Region must accompany the Red Guards when they escort Comrade Peng Dehuai to Beijing. No one can interfere or intercept the transfer. Peng's security must be guaranteed, which means no abusive language or behavior. Next," Zhou declared, "the transfer must be arranged by Military Region commanders and has to be by train, not by air. Finally, security forces in the capital will meet the train when it arrives in the Beijing railway station and personally escort Peng to his accommodations, where he will be allowed to study."

Years later, Peng's personal aide-de-camp recounted the dramatic impact that Zhou's actions had on the former minister of defense in his memoir *Beside Chief Peng*.

When no one was present I conveyed to Peng the three instructions that Premier Zhou had issued. For a moment the chief went completely silent. Then he asked, "Really?" "Yes," I responded. "And did he really call me comrade?" Peng wanted to know. "Yes! Yes! He said it twice, very clearly," I said. Peng put his head in his two hands and turned to the wall. I could see his shoulders tremble with excitement. He only finally turned around after quite a long while.

The protective reach of Zhou Enlai's tall political tree was not unlimited. After he returned to Beijing, Peng Dehuai, the former commander of the Chinese People's Volunteers in the Korean War, was dragged unceremoniously to innumerable "struggle meetings," where he was accused of having illicit dealings with Nikita Khrushchev. A rugged man of tough stock, Peng survived the physical assault and violence. He died in 1974, and, once the Chairman had left the scene, he was rehabilitated, like so many victims of the Cultural Revolution.

In one case, Mao Zedong actually joined Zhou in an effort to protect a top leader, namely Marshal He Long, another prominent military figure. The premier's ties to He Long went back forty years or more; Zhou had been a major force in his life from the very moment He Long had joined the revolution, and together the two men had been closely involved in the 1927 Nanchang Uprising, when He Long, then a disaffected Nationalist officer, had provided key resources to Zhou's military operation. Mao's relationship with He Long had been equally cordial over the years. When Mao had wanted to marry Jiang Qing back in the Yan'an days, he ran into a storm of resistance from other Party leaders, but He Long showed his rustic military bearing and stood up for Mao. "You're the Chairman," he announced. "What's this fuss over a woman all about? If any of them brings this up again I'll personally shoot 'em." He Long didn't mince words when he took the side of Mao against Wang Ming and his Soviet backers in the late 1930s and early 1940s. "Chairman Mao's direction is our Party's direction," he warned. "So just what does this man Wang Ming know? If he wants to ride herd over Chairman Mao, I'll take him out with one bullet." In the somewhat rarefied little world of Yan'an, He Long's words came as a shock.

Mao did not perceive this old soldier as a potential enemy. The problem was Lin Biao, who considered Marshal He Long a thorn in his side. Of the two military heroes, He Long had been far less successful in battle than Lin Biao, but he enjoyed stronger support and greater seniority by far in the military ranks. He Long had been the top military commander in the Nanchang Uprising, while Lin Biao at that time had been a mere company commander. He Long was much admired for his straightforward military style. He was considered a gallant leader who cared deeply for all his officers and soldiers, and over the years this had earned him a good reputation. In this sense, He Long was the only man left with real power to counter Lin Biao's still somewhat tenuous command of the People's Liberation Army.

At the outset of the Cultural Revolution, Mao had hoped to mediate the obvious conflict and tension between He Long and Lin Biao, but he had little success. Jiang Qing, at a hastily called meeting of the Party Central, made a move to line up with Lin Biao against Mao by bringing up the case of He Long, although it was not on the agenda, and Mao had been distinctly ambivalent about raising the matter at all.

"Why are we not striking down He Long?" Jiang Qing demanded to know.

"This matter is not up for discussion right now," Mao replied coldly.

"Chairman," Jiang persisted. "Are we going to inhibit the masses from rising up? If that's the case then I'm going to rebel against you."

"The meeting is adjourned," Mao replied curtly, and that was that—at least for the moment.

Zhou Enlai intended to do his best to protect He Long when he was targeted; he spoke up on more than one occasion to defend He Long, and he did whatever he could to quell anti-He Long sentiment. Very few people know that on one occasion, when Mao was reviewing Red Guard detachments parading through Tiananmen Square in front of the Gate of Heavenly Peace, Zhou made arrangements so that He Long could ride along in the military jeep with the Chairman, while Lin Biao was consigned to a follow-up vehicle. Zhou clearly wanted to show the public that He Long belonged to "the headquarters of Mao." The Central Cultural Revolution Group, under the influence of the headstrong Jiang Qing, immediately lodged a protest and tried to prevent the publication of a photograph of Mao's review because it would reflect poorly on Lin's position as Mao's new heir apparent. Two contending parties spent an entire evening trading fire over the photo before Zhou came up with a solution that pacified everyone when he finally hit on the idea of referring to Lin Biao in the photo caption as the Chairman's "closest comrade-in-arms," a phrase that would stick to Lin Biao for years to come.

Zhou's defense of He Long had its limits. The premier underwent a change of mind when the attacks on the old marshal intensified, especially when he realized that Lin Biao was doing everything in his power to oust He Long. Zhou didn't want to offend Lin Biao, who had emerged as the nation's deputy commander-in-chief, and, because Mao's attitude about the affair hadn't changed, Zhou realized that he could still rely on the Chairman's ambivalence to relieve the pressure on He Long and fend off Lin Biao and Jiang Qing, who were lurking behind the curtains, ready to attack.

By the end of 1966, the most radical faction of Red Guards, the revolutionary rebels (*zaofanpai*), were rampaging through the eastern section of Beijing where the old marshal lived, breaking into houses near his residence. Zhou tried to offer He Long protection by moving him temporarily to the western suburbs so that he could get some rest. "I'll take care of things at your home," the premier assured He Long. The old marshal decided to just go back home and wait for the Red Guards to show up. They were now hot on his heels. Zhou even moved to protect He Long by inviting the old marshal to stay in his personal residence at Western Flower Pavilion in the leadership compound of Central South Lake. That's the legend. Actually, the truth is more complicated. He Long's wife telephoned the premier on three separate occasions and pleaded with him to deal with the emergency situation that she and her husband confronted, but she could not get a reply. One evening, when He Long was passing by Central South Lake, he decided he'd drop in on the premier to report the decision he'd made to confront his fate with the revolutionary rebels. This was a hot potato for Zhou, one he couldn't afford to fumble. Zhou wasn't at home when He Long paid his call, but his secretary invited He Long and his wife to come in and wait for him. When Zhou finally returned home, He Long was his usual straightforward self. "Premier," he said. "He Long is in trouble. I came here to beg you!" Forty years earlier, when the revolution had been on the verge of failure, and the fledgling Communist movement had been close to political extinction, Zhou had made a similar plea to He Long. Now that the tables were turned, and it was He Long who was in trouble, the old marshal thought Zhou was obligated to help out. Zhou acquiesced to this pressure and agreed to provide He Long and his wife refuge under his roof.

Zhou, and Deng Yingchao, looked after He Long throughout their stay, but never once did they raise the matter of He Long's political problems, even though He Long stood by the front window of Zhou's house every day waiting for the premier to come home so that he could talk to him about his personal frustrations and feelings. But Zhou never gave him the opportunity. Ultimately, Mao was the one who determined the fate of He Long, when he finally gave Lin Biao the green light to do whatever he wanted to his nemesis (Mao needed Lin Biao's support at the time). Lin quickly denounced He Long as a "peasant bandit" and an "enemy of Chairman Mao" at a January 1967 emergency meeting of the Central Military Affairs Committee of the CCP and personally met with Zhou Enlai and pressured him to hand over his house guest.

Zhou, who above all avoided conflict with Mao, had to comply somehow with Lin's demand. He arranged to have He Long transferred elsewhere in the name of securing his personal protection. By fall 1967, however, when He Long indicated that he wanted to go back to his old residence in Beijing, as Zhou had promised him, the Party Central set up an official group to investigate the case of He Long. The final report, as per protocol, went to Zhou Enlai, who made a number of corrections and added some comments of his own. Many people later tried to relieve Zhou Enlai of any kind of responsibility for the persecution of He Long, but in his heart Zhou knew that he had collaborated. The marshal died of diabetes under suspicious circumstances in June 1969.

10

A WHIRLPOOL
OF ABSURDITY

December 26, 1966. Mao Zedong, Chairman of the Chinese Communist Party, celebrated his birthday at a specially arranged party in his Central South Lake villa. Guests included members of the Central Cultural Revolution Group who engaged the Chairman in spirited discussions on a night when Mao decided on his strategic plan for an "all-out seizure of power" by revolutionary rebels. Raising his glass, Mao shocked his honored guests with his toast to "all-out civil war in the nation."

This strategy of Mao's culminated during the 1967 "January Storm," in Shanghai, where leftist forces deposed the city's sitting Party Committee. The booming propaganda machine of the leftist Central Cultural Revolution Group called this the greatest festival in the history of international Communism, and the greatest innovation, but the geysers of ink the leftists squandered in the act of praising their own power grab couldn't mask the bloody truth. The country was, as Mao had predicted, close to civil war.

This was starkly apparent at a joint meeting of the CCP Politburo and the Central Cultural Revolution Group in February 1967, chaired by Zhou Enlai at Cherish Benevolence Hall (*Huairentang*) in Central South Lake. The pent-up anger of high- and mid-level officials exploded like a bomb. These people formed the core of the Chinese Communist Party and the People's Liberation Army. All the old and venerable cadres who had liberated China and run the country for almost two decades were now gathered in the hall, lashing out at the crimes of the leftist rabble-rousers. They were furious, but Mao's fury was even greater and ultimately it destroyed them all. It annihilated an entire generation of old cadres. Zhou Enlai was the only one who managed to safely and deftly navigate his passage through the ordeal and it took all the political skills he could muster: Taoist-like concealment and endurance were combined with obedience and strategic defense, along with a two-timing personality and the face of Janus revealed to all.

The political explosion that erupted from February 11 to 16, 1967, dramatically changed the composition of the political leadership in the CCP from the Party Central to the grass roots. It came to be known as the February Adverse Current. The conflict began the previous October within the military when the minister of defense, Lin Biao, issued urgent instructions on a number of matters that were effectively rubber-stamped by the Central Military Affairs Committee and the General Political Department of the People's Liberation Army, the body set up to ensure CCP control of the army. Rebel students had been mobilized, at China's major universities and elite middle schools, into action against Party organs, and Lin's order encouraged rebels within the military academies to do the same thing and launch their own revolutions without the leadership of the Party. Rebel military groups stormed into Beijing in the name of carrying out investigations of "black materials" that could incriminate top officers within the PLA. They surrounded the headquarters of the Ministry of Defense and rapidly pulled the army, China's last source of civil order, into the maelstrom of the Cultural Revolution.

Lin Biao's initial ploy was to eliminate his many rivals in the top ranks of the PLA by invoking Mao's call to launch attacks against all bourgeois counterrevolutionaries. It never seems to have occurred to Lin when he lit his own little bonfire that it would spread out of control into his own backyard. Soon the rebels were targeting high-ranking military officials, including many in the Ministry of Defense, who were attacked in the same manner as officials from the Party and local government organs. Rebel students dragged these military personnel onto the streets from their offices and ripped their badges and collars off and forced them to kneel. Some they killed. Suddenly, telegrams were flying in from military districts and regions all over the country pleading for help.

Officers in the highest reaches of the military hierarchy reacted with a sense of extreme urgency as chaos inside the ranks began to destroy the viability of the Chinese army. The ominous possibility occurred to some of the old PLA marshals—Ye Jianying, Xu Xiangqian, Nie Rongzhen, and others—that foreign powers might seize this time of internal turmoil within China's defense forces to make trouble. "The more chaotic the situation is in local governments," the marshals argued, "the more stable the military has to be." Marshal Ye Jianying held a position on the Central Military Affairs Committee that gave him the responsibility for running the day-to-day affairs of China's armed forces. He did everything in his power to keep the Central Cultural Revolution Group from deploying its forces within the ranks of the military. He constantly found himself facing down leftist leaders, while Lin Biao generally avoided any involvement and issued no opinion on the matter. Lin's primary purpose was to follow Chairman Mao, but he did not want to antagonize the Central Cultural Revolution Group, either. Yet Lin was a military man, and he shared a concern with Ye and the other marshals about the trouble that would follow if the army slipped into chaos.

Mao was acutely sensitive to the differences that separated government cadres and military officers. He understood what a dangerous game it was to offend the marshals. They might take matters into their own hands and rebel. He needed the military for his own purposes. The all-out seizure of power in early 1967 wasn't going all that well. Across China, established authorities were often defeating leftist groups in political struggles so that power was falling into the hands of conservative factions that wanted to terminate the Cultural Revolution, a complete reversal of Mao's aim. On numerous occasions military officials had to be called in to reduce tensions. On January 22, 1967, Mao met with top military leaders during the convocation of an enlarged meeting of the Central Military Affairs Committee of the CCP and warned them not to "live on the laurels of their past achievements." He exhorted them to make new contributions to the revolution. But Mao realized that the marshals were unhappy with the entire Cultural Revolution, and he allowed himself to sit for a while and listen to their complaints. "The military must be prepared for war," he then declared. "It should remain stable and unified without any internal splits."

Lin Biao was infuriated. He told the Central Cultural Revolution Group that if they wanted to pick a fight with the marshals they could "come right over and struggle against me." He asked Jiang Qing to come over to his Maojia Bay residence so that he could vent some of his rage at her. The liberation army that Chairman Mao had founded and led was now on the verge of turning into a force for revisionism. "How do you explain that?" he asked her. "What am I supposed to say about all this as minister of defense? If the army does indeed become a force for revisionism there's no hope for the country," he ranted. "It's finished." As Lin spewed out his anger at the situation unfolding, Jiang made the obligatory self-criticism. In his rage, Lin kicked over the coffee table in front of him, making Ye Qun, his wife, cry out and beg him not to offend Jiang Qing. Lin, however, was beside himself, and ordered his wife to throw Jiang Qing out of the house. He threatened to resign from his job.

Lin never acted on this threat. He gave in to the tearful persuasion of his wife once he had blown off steam. But Jiang Qing had seen Lin's viciousness. The seeds had been sown for the ultimate confrontation between Jiang Qing and Lin Biao three years later, when they would engage in an all-out power struggle at the August 1970 Second Plenary session of the CCP Central Committee that drove the official successor to apparently allow an ill-fated assassination attempt against Mao Zedong and ended with the disappearance of the Chairman's "closest comrade-in-arms" from the Chinese political scene.

Mao, meanwhile, made a new political move in the early months of 1967, even as he tried to smooth the ruffled feathers of the PLA marshals, when he ordered Lin Biao to send in army units to support the left. The military was Mao's last card. Factional fighting had escalated across the country far beyond the Chairman's expectations and the Party and government were utterly paralyzed. Mao knew that he had to figure out how to handle the barrage of complaints issuing from military leaders. During a February meeting of the Central Politburo he joined with other disgruntled political leaders and fired some criticisms against Jiang Qing and Chen Boda. "All you want to do," Mao railed at Chen Boda on February 10, "is to use one group to smash another group." Mao gave Jiang Qing a truly bitter tongue lashing. "You can't see beyond your own nose," he told her. "You have great aspirations but not an ounce of talent."

Whenever Mao performed an action, however, he also took a measure to counteract it. This is what he now did, as he discreetly raised the political status of the Central Cultural Revolution Group and gave it powers long exercised by the CCP Secretariat, which for years had been responsible for overseeing appointments throughout the vast organizational apparatus. When he sent off a congratulatory telegram to the newly installed leftist authorities in Shanghai, who had successfully engaged in an all-out seizure of power in January 1967, Mao listed the Central Cultural Revolution Group right alongside the Central Committee, the State Council, and the Central Military Affairs Committee. By doing so, he virtually put the leftist-dominated body on a par with the supreme institutions of the Chinese state.

Zhou Enlai was less than optimistic about where the Chairman was taking the country. Zhou was just about the only person who understood why the Chairman was promoting the Central Cultural

Revolution Group. Most high-ranking Party officials had no idea why Mao was cultivating these people. Mao appeared to be willing to calm things down throughout the country, but it was never easy to read his political moves. Zhou was convinced that Mao was putting on a big show when he staged his criticism of Chen Boda and Jiang Qing. Zhou shared many of the same worries the marshals had expressed to Mao and he hoped their counterattack would convince the Chairman to end the madness and rein in the activities of the Central Cultural Revolution Group, but he kept his own counsel and watched events unfold with a cool eye. He refused to commit himself to either side. This was his usual modus operandi. Years of one political struggle after another had convinced the premier that he had to be prepared to switch in a flash from offense to defense. In the present situation, it worried him that the marshals would go overboard when they took on the chaos and excesses of the Cultural Revolution and throw the advantage to the leftists and drag down a whole host of leaders, himself included.

Zhou Enlai chaired a meeting of the Standing Committee of the Politburo at Cherish Benevolence Hall on February 11, 1967, in the midst of a flurry of activity by the central leadership to cope with the growing crisis generated by the intensifying chaos of the Cultural Revolution. He wanted to discuss ways to maintain an even economic keel and to balance that interest with the political goals of the Cultural Revolution. The marshals, however, used this occasion to attack the leftists. They were emboldened by Mao's biting critique of Jiang Qing and Chen Boda, the titular chief of the Central Cultural Revolution Group. Marshal Ye Jianying, the first to speak, gave Chen Boda an earful. "You've made a mess of the Party," thundered Marshal Ye. "You've made a mess of the government, a mess of the factories and a mess of the countryside. And still you aren't satisfied. Now you have to make a mess of the army, too." Marshal Xu Xiangqian was next. "What is it that you want?" he demanded of Chen Boda. He banged on the table. "The army is a pillar of the proletarian dictatorship, but the way you're making a mess of it, it's as if you didn't want this pillar. Are you trying to say that none of us is worth saving?" Xu mentioned the notorious revolutionary rebel leader, Kuai Dafu, from Tsinghua University, and asked Chen Boda, point blank, "Do you want people like Kuai Dafu to command the army?"

The leftists did not have much to say in their own defense. The meeting was quickly adjourned. Zhou sat back and listened rather passively to arguments by both sides and offered few comments and very little in the way of a reaction. He let both sides have at each other and withheld his own observations until the very end, when, as chair, he noted that the discussion had veered from the intended agenda. He recommended to the participants the possibility that an opportunity to extend the argument would present itself on some later occasion.

The arguments between the two sides continued on February 16. Tan Zhenlin and Chen Yi, two vice-premiers, led the charge for the military. Tan had a reputation in the CCP as a big cannon and was best known because he had stuck with Mao during the fiascoes of the 1958–1960 Great Leap Forward. He was furious on this occasion at Zhang Chunqiao, the radical Shanghai leader who, after the all-out seizure of power in the city, had prevented Chen Pixian, the deposed leader of the Shanghai Communist Party, from traveling to Beijing, using the prohibition by the masses as his excuse. Tan aimed his big gun at Zhang and his leftist coterie. "Your aim is to purge all the old cadres," he declared, "striking them down one by one until there's not a single old cadre left. These old cadres have devoted their lives to the revolution for forty years, and now they are ending up with broken families, lost wives and sons. Of all the struggles in the Party, this is the cruelest one of all." Tan grew more and more enraged as he spoke. He fired his last barrage at the Central Cultural Revolution Group. "You people can do what you want," he announced. "I don't want to have any part of this. Cut off my head if that's what you want to do. Imprison me, expel me from the Party, but I'll fight to the end." With that, Tan picked up his briefcase and walked out of the meeting.

Chen Yi, the foreign minister and PLA marshal, followed Tan Zhenlin. He went beyond blasting the Central Cultural Revolution Group and directed his ire at Lin Biao and, by implication, Mao Zedong. "Once in power, these are the guys who practice revisionism," Chen said. "Didn't Stalin hand over to Khrushchev? And didn't Khrushchev follow a revisionist road after he got to the top?" In a display of anger that would later haunt the marshal, Chen brought up the sensitive issue of the Yan'an period and the role that several leaders had played in the political struggles and conflicts of that time. "Back in Yan'an," Chen declared, "the most energetic supporters of Mao Zedong Thought were Liu Shaoqi, Deng Xiaoping, and Peng Zhen, not to mention Bo Yibo, Liu Lantao, and An Ziwen. They never opposed Chairman Mao. In fact, they had never even met Chairman Mao. We were the ones who had opposed Chairman Mao and were criticized as a result. Wasn't the premier criticized? Didn't history prove who opposed Chairman Mao? The future will prove it again."

Zhou once again remained neutral throughout this meeting. He said very little, and avoided getting involved in any way in the argument as it thickened. He also made sure that he wasn't implicated or tied to many of the extreme remarks that had been uttered. When Tan Zhenlin finished his attack on the leftists and got up to leave, Zhou immediately, and uncharacteristically, pounded on the table and demanded Tan's return. For Zhou, this detail was absolutely crucial, and when he reviewed the documentary record of this meeting, Zhou personally altered the record to make sure that his efforts to rein in Tan Zhenlin were duly noted.

Play Safe or Die

Zhou Enlai also played it coy when it came to Chen Yi. When Chen brought up the Yan'an purges of the 1940s at the same meeting, Zhou Enlai was quick to volunteer a self-criticism. And when Chen Yi's remarks veered in the direction of Lin Biao and Mao Zedong,

Zhou immediately stepped in to observe, "That's why we're having the Cultural Revolution."

Zhou was on the verge of joining the marshals—they had dared to say in public things that for a long time he had kept to himself. This was utterly uncharacteristic, politically speaking, for Zhou. When the meeting was over he showed sympathy for the marshals. The next day, when he met with representatives of the revolutionary rebels and government cadres, Zhou made it clear where he stood when it came to the issue of leadership. He stood with the marshals.

"Old cadres," Zhou declared, "are the property of the Party. We cannot treat them like enemies and we can't struggle endlessly against them." Zhou compared the present situation to the Yan'an purges of the 1930s and 1940s. "This time around," he said, "the criticisms directed at cadres are much more brutal and involve merciless attacks. The speed at which all this has happened in the space of one year is comparable to what in the past took place over a period of seventeen years. It pains me to think about it," Zhou said. He made it clear that this approach was completely at variance with Mao's style. "It reeks of the bad behavior of ultraleftism," Zhou said. "For us not to make this clear to our comrades and to allow it to go forward would be a crime on my part."

Zhou realized throughout the course of the February 16 meeting that the Central Cultural Revolution Group was not about to let him off the hook, despite his low-key management style. Tan Zhenlin's heated departure, briefcase in hand, and the inflammatory comments of Chen Yi, contributed to the sense that participants had gone over the top. Zhou moved quickly to seize the initiative before the meeting had even concluded and called Mao personally to fill the Chairman in on what had happened. Mao's response was to dispatch an observer to keep an eye on things and report back to him. He sent over Wang Dongxing, his security chief, but the real fireworks were over by the time Wang showed up.

Members of the Central Cultural Revolution Group, including Zhang Chunqiao, Yao Wenyuan, and the leftist rhetorician, Wang Li, headed straight from the meeting to report to Jiang Qing, who had cited illness to explain her absence. They wanted to get their version of the proceedings to Mao as fast as possible, too. "Tan Zhenlin, Chen Yi, and Xu Xiangqian have all committed serious errors in political line," they informed the Madam. "Zhou Enlai and Kang Sheng took the middle way. Only Xie Fuzhi has taken the 'correct line.'" Zhang, Yao, and Wang then went directly to Mao to deliver their damning report.

Mao knew what had happened before they even got there. At first, when Mao met with the leftist delegation, he didn't think anything too serious had been said, even when Ye Jianying, who had accompanied the group, reported to Mao that he had engaged in "a battle with Chen Boda on this day." Mao seemingly dismissed the importance of the incident and expressed his support for Ye. Mao's demeanor suddenly changed, however, when it dawned on him that high-ranking CCP leaders at the meeting had collectively assaulted him and his Cultural Revolution. He concluded that the Central Cultural Revolution Group had been merely a scapegoat. For the first time since the People's Republic of China had been founded in 1949, a large group of people at a high-level Party gathering had attacked something that the Chairman had personally authorized.

Mao realized that he was going to have to act to silence this chorus of voices to prevent the early death of the Cultural Revolution and to preserve his own historical reputation. Liu Shaoqi and his people would make a quick comeback and call in political debts for all the humiliation they had endured. Mao would be wrecked overnight.

Still, Mao took his time. He calculated that success depended on two key people within the highest ranks of the CCP: Lin Biao and Zhou Enlai. Lin's control of the army was a vital asset. Once Lin and the army had pledged their devotion to the Chairman, Mao's position would be immune to whatever the old marshals and other key leaders tried to do. How, Mao asked himself, could he win the undying loyalty of Lin Biao? The answer was simple. All Mao had to do was quote to him the remarks uttered by Chen Yi and make sure that Lin understood what a serious challenge to his position of newly appointed heir apparent Chen's comments posed, and how they indicated clearly that many in the upper CCP echelons and the military opposed Lin as Mao's successor.

To secure this relationship with Lin, Mao did something very unusual and met with Lin's wife, Ye Qun, for a confidential chat.

"The old marshals have deserted me," Mao confided to Ye Qun. "And so my plan is to ask Lin to accompany me to the southern reaches of the country where we will light the fires of a new revolution, once again engage in guerrilla war and create a new liberation army." Mao sweetened this offer. He gave his permission to Ye Qun to sit in on meetings of the Central Cultural Revolution Group, and he authorized Jiang Qing to meet and talk with Lin.

Jiang Qing, in her previous awkward encounter with the minister of defense, had received a taste of Lin's temper, but, even so, she understood how important Lin was as an ally. Metaphorically, the army and the Central Cultural Revolution Group were Chairman Mao's right and left arms, and they could not be allowed to conflict. Jiang Qing put aside the personal humiliation she had suffered in the presence of Lin and agreed to have another meeting with him.

Zhou Enlai was the other key player in Mao's scheme. The Chairman was perfectly aware of the role that Zhou had played as the chair of those meetings at Cherish Benevolence Hall. He was unhappy that Zhou had allowed Mao's critics to explode and go "overboard," but Zhou, at this stage of the game, was indispensable to Mao. Zhou was the only person who could handle the chaotic situation in the country. That's why this time the Chairman gave him a pass. Mao knew he would be lost at sea without Zhou's superb managerial skills. He needed a loyal and capable servant. The Chairman immediately ordered the Central Cultural Revolution Group to stop circulating documents that were critical of the premier. Zhou was extraordinarily clever. Mao knew that once he had revealed his basically favorable position to Zhou the premier would be on board.

At midnight, on February 18, 1967, Mao summoned key members of the Politburo to his Central South Lake residence. Zhou Enlai, Kang Sheng, Li Fuchun, Ye Jianying, Li Xiannian, Xie Fuzhi, and Ye Qun, who was there to represent Lin Biao, were among those present when the Chairman flew into a rage and declared that the meetings at Cherish Benevolence Hall were all targeted at him and Lin Biao. These meetings weren't just an attempt by Liu Shaoqi and Deng Xiaoping to make a political comeback. They were a reversal of the historical verdicts on political foes. The Chairman ranted at length. Zhou's revision of this tirade as the official note-taker toned it down somewhat, but Mao's statements were very direct.

"If someone opposes the Central Cultural Revolution Group I will resolutely oppose him," thundered Mao. "The Central Central Cultural Revolution Group has been implementing the line adopted by the Eleventh Plenary Session. Its errors amount to one, two, maybe three percent, while it's been correct up to ninety-seven percent. You can try to negate the Cultural Revolution Group but you'll never succeed. Comrade Ye Qun, you tell Lin Biao that he isn't safe either. Some people are trying to seize his power and he should be prepared." Mao really laid it on the line. "If this Great Cultural Revolution fails," he roared, "Comrade Lin Biao and I will withdraw from Beijing and go back to Well Ridge Mountain to fight a guerrilla war. Let Liu Shaoqi and Deng Xiaoping take center stage, execute Chen Boda and Jiang Qing and send Kang Sheng into exile. Go ahead. Reorganize the Cultural Revolution Group, I say, and put Chen Yi in charge and make Tan Zhenlin his deputy and recruit Yu Qiuli and Bo Yibo as members. And if that's not enough, invite Wang Ming and Zhang Guotao back and if you're still unsatisfied bring in America and the Soviet Union and join hands with them."

The Chairman stunned everyone present at the midnight meeting with his threatening remarks. "In all the years I've been with the Chairman," Kang Sheng, who attended as a representative of the Central Cultural Revolution Group, was later heard to say, "I've never seen him this angry. The Chairman was in a proletarian rage." But it was just another show that Mao staged to stop the criticism that was emanating from the Party. Mao deliberately and shrewdly separated Zhou Enlai from any of his implications. This way, the Chairman hooked Zhou and kept him at his side and at the same time made a clear warning. It was now up to Zhou to behave accordingly.

Zhou could either break with the old cadres and follow Mao, or cut himself off from the Chairman and stand with the rest of the cadres. The choice was obvious. Opposing Mao was utterly futile.

Zhou also wanted to soothe tensions on all sides. In a self-criticism he blamed himself for the failure of the old cadres to completely understand the Cultural Revolution. He also begged the Chairman to calm down. Mao eventually did, but not before he commanded the Politburo to consider this incident as a serious matter deserving of full discussion. "If one discussion proves to be insufficient," Mao insisted, "then have another one. If it's still not resolved, then take another month. And if it still isn't resolved, call out members of the entire Party to take part in the discussion." At the same time, Mao issued an order that Chen Yi, Tan Zhenlin, and Marshal Xu Xiangqian would have to "take leave and engage in self-criticism." And so it was that on the one and only occasion when high-ranking officials of the CCP joined together in a collective retaliation against the chaos created by Mao, the Chairman was able to turn it aside with his shameless threats. His helping hand was Zhou Enlai, his ever-loyal servant.

FAILING HIS COMRADES

Zhou came under considerable fire in later years for being too submissive and exhibiting an excessive desire to please. Although his supporters were always quick to claim that Zhou had no other choice, his critics insisted that Zhou encouraged Mao in his madness by yielding to the Chairman time after time and that by following him, he too was responsible for the disaster that befell China.

This kind of criticism had been a common refrain among high-ranking Party officials over the years. At the Mt. Lu Conference in 1959, Marshal Peng Dehuai told the premier to his face that he was "too sophisticated, too smooth." Zhou's comportment in February 1967 at Cherish Benevolence Hall aroused similar reactions among the old cadres. In a rage, Tan Zhenlin shot off a letter to Lin Biao, with whom Tan had worked during the Central Soviet period in the 1930s at Well Ridge Mountain in Jiangxi. He tore into Jiang Qing for a "viciousness unsurpassed within the Party," and claimed that the Madam was "worse than Wu Zetian," the infamous Tang Dynasty (618–906 A.D.) concubine, who proclaimed herself "emperor" and ruled as sovereign of China. Then Tan expressed views of Zhou Enlai that were less than flattering:

> Now that I've pondered my decision for quite some time, I am ready to sacrifice myself. While I will never commit suicide and certainly won't betray my country I absolutely will not allow these people to behave so ruthlessly. They've knocked the premier around so much it's beyond description. He has a broad heart and an enormous capacity for tolerance and endurance and he keeps on waiting and waiting. How long does he plan to wait before he's willing to speak out? Until all the cadres have been struck down? No way, no way, ten thousand times no way. I must rebel. I must. I've made up my mind to rebel. I'm prepared to die, to fight to the end, to oppose them to my last breath. Please don't worry about me. I won't commit suicide.

When he was examining the role Zhou Enlai had played in the Cultural Revolution, Deng Xiaoping noted: "Without the premier the Cultural Revolution would have been much worse. And without the premier the Cultural Revolution wouldn't have dragged on for such a long time."

Such is the criticism we have to note when we assess the role Zhou Enlai played in the Cultural Revolution. In his subservience to Mao he effectively promoted the Chairman's campaign, but as demonstrated by his efforts to protect old cadres, he was affecting some sort of middle ground.

Mao followed his outburst of "proletarian rage" in early 1967 with an all-out effort to snuff out the rebellion by top Party leaders, and he also tried to apply the torch to anyone in the Party Central who opposed the Cultural Revolution. This began with a series of struggle meetings against Tan Zhenlin and marshals Chen Yi and Xu Xiangqian. These were carried out continuously on seven different occasions from February 25 through March 18 at Cherish Benevolence Hall, where the victims had spoken out against the Cultural Revolution. Mao ordered Zhou to chair these so-called political life meetings. The premier considered this a direct slap in the face, since he not only shared many of the same feelings these old cadres had expressed, but had enjoyed good relationships with them over the years. The old cadres considered Zhou their "general supporter behind the scenes," but Zhou was not about to stand up against the vociferous demands of the Central Cultural Revolution Group. Once again, he gave into Mao's indomitable will and performed the embarrassing part Mao had assigned him to play as the organizer and chair of these meetings.

Zhou did his best to limit his comments and remained low-key in the course of these gatherings. He recapped the various self-criticisms and provided an overall summary before they adjourned.

> I am not all that sensitive to the internal affairs of the Party, though my stand has always been in line with basic principles when it comes to the most important issues, first of all those that involve dealing with the Party's enemies and differentiating between right and wrong. The same thing is true when it comes to the second major issue, organizational discipline. My duty as a Party member requires me to abide by this basic principle. I've never been ambiguous about this.

Zhou cited as an example how he had refrained from voicing any agreement with the excessive statements made by Chen Yi, Tan Zhenlin, and others at Cherish Benevolence Hall.

The collective resistance by high-ranking Party members in February 1967 was followed almost immediately by a collective collapse. Members of the Politburo Standing Committee, who for years had run the daily business of the Party, government, and military were dispersed and generally paralyzed. The Central Cultural Revolution

Group now assumed direct command of the Chinese polity. This development was exactly in keeping with Mao's strategic plan for seizing power from the Party Central. It was all he had hoped for. Zhang Chunqiao and Jiang Qing held feverish discussions that focused on how to implement Mao's instructions that the Central Cultural Revolution Group in the ultimate coup d'etat had to replace the Party Secretariat. They consistently reminded Zhou that from now on the Central Cultural Revolution Group had to be involved in any discussion about important issues as if it were the Secretariat. They pressured Zhou to send out instructions to government authorities at every level to hand over authority to local branches of the Central Cultural Revolution Group.

Zhou had done his best to maneuver his way covertly around Jiang Qing with some apparent success as she conspired to take power. But once Mao made clear his intention to reassign the key role of the Secretariat and the Politburo to the Central Cultural Revolution Group, Zhou had no room to maneuver. Jiang Qing was now the "big female boss," with awesome political power and force. That was the bitter pill that Zhou now had to swallow. "From now on you make all the decisions," he told the Madam, "and I'll make sure they're carried out."

11

NO EXIT

IN THE EARLY STAGES OF THE CULTURAL REVOLUTION, ZHOU HAD revealed a minimum of support and sincerity for the campaign, but after Mao assigned the Central Cultural Revolution Group to power, his entire approach was to follow the Tao of obedience and strategic defense. He replaced the dreary and worried expression he had habitually displayed with songs of praise and flattery. As old cadres went down for the count, Mao replaced Chen Boda, the former chairman of the Cultural Revolution Group, with Zhou. Mao's decision incensed Jiang Qing, the real boss and power in the Cultural Revolution Group. The last thing she wanted was to have Zhou Enlai invade her turf. Jiang mustered all the malevolence and bile at her command over the next several months to create a living hell for Zhou Enlai. Zhou had no desire to offend Mao by doing something that would upset his wife. The premier realized that the Cultural Revolution was little more than a mom and pop show run by Jiang and Mao. Even "Vice-Chairman" Lin Biao had to heel to Jiang Qing.

Zhou Enlai had long realized that if he departed on his own from the inner circle of power it would be a form of political death. The premier believed that as long as he remained on the inside, his presence could make some difference. Someone had to hold the fort and maintain a semblance of order while turbulence spread throughout the country. Zhou was indispensable. In this sense, he played the part of the Confucian-scholar, a tradition of national service that along with his sense of loyalty as "minister" to his "emperor" heavily influenced his political outlook. Jiang Qing would do her best to turn the country upside down, but, as long as he remained firmly anchored to the basic principles of the Cultural Revolution, Zhou would remain in the inner circle of power, where he would be a stabilizing presence.

In the years to come, this was the essence of Zhou Enlai's political life.

In late April 1967, Mao quickly shifted gears and decided that it was time to ease up a bit on the old guard of the Party. He had succeeded beyond his wildest dreams in his effort to blunt the effort the old cadres and marshals had mounted to negate the Cultural Revolution. In a series of conversations with Party elders, Mao now showed a new willingness to pursue "unity." "At the meetings in Cherish Benevolence Hall," he told these old soldiers, "some among you expressed objections to the Cultural Revolution. Some of you old marshals got visibly agitated and vented your anger. This," Mao declared, "is yang conspiracy. It's open like sunshine, unlike yin conspiracy, which like darkness is hidden." Tan Zhenlin was among those present. Mao turned to Tan and smiled. "Dear old Tan," he said, "have you finished venting your rage? I certainly have. Let's make a gentleman's agreement and pledge that we won't curse each other's mother." Zhou Enlai quickly seized on this improved state of affairs to put a list together of people to review the annual May Day celebrations and included all the major participants from the February confrontation. He then submitted the list to Mao for the Chairman's approval. If the marshals could make an "appearance" on the top of the Gate of Heavenly Peace their status would somewhat improve.

Ever the cautious player, Zhou shot off a letter to Chen Yi, Tan Zhenlin, and others in the afterglow of good feelings everyone experienced on May 1. He wanted to make sure they understood the situation and warned them against any errant behavior that might set back the incremental improvement in the political climate. In it he wrote: "The unity displayed on May Day should not be taken as an indication that the denunciation of the February Adverse Current has been reversed. Nor is it a green light to try and suppress the rebels, support the conservative faction or carry out acts of revenge. To do so will only bring out another reversal of your fortune because you will lose all your credibility with the people and the Party. This would not constitute a major loss for the Party and the revolution. It would be instead a reflection of continuing class struggle within the Party and a significant lesson for revolutionary youth." Zhou dated the letter May 5, 1967.

Chen Yi, Tan Zhenlin, and the other three cadres who received this letter realized that the premier had taken great pains to write them a serious, direct message. They were all aware that any overboard comments they made would make matters worse. They had now all endured the confrontations at Cherish Benevolence Hall that had led to Mao's rage and they had also witnessed the increasingly aggressive impact that the Cultural Revolution had made on the Party. After receiving Zhou's letter of warning, each of them displayed the highest level of caution in everything they did and said.

Confronting Political Oblivion

In May 1967, Zhou Enlai faced perhaps the most vicious threat to his political survival at the hands of Jiang Qing. At the time, Mao Zedong was driving Liu Shaoqi to his final political demise and, ultimately, an ignominious death. Not unrelated to Mao's zealous persecution was the frenzy that swept through the entire nation as people tried to dig up "traitors" from the country's political history. That May, rebel groups at Nankai University, Zhou's old institution in the northeastern city of Tianjin, unearthed a newspaper article titled "Announcement by the Fifth Warrior and Others on Their

Departure from the Communist Party." Students quickly figured out that the Fifth Warrior (*Wu Hao*) was the nom de guerre that Zhou Enlai used during the years when he worked in China's urban areas in the Party underground. Aware that they had unearthed a piece of serious evidence, student rebels sent the newspaper article to Mao via Jiang Qing. On May 7, Jiang sent a copy of the article along with a cover letter to Lin Biao, Zhou Enlai, and Kang Sheng. She wanted the entire matter formally exposed, and she called on Zhou to come forward with his confession. Full of bravado, Jiang made her declaration. "They've discovered this announcement with all its anti-Communist sentiment by someone named the Fifth Warrior, a leading figure," she crowed, "and I am requesting a meeting in person with all of you."

The purported announcement contained in the article was, in fact, a forgery concocted by the Nationalist security services to stir up trouble and create distrust among CCP members during the battles of the 1930s. This hoax was part of a war waged against the CCP underground by the Nationalists. In 1931, the Nationalists arrested two members of the fledgling CCP resistance, Gu Shunzhang and Xiong Zhongfa, who had immediately revealed the names of many members of the CCP underground personnel in Shanghai. At that time, Zhou had moved quickly to disperse Party members before the Nationalists caught up with them, and, in an act that sent shock waves through Shanghai, he killed Gu Shunzhang's entire family. The Nationalists concocted the story that this person known as the Fifth Warrior had supposedly deserted the CCP to discourage others in the CCP underground. The article was printed in all the Shanghai newspapers in February 1932. In fact, Zhou had already secretly left Shanghai two months earlier for the Central Soviet in Jiangxi Province, where he had already assumed the position of Party secretary of the all-important Central Bureau.

Forty years later, the reappearance of the article caught Zhou by surprise. He wouldn't have any trouble clarifying the facts surrounding the announcement because he'd already been through this crucible in Yan'an during the purges in the 1940s when historical "mistakes" were dredged up. Everything now depended on Mao, and his reaction. If Mao decided he wanted to use the article as a weapon to purge Zhou Enlai, there was nothing the premier could do to defend himself.

Zhou had every reason to believe that Mao had no desire to destroy him now. The affair of the Announcement by the Fifth Warrior was nevertheless swiftly becoming a life-or-death issue in his political life, and Zhou now had to act without delay to smother it, so on May 19 he appealed to Mao directly. Zhou rejected the claims that Jiang Qing had made in her letter. He reminded Mao that the newspaper report about the defection of the Fifth Warrior was a pure forgery put out by the enemy.

On the same day he appealed to Mao, Zhou put aside all his other work and visited the Beijing Library, where he and his staff personally checked out all the Shanghai newspapers from that era, and compiled a "chronicle of the big event." Additionally, Zhou Enlai asked his staff to photograph all the related newspapers and make multiple copies just in case someday the originals happened to "disappear."

That very night on May 19, Zhou sent the collection of newspaper articles and a "chronicle of the big event" that he had compiled to Mao Zedong, along with a letter in which he clarified the facts surrounding the entire incident and presented a straightforward defense of his role in the affair. "The necessary measures taken to deal with the forged Announcement by the Fifth Warrior (and the situation involving the Party Central) were handled by the reporting authorities," Zhou wrote, "all of which transpired after I had already arrived in Jiangxi Province." Zhou concluded, "If a special report is required on this matter, I will await word from the Chairman after he and Lin Biao, Kang Sheng, and Jiang Qing have had a chance to review these enclosed materials. Arrangements can be made to discuss it and then a decision can be rendered."

Mao had absolutely no intention of purging Zhou Enlai at this time, but now he saw a golden opportunity: he would keep the materials on the Announcement by the Fifth Warrior in his back pocket. After he received the hasty letter that Zhou had dashed off to him, Mao deliberately concealed his reaction, made no official response to Zhou, and simply ordered his staff to "forward it to every comrade serving on the Central Cultural Revolution Group and then file," after first sending the letter to Lin Biao "for review."

Zhou was crushed by Mao's attitude. He had believed that the Chairman in all fairness would utter one or two dismissive words about the incident and the matter would end there. Instead, his response offered Jiang Qing a weapon she could pull out at any moment she wanted to launch an attack on Zhou Enlai.

ON THE DEFENSIVE

Mao Zedong had hoped that his nationwide criticism of Liu Shaoqi would unify all the new mass organizations that had sprung up after he'd dismantled the formal Communist apparatus. Despite the Chairman's call for unity in April 1967, and his efforts to make do with the Party's core of old cadres, factional fights continued to rage all over the country. Too often, the masses could care less about achieving a semblance of national unity; they were mostly interested in seizing power. Mao's decision to order the army to give the leftists critical support also began to backfire. Clashes between military units and rebel forces had broken out in a number of places, and in several provinces military units dispersed some mass organizations and arrested their leaders. Mao feared that this sort of unrest would effectively weaken the Cultural Revolution.

By June 1967, hostile forces were waging bloody combat with weapons they'd seized from the military. The Chairman had no choice but to seriously consider a timetable for ending the Cultural Revolution. He outlined a two-year plan: the following year would establish a new political framework and an institutional foundation; the next year, according to Mao's calculations, would wrap up the entire affair.

In mid-July Mao took matters into his own hands and visited the central China city of Wuhan located on the Yangtze River, the site of one of the most vicious of all the conflicts that had broken out all over China. The Chairman decided that in Wuhan he would set an example for the entire country.

Zhou immediately ordered personnel from army, navy, and air force units to accompany the Chairman for his protection when he traveled to Wuhan. The night before Mao was scheduled to arrive, Zhou slipped into the city to take a personal hand in the preparations. Zhou's motivation for taking these extra precautions was fueled, in part, by his desire that Mao forget the Announcement by the Fifth Warrior. He hoped that the Chairman would reward his demonstration of loyalty by dismissing the affair altogether. Zhou also knew that the battles tearing Wuhan apart were all being orchestrated by Lin Biao and Jiang Qing.

Lin Biao and Jiang Qing were out to sabotage Chen Zaidao, the general in command of the Wuhan military region. Lin Biao had a long-standing loathing for Chen Zaidao that dated back to the civil war, when Chen, who led forces in the Fourth Army commanded by Lin, refused to acquiesce to him. When the Cultural Revolution broke upon China, Chen Zaidao did everything he could to protect Liu Shaoqi. The Central Cultural Revolution Group immediately blacklisted him.

Mao didn't like the way the military was suppressing rebel forces in Wuhan, but he could not go along with a purge of Chen Zaidao. He was the rustic kind of man Mao liked, not someone who would naturally align himself with Liu Shaoqi. Mao wanted Chen to acknowledge his mistakes, but he also thought he could persuade the general to support the revolutionary rebels, who would, in turn, offer him their support. Zhou agreed that the military in Wuhan could solve the political problems and that Chen Zaidao would ultimately control the situation.

All this was wishful thinking. The fighting in Wuhan escalated even after Mao arrived in the city to resolve the crisis. The Chairman's safety was now seriously at risk. Zhou made arrangements so that Mao could fly to Shanghai.

It was a blow to Mao's ego to admit that his presence in Wuhan had absolutely no effect whatsoever on the fighting. He decided that he had to radically alter the timetable he'd constructed for the Cultural Revolution, to bring it to a definitive conclusion. To close, he would allocate even more power to the leftist rebels at the expense of the conventional forces of the army and the police. Across the country, rebel groups began to arm themselves. Some even commandeered tanks to use against their political rivals in factional battles. Civil war was at hand.

Zhou never had a moment's rest or relaxation during this entire period. That summer, when Chen Yi, the foreign minister and PLA marshal, was singled out for intense criticism and attacks, Zhou realized that as the man responsible for running China's foreign policy, he was the real target. The Central Cultural Revolution Group now held the premier's fate in its hands. If Chen Yi were struck down, Zhou knew that he would surely follow. He wanted to survive, and he knew instinctively that the crisis would blow over if he followed Mao closely. On several occasions, Zhou addressed rebels who had virtually taken over the Foreign Ministry. "Am I afraid of being targeted in the struggle?" Zhou asked the rebels. "You bet your life I'm not. Why should I fear this when I've endured the revolutionary struggle over several decades? The one thing I do not want to do is self-destruct by going against the tide." Zhou went on to show the same verbal and political steel that had saved him on so many occasions. "If I fail to follow Chairman Mao," Zhou told the rebels, "then my downfall would be a foregone conclusion whether or not you decided to strike me down. But the opposite is also true. If I continue to obey Chairman Mao and follow him closely, no matter how hard you try, you can never destroy me." Zhou followed up on this two months later when he made a direct response to rebels while the Central Cultural Revolution Group looked on.

I know some people have conducted research on me and looked into my background of many years past. I give you my profound gratitude. I've been a Party member for some forty-six years, and during that time I have made many mistakes. Ultimately, however, I've made the decision to walk behind Chairman Mao, and I'll do this until the day I die, just as I will continue to learn and I'll continue to reform myself until I reach death's door. Because my efforts will persist to the very last minute of my life and beyond.

Zhou's days were far from easy. The rebels constantly caused him embarrassment. In his usual tactful way, however, Zhou somehow guarded his political backside. The events that occurred on September 9, 1967, well illustrate Zhou's ability to operate in difficult conditions. On this occasion, representatives from various rebel groups had gathered in Beijing's Workers' Stadium to celebrate Mao's leadership of the 1927 Autumn Harvest Uprising. August 1, the date in 1927 when Zhou had launched the Nanchang Uprising, had long been set aside to celebrate the birth of the Red Army, but now, forty years later, the rebels, in deference to Mao, wanted to shift Army Day in China to September 9. Chants of "down with August 1" rang through the stadium during Zhou's speech to the gathering, while Zhou was the target of catcalls as rebels tried to shout the premier off the stage in favor of Jiang Qing and Mao Zedong. Zhou responded with political deftness. "Comrades, I understand all of you," he said with a voice shaking and weak. "You love Chairman Mao and you love Comrade Jiang Qing, all of which is entirely correct. But I must tell you that I, Zhou Enlai, love Chairman Mao just as much as you do. I must also tell you that Vice-Chairman Lin Biao, not I, led the August 1 Nanchang Uprising. Chairman Mao canonized August 1 as Army Day and this cannot be stricken down. I, Zhou Enlai, have made many mistakes, but I support Chairman Mao and Vice-Chairman Lin. If you don't believe me, you can take a look. My heart is red." And with this Zhou suddenly ripped open his shirt exposing his chest for all to see.

So it was that Zhou survived politically by expressing his eternal deference to Mao. At the same time, Zhou also did everything it took to avoid any kind of confrontation with Jiang Qing. Twenty-four hours a day, seven days a week, groups of rebels blasted their ongoing messages of political struggle and hate over loudspeakers set up outside the Central South Lake leadership compound. Zhou, isolated among the frenzied leftists who dominated the Central Cultural Revolution Group, was in a constant battle to save his political neck. Jiang Qing was relentless in her pursuit of Zhou, repeatedly insulting him in front of other leaders, many of whom could not bear to watch this humiliation. Zhou concealed his feelings behind closed lips and an impassive mask, and bore the torment in silence. Never would he indulge in a single casual remark that might give Jiang Qing ammunition for some future attack.

Sometimes, even Mao concluded that Jiang Qing had gone just a little too far. "Don't be afraid of Jiang Qing," the Chairman quietly advised Zhou. "When she blunders and makes a mistake you've got to stand up and fight her. It's true. I do support Jiang Qing when she's in the right, but I also oppose her when she's wrong. Why should you, the premier, be afraid of her just because she has a few pieces of paper on you?" But Zhou knew better than to ever follow Mao's advice and "fight" Jiang Qing.

Zhou Enlai made a herculean effort to rescue Chen Yi, the PLA marshal and foreign minister. He realized that if Chen Yi were struck down he wouldn't be far behind.

Chen Yi was popular within the Party. Throughout the Cultural Revolution Chen had earned the affection and respect of people inside and outside the Party time and again by firing off comments criticizing the current state of affairs. This sort of candor didn't go over very well with Mao, who decided to teach Chen a lesson by throwing him to the revolutionary rebels known as the *zaofanpai*.

When the rebels gathered outside the Foreign Ministry and clamored for Chen Yi so they could carry out their intense criticism, which in many cases during the Cultural Revolution resulted in death to the victim, Zhou made a deal with them under considerable pressure before they could take any action. The rebels agreed that slogans like "Down with Chen Yi" could not be shouted out, that they wouldn't physically abuse the aging marshal, and they agreed that Zhou could attend every struggle session. Zhou stood his ground under the hot sun of the midsummer day, arms folded across his chest, for an entire hour, until the rebels removed a banner inscribed with the words "Down with Chen Yi." A few days later it happened again. Tens of thousands of people had assembled for a planned struggle meeting inside the Great Hall of the People in Tiananmen Square. Zhou grabbed Chen Yi and together the old comrades left the meeting without saying a word.

The attacks against Chen Yi continued, and, by August 17, 1967, Zhou had gone for eighteen hours without a break when another meeting was scheduled with Cultural Revolution rebels from the Foreign Ministry, who wanted to hold a discussion about launching a struggle meeting of their own against Chen Yi. This time rebels aimed their threats at Zhou Enlai. They promised that if he did not meet their demands they would intercept Chen Yi's car and organize the masses to attack him. Zhou Enlai was furious. He made sure the rebels understood that they were playing with fire. "If any of you intercept Comrade Chen Yi's car, I will oppose you," he told them. "If any of you carry out planned attacks at the meeting, I swear I will stand in the entrance to the Great Hall of the People so that you'll have to walk over me." That day, exhausted and enraged, Zhou Enlai suffered a heart attack.

Once Zhou was temporarily sidelined, the foreign policy of the People's Republic spun wildly out of control. On August 22, Red Guards assaulted the British mission in Beijing, setting the building on fire and physically abusing embassy staff. Zhou, despite his weakened state, immediately dispatched security forces from the Beijing garrison command to restore order and to provide protection to the embassy staff. Knowing that his name would not carry much weight with the rebels, Zhou invoked the names of Jiang Qing, Chen Boda, and Kang Sheng in a speech aimed at persuading the rebels to leave the compound.

That night, Zhou Enlai and Chen Boda met with rebel representatives from different organizations and announced that it was "illegal" to seize power at the Foreign Ministry. The Central Cultural Revolution Group realized that a huge blunder had been committed, and that they would plead ignorance if Mao inquired about the incident. Chen Boda then made a statement to the effect that from then on any decisions involving foreign affairs were the exclusive preserve of the premier.

Zhou decided to make an effort to convince Mao that he could start to wind down the Cultural Revolution. Mao, who had managed to escape from the violent atmosphere in Wuhan, was in Shanghai. When Mao received Zhou's report on the situation, he understood the severity of the confrontations. He realized that if the rebels continued to battle each other and the country began to spin entirely out of control that he really would have to act on his threat and retreat to Well Ridge Mountain in Jiangxi Province and start the "liberation" of China all over again.

One year and three months of national chaos was enough. By late 1967 the shop began to close on the Cultural Revolution. At the same time, the political environment in which Zhou Enlai operated began to improve dramatically. One political storm after another had flown Zhou's way, but the premier had held his ground. Mao alternately had softened his attitude, finally managing to send words of concern to Zhou about his recent heart attack. Soon after that, the Chairman broke his silence on the matter of the Announcement by the Fifth Warrior. "This was cleared up a long time ago," Mao informed Zhou. "It was nothing more than Nationalist rumor-mongering, a smear job." Zhou was flattered by Mao's comforting words, but he knew, instinctively, that the Chairman needed him to clean up the mess left over from the Cultural Revolution.

Gangs of revolutionary rebels still roamed many parts of the country like packs of wild dogs, utterly beyond the control of any authority. Tensions along the Soviet border began to simmer (they would eventually result in an armed clash in 1969 along the Ussuri River in the far northeastern region of China). Despite these obvious challenges, the situation was much better than it had been at the height of the chaos, and Zhou knew that he was the indispensable man who could manage the situation and bring order back to the Chinese nation.

Thus it came to pass that over the next year, Zhou followed Mao's directive to replace "great chaos under heaven" with "great order under heaven," to clean up the mess, ever mindful that he had to proceed with great caution. Zhou also devoted considerable energy to preparations for the upcoming Ninth CCP Party Congress, when Lin Biao would officially be anointed as Mao's successor and the Chairman would begin to bring closure to the entire affair of the Cultural Revolution by declaring "victory." Throughout 1968 and into early 1969, Zhou would issue orders in the name of the Party Central to halt all factional fighting so that factories caught in the crossfire could resume production and the government could restart the transportation system. (Transportation had been hard hit by the Red Guards, who had commandeered the rails and destroyed the trains.) Zhou ordered the PLA to restore law and order in areas especially ravaged by persistent factional fighting. The PLA also assumed control of the heretofore paralyzed Public Security units.

Not surprisingly, the chaos of the Cultural Revolution didn't vanish overnight. Indeed, it continued largely unhindered for two more years, thanks to incidents involving the purge of the major military men Yang Chengwu, Yu Lijin, and Fu Chongbi from the ranks of the People's Liberation Army as part of Lin Biao's struggle to secure control over the army. A nationwide political campaign begun in March 1968 attacking the "right deviationist attempt to reverse correct verdicts," purportedly led by Liu Shaoqi and Deng Xiaoping, perpetuated the sense of continuing conflict and mayhem. Through the ongoing turmoil, Zhou kept his eye on the political bottom line, never once jeopardizing the Cultural Revolution. No one engineered any fundamental single reversal of the Cultural Revolution, but by September 1968 revolutionary committees—the "three-in-one alliances of revolutionary leading cadres, revolutionary mid-level cadres and representatives of revolutionary masses"—had been established at the provincial and municipal levels with a large number of military personnel to ensure order. The day had finally come when all corners of the country had become a shire to Mao Zedong Thought.

Now that Mao had decided to shut down the Cultural Revolution, his thoughts turned to the case against Liu Shaoqi. Mao had dragged the country to the brink of civil war in an act of unprecedented conflict and chaos. To justify his actions politically, he now had to pull some kind of hat trick and show all of the "achievements" of the grand movement he'd started. Mao decided that the only way to demonstrate that all the disorder of the Cultural Revolution was "completely necessary" and "utterly timely" was to continue the onslaught against Liu Shaoqi and to consider even more deeply the outstanding "historical problems" involving the now disgraced but not yet defeated state chairman.

When Mao returned to Beijing in late September 1967, he immediately called a series of meetings to discuss the case of Liu Shaoqi and probe his history in the CCP. The Chairman kept his eye trained on the situation as it developed, and he made clear that before the Ninth Party Congress even convened the Liu Shaoqi case had to be resolved.

Not unsurprisingly, the task fell to Zhou Enlai. The premier was required to chair the special committee to investigate all matters involving the state chairman, but Zhou did whatever he could to slow the whole process down. Whenever the group met, Zhou had a tendency to speak out of both sides of his mouth, and he insisted that all pertinent materials be scrutinized, and that documents should not be circulated widely. Zhou's instructions slowed the work down to a snail's pace. Under Zhou's leadership, there was no major breakthrough in the case.

Unhappy with the slow pace of Zhou Enlai's performance, Mao replaced him as head of the special investigative group with Jiang Qing and appointed Kang Sheng, the security chief, to assist the Madam. The special investigative group operated under the highly secretive Central Case Examination Group (which employed a staff

Zhou Enlai in Japan with fellow Chinese students in 1917. Zhou is on the far right (standing).

In July 1920, Zhou Enlai was arrested as the leader of Tianjin Student Union during the May Fourth Movement. This photo was taken at his release from prison in Tianjin. Zhou Enlai is fourth from left in the fourth row. (Zhan Ruoming, Zhou's first love, is pictured here sitting on the left in the front row.)

Zhou Enlai (second from left) with Zhan Shengfu (far right) and Liu Qingyang (second from right) in Berlin in 1922. Zhang and Liu first introduced Zhou to the CCP.

In 1924, Zhou was appointed director of the Political Department of Whampoa Military Academy in Guangdong Province.

Zhou and Deng on their honeymoon in 1925 in Guangzhou.

In October 1935, Zhou arrived in the northern Shaanxi Province at the end of the Long March.

Zhou Enlai (second from left) in 1938 in Wuhan with Western friends. (The American writer Agnes Smedley is in the middle).

In July 1939, Zhou Enlai fell off a horse in Yan'an and permanently injured his right arm. He is pictured here with Liu Shaoqi.

Zhou Enlai in flying gear in front of an airplane after returning from Xi'an, date uncertain. IMAGE COURTESY OF HUMANITIES AND SOCIAL SCIENCES DIVISION, NEW YORK PUBLIC LIBRARY

Zhou Enlai at the grand ceremony in celebration of the founding of the People's Republic of China on the Tiananmen rostrum, October 1, 1949. IMAGE COURTESY OF HUMANITIES AND SOCIAL SCIENCES DIVISION, NEW YORK PUBLIC LIBRARY

Zhou Enlai with Jiang Qing during the Cultural Revolution.

In 1954, Zhou attended the Geneva conference (It was his first appearance at an international convention representing the newly founded People's Republic of China). At the conference, U.S. Secretary of State John Foster Dulles refused to shake Zhou's hand. Another eighteen years would pass before a handshake between the United States and China was exchanged.

Zhou Enlai accompanying Mao in reviewing the Red Guards atop the Gate of Heavenly Peace in Tiananmen Square in 1966.

Zhou Enlai, surrounded by soldiers of the Chinese Army, addresses a meeting in support of the Cultural Revolution, probably in 1966. AFP/GETTY IMAGES

Mao Zedong with Vice Chairman Lin Biao and Zhou Enlai, January 26, 1968. J. A. Fox
Collection/Magnum Photos

Zhou Enlai at the Second Plenary Session of the Ninth Central Committee of the Chinese Communist Party, August 1970. Image courtesy of Humanities and Social Sciences Division, New York Public Library

Zhou Enlai in September of 1973. Keystone/Getty Images

Zhou Enlai and Richard Nixon sharing a toast at a banquet in the Great Hall, 1972. JOHN DOMINIS/TIME LIFE PICTURES/GETTY IMAGES

Zhou Enlai waits at Beijing airport for the arrival of the French President G. Pompidou in September 1973. AFP/ GETTY IMAGES

January 1975, Zhou delivered his last, legendary speech at the Fourth National People's Congress, in which he reaffirmed the "Four Modernizations".

Deng Yingchao, widow of Zhou Enlai, is offered consolation at a memorial service after Zhou Enlai's death. Party and state leaders pictured include Wang Hongwen, Ye Jianying and Deng Xiaoping. IMAGE COURTESY OF HUMANITIES AND SOCIAL SCIENCES DIVISION, NEW YORK PUBLIC LIBRARY

of thousands, including military personnel) and at Jiang Qing's feverish command used everything from forged materials to forced confessions. By the middle of September 1968, they had compiled three volumes of so-called criminal materials on Liu Shaoqi that, among other things, revealed that in his revolutionary days as a leader of the underground Party in the white areas controlled by the Nationalists, Liu had been arrested on three separate occasions. Each time he had betrayed the CCP.

Zhou Enlai could feel the pressure. Jiang Qing and Kang Sheng had written comments that put him on a political hot seat. Zhou easily could have punched holes in the so-called criminal materials that had been gathered to make the case against Liu Shaoqi. But Zhou Enlai was no fool. He was the last person who could be swayed by such a clumsy attempt to nail Liu Shaoqi. Zhou had just emerged from the political dust storm over the historical problem created by the Announcement by the Fifth Warrior. He could easily see what Mao was doing. Mao had an unquenchable desire to drive the state chairman to his grave and he was using historical records to strike the final blow.

Caving to Power

Since he had headed the special investigative group on Liu Shaoqi, Zhou vowed that he would do nothing that assaulted his own conscience. He knew that the materials on Liu were not worth the paper on which they were written and that's why he had avoided coming to any quick conclusions about the Liu case. It led to a series of face-to-face arguments with Jiang Qing and Kang Sheng, foremost among others, during which the rabid leftists pounded the table and shouted at Zhou and then immediately scurried off to see Mao to "make a report." They got through to Mao, who put pressure on Zhou, who finally caved in. "If you want to make a change," Zhou conceded, "then make a change." Zhou had initially hoped, and believed, once the reins of power had been handed over to Jiang Qing, that he could avoid the situation entirely, but before long he realized that he was going to have to make a choice between his conscience and his political survival. No one can be sure exactly what Zhou was thinking when he came to this fateful decision, but it is undoubtedly true that the premier suffered his worst inner torment and his most soul-searching moment over the decision he had to make. Deng Yingchao, his wife, once related to Zhou's biographer that the entire matter was so painful for him that for days he paced back and forth by himself in his room until late at night with the lights burning. In the end, under enormous pressure from many sides, Zhou considered the "whole picture and in the name of serving the interests of the Party while also aging gracefully," he finally decided to make the big break with Liu and endorse the so-called criminal materials compiled by Jiang Qing and her relentless gang.

"Enlai signed off on the documents used to expel Liu Shaoqi from the Party," Zhou's widow confided to the author Han Suyin nine years after her husband's death. "Can we just simply apologize for this? The whole affair caused Enlai so much pain. But he had no choice," she told Han Suyin. "He did it for the benefit of the whole picture." Indeed, ten days after he had received his copy of the so-called criminal materials, Zhou broke his silence on the matter and delivered his formal decision on Liu's case by drafting his own statement, dated September 25, 1968, and signing his own name on the official report next to those of Chen Boda, Kang Sheng, and Jiang Qing. Once the report was sent to Mao and Lin Biao, immediate action was taken in October 1968. Liu Shaoqi was officially "expelled from the Party forever, and stripped of all his positions in and outside the CCP." Case closed.

Zhou was more than aware that Mao had made his premier's attitude toward the Liu case another test of his loyalty. The harangues by Jiang Qing were actually communiqués from Mao. To make sure he passed this test, Zhou decided to use virtually the same language and tone that Jiang Qing had used in her personal statement, when he submitted his personal reply to the Madam. "I fully endorse your comments and opinions on this case," he wrote.

I too am filled with great hatred as I read and considered the materials and checked off the various examples contained in the three volumes that document how the traitor Liu betrayed our Party and sacrificed our comrades.

The criminal Liu is a big traitor, big scab, big spy, big foreign agent, and collaborator who sold out the country. He is full of the five poisons and a counterrevolutionary guilty on more than ten accounts!

We must fervently support the Great Proletarian Cultural Revolution launched and led by our great leader Chairman Mao. Without such a great revolution, how could these criminal materials on the traitor Liu and his people who committed treason against the Party and the country and killed our comrades get dug out so deeply and thoroughly?

Of course, we must continue this probing without the slightest delay, and without losing sight of our goals. If the task cannot be finished in our lifetime, then it should be passed onto our descendants!

We must also be extremely grateful to Vice-Chairman Lin for raising high the great red banner of Mao Zedong Thought, for widely disseminating Mao Zedong Thought and spreading the Chairman's voice (*Quotations from Chairman Mao*) to millions of liberation army soldiers and hundreds of millions of laboring people. Without these great numbers of laborers and liberation army soldiers fully grasping Mao Zedong Thought, could this Cultural Revolution have been launched with the participation of tens of millions of revolutionary masses taking part from bottom to top and from top to the bottom? To spread Mao Zedong Thought and Chairman Mao's voice and to carry out Chairman Mao's instructions is the preeminent test of our qualifications as Party members and of whether we can maintain revolutionary integrity to the end. On this point, we must learn from you! I even more learn from you!

(After reading the above, Jiang Qing wrote: "Learn from Comrade Enlai! Encourage each other, age gracefully to the end!")

Zhou gave a hard kick in the stomach to Liu in his statement on the issue of the state chairman's historical problems. Like the

Madam, Zhou followed along with his own voluminous and disgusting flattery of Mao and the Cultural Revolution, icing the cake with obsequious remarks directed at Jiang Qing and Lin Biao. Despite his efforts at elusive praise, however, Zhou did not altogether relieve Mao's suspicions, and the Chairman immediately ordered Zhou to deliver on behalf of the Party Central the official report of the special investigative group on Liu to the upcoming Twelfth Plenum of the Eighth Central Committee held in October 1968. Zhou was now effectively forced to carry Mao's execution knife and play the role of cohort in Mao's strategy.

In the history of the Cultural Revolution, Zhou's handling of the Liu case gave the premier a black mark. Later, some old cadres within the Party wanted to "promote Zhou and overthrow Mao." Deng Yingchao begged them to hold off. "Don't do this," she advised them. "When did Enlai oppose Chairman Mao? Zhou, this man you all know, if the Party line was right, he was right. If the Party line was wrong, he was wrong. If you do that, and say that, there won't be any way to make history clear for our descendants."

History has a way of playing cruel jokes on people. Mao had finally gotten rid of Liu Shaoqi only to discover that Lin Biao, the man he had cultivated with such care, was an even more difficult choice. The day the Ninth Party Congress opened in April 1969, the split between Lin and Mao would begin. Despite all claims of "unity and victory," another even more dramatic power struggle began quietly to unfold. Without a moment of rest or relief after the tormenting years of the Cultural Revolution, Zhou Enlai would be dragged into yet another life or death battle between two forces—from which there would be no exit.

12

HEIR PRE-EMPTIVE

The Chinese Communist Party held its Ninth Party Congress in Beijing in April 1969, and proclaimed it the Congress of Victors. Chairman of the Communist Party Mao Zedong waltzed into the grand auditorium of the Great Hall of the People followed by an entourage of leaders who had either thrived, or, at least, survived, the "great chaos under heaven," while members of the audience waved their copies of the Little Red Book, a collection of the quotations of Mao, and all the while chanted "Long Live Chairman Mao." Young female Red Guards in the throng overwhelmed by the emotion of the moment could be seen breaking down in tears. It was a classic Stalinist show. It was a secretive gathering, and, unlike other Party congresses, it was not announced in advance. Mao's "profound" comments about "unity" and "victory" to this top-secret conclave were followed, according to the official transcript, by "prolonged enthusiastic applause," and shouts of "Long Live Chairman Mao."

To all appearances, years of conflict and struggle had finally culminated in a united central Party leadership that, in Mao's words, would go about the still unfinished business of completing the Great

Proletarian Cultural Revolution in a "meticulous, down-to-earth, and conscientious way." Over the course of three weeks, various leaders addressed the assembled Party veterans, Red Guard and revolutionary rebel leaders, and members of the People's Liberation Army who comprised the Congress delegates. Lin Biao reported on the need for "struggle and transformation," Mao Zedong spoke about how "apparent leftism may conceal real rightism," and the entire lineup of leftist leaders, from Kang Sheng to Wang Hongwen, all fell into line, proclaiming the "victory" of the moment. Lin Biao's name was inserted into the new Party constitution to avoid any misunderstanding about his designated role as the Chairman's official successor. The words "unity" and "victory" were broadcast everywhere against a background of growing tensions along the northern border with the Soviet Union that added yet another layer of militancy to the gathering.

But it was a façade. Behind the scenes, the revolutionaries were beginning to turn on each other. Mao's major goal in the immediate aftermath of the "historic" and "transformational" Ninth Party Congress was to strengthen the impact of the Cultural Revolution on politics, ideology, and organizational structure. He intended to carry out to the very end the struggles against all who thought the old politics of the 1950s that Liu Shaoqi represented could somehow still be retained. Mao called for criticism and rectification of all diehard revisionists, and the Chairman pursued his lofty ideal of purging and purifying the CCP so that revisionist thinking could never sink back into the Party foundation. Yet as he did so, members of the pro-Cultural Revolution camp had already begun to turn on each other. What began as a magnificent effort to transform the Chinese political scene and create a new, more radical politics, rapidly began to deteriorate into a confusion of animosities, and in the swiftly worsening climate of loss, the Chairman confined himself increasingly to a state of sorrowful isolation as all his revolutionary dreams began to drain away.

Two contending forces emerged in conflict. Lin Biao, the official successor and his followers, now faced off against Jiang Qing and those who supported her as the de facto leader of the Central Cultural Revolution Group. These were the right and left hands of Mao whom the Chairman had relied upon to launch his Cultural Revolution, even though, as political groupings, they had neither historical ties nor any current relationship. Their alliance was the product of Mao's purge of Liu Shaoqi. It was a true political honeymoon, but it was utterly superficial. Both scrambled up the political ladder, crossing each other at every opportunity, until, at last, they were confirmed enemies.

Lin Biao, like Zhou Enlai, was a rare breed in Chinese politics, not at all a creature of the political culture of the Chinese Communist Party. As a military man, Lin had been a brilliant commander. He had been indispensable to the Chinese Communist victory in the civil war that, in 1949, brought the Communists to power. As a political animal, Lin was also quite adept; careful and meticulous as he was in his political calculations, he came to possess real insight into and understanding of Mao's political nature. Soon after the CCP seized power, Lin deliberately distanced himself from the political scene throughout the 1950s and often used poor health as an excuse to avoid deep involvement in matters of state. When he was offered supreme command of the Chinese People's Volunteers in the Korean War, Lin turned it down, and, it could be said, he was given "a severance check for transfer."

Lin had another plan for himself. He wanted to be transferred to a remote province where he could be the local supreme leader and big boss. That was before he realized how vicious Chinese politics were, and how absolutely unpredictable the nature of Chairman Mao's leadership style was. Gao Gang, a powerful leader in the northeast, and Rao Shushi, the prominent Shanghai leader, were accused, in the mid-1950s, of operating at odds with the central leadership and ultimately purged over accusations that they had turned their local bailiwicks of authority into "independent kingdoms." Gao committed suicide while Rao was run out of the Party and died in prison. Lin barely managed to avoid being implicated in this incident. He beat a quick retreat, once again citing poor health.

Lin subsequently avoided politics altogether, remained in virtual seclusion, and bided his time, waiting for the most opportune moment to make his move.

Lin was destined for the political fray, if only because Mao had cultivated him for years as his favorite general. The Chairman was not at all happy that Lin seemed to stay at home enjoying leisure time when what Mao really wanted was to get Lin back into the political limelight. "Break out of your depression," Mao once remarked to Lin. He instinctively knew that Lin was a valuable card in his political poker game, one that might turn out to be decisive. For in the late 1950s, another major military figure, Peng Dehuai, then minister of defense, had begun to weigh heavily on Mao's mind.

Mao thrust Lin Biao into the political limelight just before the eventful August 1959 conference at Mt. Lu, where Peng would launch his criticism of the Great Leap Forward and pose serious questions about the Chairman's leadership and his program of radical economic change that had created a food supply crisis in many areas of the country. Mao promoted Lin in 1958 to a position of extreme political prominence on a par with Deng Xiaoping when he made him a vice-chairman of the CCP and a member of the all-powerful Standing Committee of the Politburo. Lin was ranked only third in the hierarchy of the People's Liberation Army, but now Mao promoted him to a position in the Party higher than Peng. Mao's sudden promotion of Lin Biao went almost unnoticed, but with this act the Chairman placed Lin in a strategic salience where, when needed, he could challenge Peng and even replace him if it came to that. Peng sensed the danger to his position posed by Lin, and he offered to resign, but for the time being was persuaded to stay on as minister of defense. Lin still wanted to remain on the sidelines, and although he'd been promoted to the political limelight, he called in sick, to avoid any real involvement in the high stakes game. When Peng challenged him at the Mt. Lu Conference, Mao made a frantic call to Lin and dragged him onto center stage to join the criticism of Peng that Mao had authorized. After years of hiding out and watching from a safe distance, Lin now rode to the rescue. He hurled himself into the vicious attacks on the minister of defense, and accused the now isolated Peng of being overly "ambitious, conspiratorial, and hypocritical," another version of Feng Yuxiang, the early twentieth-century warlord whom the Nationalists had courted to no avail. Lin also managed to demonstrate a certain fawning flattery of Mao, as he was to do often on many occasions thereafter. "In China," Lin declared to the Mt. Lu crowd, "Mao is the greatest hero, a role to which no one else should dare to aspire."

Mao could not control the delight he felt over Lin's performance. As soon as the Mt. Lu Conference ended, Mao dismissed Peng, and arranged for Lin to be given the old marshal's prime job of running the daily and routine affairs of the CCP Military Affairs Committee, which oversaw and controlled all the forces, three million men strong, of the People's Liberation Army. In a flash, Lin Biao had emerged from virtual political obscurity to the forefront of political power, which, as Mao had famously noted, "grows out of the barrel of a gun." Lin was profoundly aware of the limitations of Peng's naïve belief that, somehow, if you told the "truth" about conditions in China, you would win political points. Lin acted on the principle that "those who don't lie are bound to fail." Lin was altogether preoccupied by the task of reinforcing his newly acquired power. He showed no concern whatever with conditions on the ground. Instead, he devoted himself to showering Mao with flattery. He wooed the Chairman in every conceivable way, and immediately launched his fevered campaign among the ranks of the PLA to worship Mao Zedong Thought by studying the *Quotations from Chairman Mao*, which was now distributed throughout PLA ranks.

Such was the public face of Lin Biao. Privately, he held an entirely different opinion of the Chairman and his critique of Mao's leadership went far beyond anything Peng Dehuai voiced in 1959, or even criticisms later made by Liu Shaoqi and other high-ranking Party officials. Under the entry "personality cult," for instance, in his private dictionary, Lin wrote: "For Mao one must always take care of his needs so that he doesn't feel the necessity to surround himself with any kind of gang. On political matters, it's essential to take the initiative to point out his creations and achievements so that he won't have to boast about any of this himself."

When it came to the Great Leap Forward, and his judgment of it, Lin's private belief was that the entire campaign was "based on fantasy, and a total mess." He agreed with the criticisms of Peng Dehuai, and thought they were undoubtedly correct, although he also thought that his predecessor's actions had been "too hasty." After Mao attacked Peng for pursuing the ultimate political crime of revisionism, Lin observed that whenever the "language and the deed are too extreme, then mistakes are unavoidable." The distance that separated the private Lin Biao from the Lin who flattered the Chairman with unrestrained obsequiousness came as a shock to his daughter. When she learned of Lin's blistering denunciation of Mao behind closed doors, Lin Liheng, Lin Biao's daughter, also known as Doudou, fell into a deep depression, and made a botched attempt at suicide.

Lin's private disapproval of Mao's policies continued unabated in years to come when the Chairman first launched the Cultural Revolution. Lin was decidedly unenthusiastic about the entire effort, but he could say little in opposition, publicly, because he had firmly secured his line to the Maoist ship, even as it began to sink deeper and deeper. Years later, when she recalled these days, the daughter, Lin Liheng, described how Jiang Qing had demanded that Lin Biao pay more attention to propaganda work in the army to show unequivocal support for the Cultural Revolution. The concept left Lin cold. "I don't know," was all he could say, and this almost provoked an argument between the Madam and Lin. Later, Jiang pressed Lin again, and used the words of Mao to goad him. "The Chairman has asked me to invite your esteem and respect," she told him, but Lin, as he so often had done in the past, once again pleaded poor health. Jiang and Lin parted without further word, and in a state of considerable discontent.

At the crucial August 1966 Eleventh Plenary Session, when Liu Shaoqi was effectively removed as heir apparent, the Chairman decided to turn Lin into his anointed successor. Lin was horrified. He repeatedly declined Mao's offer, and was profoundly aware that if he accepted Mao's proposal he would be Mao's right-hand man, which would be like walking next to a tiger. Lin was afraid that he would share the fate of Liu Shaoqi, whom he was being called upon to replace. "Liu Shaoqi and Deng Xiaoping are good comrades," Lin observed in confidence to his daughter, Lin Liheng. "There was no reason to get rid of Liu."

The Reluctant Suitor

Lin took yet another sick leave to avoid the political thickets during the August 1966 Eleventh Plenum and retreated to the northeast seaside city of Dalian. Once he had made his decision in the course of the plenum to dismiss Liu Shaoqi, however, Mao quickly dispatched Wang Dongxing, his security chief, to fetch the minister of defense, and he ordered Zhou Enlai to make the arrangements to send a plane to bring Lin back to the capital. Lin had no choice. He had to return, but he did so with no show of elation. When he arrived at the Great Hall of the People, Lin bowed to Mao, who had come out to greet him in person, but he almost immediately revealed the displeasure he felt about the entire business, and told Mao once again that he was not willing to take on the role of the Chairman's successor, citing the usual health problems.

Lin had failed to live up to the Chairman's expectations. Mao cornered Lin. "I don't believe for a minute that you don't want to take part in the Communist movement," he muttered, and Lin had no real answer. The Chairman had cut straight to the heart.

Lin had almost no room to maneuver under the circumstances; basically, he had to follow the Chairman's orders. Once he had accepted Mao's offer to be his successor, Lin was more terrified than flattered. He found it necessary to assist Mao and promote the Cultural Revolution with a battery of horns and whistles. Lin took on the task with aplomb and outperformed the best of the Chairman's followers as he ascended to the political stage. This was the way Lin dealt with his personal terror. He expressed his unequivocal support for the Cultural Revolution and talked it up as if it were the greatest political movement in human history. "We must stir up the heavens and the earth for everyone to hear, rile the oceans and waves, high and low," he declared. "In half a year, we must make both the bourgeoisie and the proletariat sleepless." He was effusive as he exhorted everyone to toe the line and follow Mao's instructions. "We must follow each and every word of the Chairman whether or not we understand them," he called out.

As it turned out, serving as Mao's successor amounted to little in the central power structure. Lin had no real organizational or political support base, unlike his predecessor, Liu Shaoqi, or Zhou Enlai, both of whom over the decades had built up a following within the CCP. The way the whole system operated, Mao was the "decider," and Zhou was the executioner. Lin Biao was thus nothing more than a political mannequin, out on display, but with virtually no influence on the operations of the Party or the government apparatus.

Lin had every reason to be filled with apprehension and suspicion as he entered this new situation: Mao made key decisions as the Cultural Revolution unfolded without consulting Lin, whom he kept totally in the dark most of the time. But for Lin there was no going back. He detested his role as the supporting actor in Mao's political drama, assigned to hunt down supposed enemies of the Communist Party and the state apparatus, yet he was now the designated successor. As Mao exulted in the adulations of masses of Red Guards while he stood atop the Gate of Heavenly Peace, Lin Biao found the ordeal excruciating. Lin, whose health was failing, realized that he couldn't extract himself from his position, though he did try to relieve himself of commitments whenever possible. Lin wanted as little direct association with Mao as possible. Whenever people wished "salutations and wishes of longevity for Vice-Chairman Lin," Lin's response was of discouragement. He sent a letter to Zhou Enlai and the Central Cultural Revolution Group in which he declared, "from now on, the sole emphasis at public events and in meetings, documents, newspapers, and magazines and any and all media outlets should be on Chairman Mao. Do not mention me in the same line with the Chairman."

Lin's message was clear: Mao was still in charge and the propaganda should portray it that way. Lin also wanted to disguise his political passivity, however. He did everything he could, therefore, to cultivate the impression that in all his words and actions Lin was closely following Mao. For that reason, Ye Qun, Lin's wife, prepared a list of rules for Lin's staff to observe, among them that "all Lin's speeches must include references to the Chairman, that Lin must never be seen without the *Quotations from Chairman Mao*, that whenever they appear together Mao must always be allowed to take the lead and that Lin must also circle whatever item the Chairman denotes on a document." Whenever Lin and the Chairman appeared together in public, the staff was directed to make sure that Lin always followed the Chairman, but that while he must never move ahead of the Chairman he must also never fall back very far. Lin and his wife choreographed the successor's every movement vis-à-vis the Chairman down to the most minute detail. In doing so, Lin made it clear that he did, indeed, aspire to become the true successor to Mao. The Cultural Revolution in this sense provided the perfect opportunity for Lin to expand his power within the Chinese army.

In January and February 1969, Mao suggested to Lin Biao that he might deliver the Political Report to the Ninth Party Congress. The question of just who would actually draft the critical document naturally followed. Zhang Chunqiao, the Shanghai political leader and Jiang Qing's ally, thought that his name, along with those of his assistants, and his cohort of Shanghai supporters, belonged at the top of the list. But then the self-proclaimed "top pen" of the Party, Chen Boda, disagreed. Chen could not stomach the idea that all the glory might be handed over to the Shanghai upstart Zhang Chunqiao, and he pleaded personally with Mao for the right once again to wield the pen. Lin Biao wanted to stave off any interference from the Central Cultural Revolution Group, outline the essence of the speech on his own, and have a summary report prepared following his delivery to the Congress. He moved to keep the entire process under his personal control by forming a writing pool that consisted of his personal secretary; his wife, Ye Qun; and his son, Lin Liguo.

Mao, as always, was thinking strategically. He was principally concerned with maintaining a balance of power between Chen Boda and Zhang Chunqiao, the two contenders for ideological supremacy, warning the chronically ill Lin the task might be too "tiring" for him. Mao, in his effort to achieve balance, called for Chen Boda to oversee the composition, and designated Zhang Chunqiao and the equally polemical Yao Wenyuan to help in drafting it.

Chen Boda, a native of the southeastern Fujian Province with a heavy accent, was the head of the Central Cultural Revolution Group that had been at the vanguard of promoting Mao's vision for radical political change in China. Nevertheless, Jiang Qing and Kang Sheng, and even members of the "younger generation" of leftist leaders like Zhang Chunqiao and Yao Wenyuan gave him little respect. Jiang thought nothing of yelling at Chen Boda, and on just about any occasion she subjected him to all kinds of personal humiliation. Zhang and Yao joined the fray, "shitting and peeing on his head," as Chen put it, despite his formal position as a leader of the radical left. On a number of occasions, Chen contemplated suicide. As he cast about for a possible ally, Chen realized that Lin Biao was probably the most likely candidate. For his part, Lin Biao reached out to Chen as someone whom he could use as a counterweight to the awesome power of Jiang Qing. Ye Qun, Lin's wife, like Chen, was a native of Fujian Province, and Lin relied on that powerful connection—regional affiliation is always an important link between politicians in China—to draw Chen to his side in his effort to block the Madam. "Chen Boda is a good man," Lin said, "and we all have to remember that it's never easy for a man of letters to handle such a major political situation." After years of fending for himself in the cauldron of leftist politics and without even batting an eyelash, Chen shifted his allegiance to Lin Biao's camp.

Chen by now was deeply involved in the work of drafting the all-important Political Report that was to be delivered at the Ninth

Party Congress. He broke with his previous allies on the left and made almost daily visits to Lin's personal residence, where they discussed the outlines of the report. This left Zhang Chunqiao and Yao Wenyuan in the political dust.

Lin Biao had been dragged against all his instincts into the maelstrom of the Cultural Revolution; all he wanted to do now was to bring the entire episode to a close. As the designated successor to Mao, Lin's power was firmly established, at least within the inner circles of the CCP central leadership, and he made it his goal to end the Cultural Revolution on good terms. Lin believed that Mao had expressed his greatest trust in him as his successor, and so he approached the drafting of the Political Report with the utmost seriousness.

Deep down, Lin entertained a vision for the future of China that was entirely antithetical to Mao's. He believed that once the Cultural Revolution had been brought to a close, China should focus on its economy, and do its best to achieve the long-sought-after goals first enunciated in the nineteenth century to achieve wealth and power for the Chinese people. Lin believed that improving the lot of the Chinese people and the country should be the main thrust of his Political Report. In this respect, Lin's ideas closely resembled those of Zhou Enlai. Privately, Chen Boda had asked Zhou for his opinion about Lin's plan, and Zhou had tacitly indicated his support. Chen was assigned to produce a draft of the Political Report, and he drew on Lin's basic line of thinking and called it "Strive to Build Our Country into a Powerful Socialist State," but he made very little progress on the document, perhaps because he was getting old and his energy was running out. He also may not have wanted to offend Mao, as he might have done by giving full expression to Lin's ideas. Mao badgered his former secretary to get the job done, but three months passed and Chen had managed to complete only three out of the projected ten sections of the planned speech. Jiang Qing and her leftist sidekicks, Zhang Chunqiao and Yao Wenyuan, constantly ambushed Chen at one discussion meeting after another. Yao accused the bookish Chen of crafting a report that focused too much on the role of "productive forces" at the expense of the political issues that had dominated the Cultural Revolution. Mao grew increasingly irritated as time went on and Chen failed to deliver a final draft. He finally took it away from Chen and put Kang Sheng in charge of the speech and assigned Zhang Chunqiao and Yao Wenyuan to the task. Once Mao had made his position clear on the matter, neither Lin Biao nor Zhou Enlai said a word.

Zhang produced an acceptable draft, one that focused much more on politics, and immediately Chen Boda issued a counterattack. The time had come, Chen insisted, to "develop and improve our economic production and raise the productivity of the labor force. We cannot continue," he said, hewing to Lin Biao's line, "simply to launch one movement and political campaign after another." Chen, the consummate political theorist, displayed his credentials by citing the comments of Eduard Bernstein, the nineteenth-century German revisionist, complaining that the draft, because it focused only on political movements, lacked "any sense of direction or overall goals and is completely lost." Mao, who decided that Chen was nothing more than a political opportunist, was enraged.

He rejected Chen's draft of the Political Report in favor of Zhang's version. Chen Boda was devastated. After Mao's outright rejection, Chen increasingly sided with Lin Biao on important matters.

Lin Biao kept his peace and uttered not a word on the entire matter. He was aware of the hidden firecrackers that were now exploding in Mao. From then on, however, the designated successor felt only hatred for Zhang Chunqiao. "Zhang and Yao Wenyuan are nothing more than unknown newspaper reporters," Lin declared with disdain. "They can write whatever they want, but I, Lin Biao, won't touch any of it." Lin remained true to his word—refusing to review the Political Report before he went on stage to deliver it to the audience at the Ninth Congress. When the conclave came to a close, Zhang politely urged Lin to sign the document before it went to press, but he refused.

In the afterglow of his Congress of Victors, Mao had planned to reverse his call for "great chaos" with a new policy whose end-goal was to "achieve great order under heaven." To his dismay, Mao realized that all his energy was being called upon to stamp out a series of major political brushfires that had broken out between Lin Biao and Jiang Qing. To his credit, Mao showed little, if any, favoritism to Jiang Qing as he tried to resolve their discord. Increasingly, he grew annoyed with his wife and her tendency to foment trouble whenever she could.

The Ninth Congress propelled Lin Biao to center stage in the theater of national politics. Lin's strength was substantially enhanced. As he began to spread his political wings, Mao was put on guard. Mao, who had never really planned to hand over any real power to Lin Biao, only ordained Lin as his official successor in order to rid the Party leadership of Liu Shaoqi. Lin, despite the years he'd spent in the political wilderness, turned out to be far more politically adroit than anyone had supposed, or than his polite and obedient demeanor had suggested. His appointment was something the Chairman would never cease to rue.

"WILL NO ONE RID ME OF THIS TURBULENT PRIEST?"

Particularly troubling to Mao was Lin's sway over the army. Lin's cronies included members of the crucial Central Military Affairs Committee and most of the leading figures in the Party committees throughout the country, as well as military officials originally dispatched to the central government ministries to support the leftists, but who now served the interests of the official successor. Lin had an immense power base. He commanded the influence of the so-called four golden pillars of steel: General Huang Yongsheng, former commander of the Guangzhou Military Region and army chief of staff; General Wu Faxian, commander of the PLA Air Force; General Li Zuopeng, deputy chief of staff and first political commissar of the PLA Navy; and General Qiu Huizuo, head of the PLA logistical arm. Lin could now claim the steadfast loyalty of Chen

Boda, who would command the pen, and he also had a great asset in Ye Qun, his wife, who was known to be able to coordinate events as if she were running a thread through the eye of a needle. This co-hort, which could operate as defense and offense, far surpassed in strength the independent kingdom assembled by Liu Shaoqi, for which Liu had been purged. Once he realized that Lin's power was now strong enough to counter his own, Mao retreated to his resi-dence, where he lay in bed for hours on end to mull things over un-til he could come to a solution.

In the end, Mao decided to exploit the emerging conflicts between his wife and Lin Biao, and to throw his weight behind Jiang Qing. The Chairman, aware that Lin had built up his political credits by pi-oneering an effort to deify Mao and his Thought, then moved to re-duce the attention paid to his own personality cult. Once the Ninth Party Congress had ended, Mao ordered Zhou to take down all the huge banners with the Chairman's famous quotations from the Great Hall of the People and once actually said to Lin's face, "Things created by these bastards have to go." Lin knew right away that Mao was refer-ring to him, but he kept his composure. He resented Mao's approach and he issued an order of his own that decreed that the Jingxi Guest House in Beijing, which the PLA operated, had to keep all the ban-ners with their Mao quotations on display.

On a trip with Zhang Chunqiao soon after the Ninth Congress to Suzhou in central China where Lin Biao maintained a residence, Mao made it clear to Lin that he was reconsidering his choice of suc-cessor. (The ostensible purpose of this meeting was to talk about how to prevent the reemergence of revisionism in Chinese politics and society.) According to inside accounts, during the course of their conversation, Mao mentioned that Lin was getting on in years and asked him what thoughts he'd had about who his successor might be. Mao put it to Lin bluntly: "I am old, and you are not in good health," he said. "Who do you think would want to be your succes-sor?" Lin said nothing, so Mao pressed on. "What do you think of Little Zhang?" he asked him, using a term of endearment for the

Shanghai politico. Lin was struck dumb. When he found his voice, he avoided a direct answer. Instead, he noted that people like Huang Yongsheng, Wu Faxian, Li Zuopeng, and Qiu Huizuo had from a very early age followed Mao's revolution, which made them much more reliable. "We must prevent the bourgeoisie from seizing power," Lin asserted, in a not-so-subtle jab at Mao's favorite candidate, Zhang Chunqiao.

Disaster loomed before Lin as he contemplated his future. Lin and his wife locked themselves behind closed doors and wept for one another. But Lin was unwilling to sit back and let Mao toy with him. Instead, he decided to launch a defensive campaign to protect his position as Mao's officially anointed successor. According to conventional wisdom, Lin Biao could not wait to seize power. Not so. This is the fiction that subsequently emerged to explain the ensuing conflict. Lin acted out of fear in a preemptive display of self-defense.

Zhou Enlai, tactful as ever, observed from the sidelines as the sparring match between the forces of Lin Biao and Jiang Qing heated up over the subject of Mao's successor. Zhou never liked to commit himself to one side or the other in political disputes, but here he leaned somewhat in favor of Lin Biao. (Zhou thought the Madam was arrogant and intolerable, and over the years the officers in the army who backed Lin Biao—generals Huang, Wu, Li, and Qiu—had shown Zhou Enlai respect and supported his work.)

Lin Biao also had a bond of sorts with Zhou Enlai that went back to the 1920s, when Lin had been Zhou's student at the Whampoa Military Academy. Lin demonstrated enormous military prowess in the years that followed, and he rose rapidly in the ranks of the PLA, but he never achieved the Olympian status occupied by Zhou in either the CCP or the military. Lin' s four golden pillars of steel, the generals Huang, Wu, Li, and Qiu, were subordinate to Zhou, who in the 1930s had already risen to the rank of general political commissar of the Red Army. Age and rank have always mattered in military tradition, and these men continued to pay Zhou Enlai the respect that he had always commanded as their superior.

Lin Biao sought out anyone he could enlist who happened to be on the wrong side of the Madam so that he could expand his power base in their political rivalry, and he overtly went after the support of Zhou Enlai. On more than one occasion during the most politically heated days of the Cultural Revolution, Lin Biao stepped up to defend Zhou Enlai. In the summer of 1967, when Mao Zedong was on one of his sojourns in southern China, and Lin Biao had been put in charge of the government in Beijing, Jiang and her minions ganged up on Zhou during a series of meetings of the Central Cultural Revolution Group. Lin came to Zhou's defense and conferred on the premier the power to chair the gatherings and take charge of matters and sent word to the military to extend its full support to Zhou.

At the Ninth Party Congress of April 1969, Kang Sheng and Zhang Chunqiao had provoked the unsuspecting General Wu Faxian to speak out against Zhou Enlai for his approval of an editorial that called for "exposing the small gang within the military." Lin Biao, as soon as he heard about this mischief, immediately sent a warning to Wu. "Tell fatty not to be fooled," was Lin's advice. "We cannot do without the premier in our Party. The Chairman handles policy and politics, but I am not in good health and no one else except the premier can handle the routine work." He added, "If you bring this matter up, you're finished." To make sure that Zhou got the message, Lin told his messenger, his wife Ye Qun, to deliver it to him in person.

Zhou Enlai was grateful to Lin Biao for the concern that he showed. Mao had promoted Lin to his present prominence, and Lin was regarded as Mao's man, but Zhou had watched Lin grow and mature as Mao's designated successor. Zhou displayed the utmost precaution. He made every effort to avoid any suspicion that, just because he happened to have had more political experience than Lin, he wasn't about to show him proper respect as the official successor. Zhou went out of his way in his own speech at the Ninth Congress to describe Lin as "a glorious representative figure" who had brought together Red Army forces during the period of struggle in the 1930s on Well Ridge Mountain. Lin got so excited when he heard the effusive praise for his past exploits that he stood up in the middle of the speech, interrupted Zhou Enlai, and blurted out, "I, Lin Biao, am nobody. Everything belongs to Chairman Mao. If I had followed He Long and Zhu De, I would have been finished long ago and there would be no today." As Lin made his declaration, he broke down into tears.

Lin and Zhou also developed an affinity of sorts after the Ninth Congress, when they both showed a serious interest in paying greater importance to the development of China's national economy. As Zhou put it, "On entering the 1970s, all our struggle, criticism, and rectification should be focused primarily on economic work." Zhou never openly came out in favor of Lin Biao in his ongoing struggle with Jiang Qing, but on most major issues, clearly the premier and Lin Biao were on the same page.

According to the memoir of Chen Boda, in late April 1969, the Chairman invited the premier, Lin Biao, Kang Sheng, Xie Fuzhi, and Chen to discuss just how long the Cultural Revolution should continue. Zhou immediately talked about the economic problems confronting the country and the need to bring an end to social anarchy and the sacrifice of so many cadres to rebel forces. "I agree with the premier's view," Lin Biao chimed in. "We must develop the economy, strengthen national defense, and put an end to factional struggle. Chairman Mao's revolutionary line has won a thorough victory, and so now we must develop the economy and unite the people." Mao was still troubled by the possibility that his Cultural Revolution was going to end prematurely. "The struggle has just passed through its initial stages," Mao retorted. "Don't we want to continue with the revolution? I can see I am in the minority today." As usual, Kang Sheng and Politburo member Xie Fuzhi voiced their immediate support for Mao's view, while the premier beat a quick retreat by suggesting he was "deficient in his studies and understanding of Chairman Mao's teachings and thoughts." Mao seemed to calm the situation by proclaiming, "The premier had no need to engage in self-criticism as different views and standpoints within the Party were expected," but the Chairman made his real views known when he suddenly walked out of the meeting and canceled plans to dine with Zhou. That gave Lin Biao the opportunity to express his concern that the Chairman was utterly unable to tolerate alternative views. "He is more of a dictator than Stalin," the vice-chairman observed. "And for this the country is sure to suffer."

Zhou, realizing that Mao was growing increasingly unhappy with Lin Biao, sent word to Lin through others that he should break his habit of staying home all the time. He urged him to travel around the country conducting some kind of research and investigation. Lin thanked Zhou Enlai for the words of warning, but he declined the advice. He claimed that ill health did not permit him to embark on such activities.

Lin Biao was never really very sick. (It's true that he feared contact with water and didn't like to be exposed to the wind because he caught cold easily, and often broke out in sweats.) But this wasn't why he stayed at home in his Maojia Bay residence in Beijing: Lin stayed to avoid arousing Mao's suspicions. Unfortunately, Lin's reclusive behavior could not save him. He fell into the first trap that Mao set for him. He did not have what it took to maneuver around the Chairman.

13

NIGHT FLIGHT

Mᴀᴏ ʜᴀᴅ ᴅᴇᴄɪᴅᴇᴅ ᴛᴏ ʀᴇᴏʀɢᴀɴɪᴢᴇ ᴛʜᴇ Pᴀʀᴛʏ ᴀɴᴅ ɪᴛs ᴛᴏᴘ leadership. This was the motive behind preparations that, by March 1970, were in full swing for the Fourth National People's Congress. Following the departure of Liu Shaoqi, the top position of state chairman (i.e., head of state) was vacant. Mao had absolutely no interest in holding this position, which called for the kind of ceremonial activities and protocol he always wanted to avoid. But he was very reluctant to give the post to anyone else—in so doing he would have to confront the nightmare that in China two people would hold the title of "Chairman" (*Zhuxi*). A China with two chairmen—one of the Party and one of the state—was anathema to Mao. He particularly did not want Lin Biao to occupy this position. Mao decided that the Fourth National People's Congress would modify the state constitution and eliminate the position altogether.

At least this was how most accounts of this affair published in mainland China describe the conflict. But in his account of the March 8 Politburo meeting, General Wu Faxian suggested that Mao had left an opening for Lin Biao: "On March 8, 1970, Chairman

Mao dispatched Wang Dongxing to convey his ideas to prepare for the Fourth National People's Congress. The Chairman's proposal went something like this: 'The time has come for the Fourth Congress to select the leadership of the government and modify the state constitution. The Politburo must consider whether the government needs to retain the post of state chairman and if so who is qualified to fill the position. As of now, it appears that Lin Biao would be the right choice, if, that is, the position of state chairman is necessary. In my opinion, it is better not to retain this post.' When this message from Mao, via Wang Dongxing, was delivered to the Politburo meeting, the meeting was coming to a close and there was little time for discussion. Ye Qun, Huang Yongsheng, and I all made a beeline to Wang's residence. There, the security czar repeated Mao's message almost word for word. Ye Qun was delighted because Mao's words seemed to suggest that Lin might be allowed to assume the post."

This was hardly the first time that Mao had uttered contradictory words. Before the formal opening of the Ninth Congress, during the discussion about who would chair the congress, Mao declared, "I nominate Comrade Lin Biao to serve as chair." Lin, at the time, understood exactly what Mao really wanted—he was testing Lin's loyalty. Lin stood up and immediately responded, "The great leader Chairman Mao should serve as chair." "Comrade Lin Biao should be the chair and I'll be the vice-chair, how about that?" Mao retorted. Lin Biao waved his hand back and forth repeatedly and shot back, "No good, no good, Chairman Mao is the chair. Everyone agree. Raise your hands, please." Hands were raised high all round the room. Seeing this, Chairman Mao said, "Ah, you are such a good guy. Too polite."

This time, however, prodded by Ye Qun, Lin Biao took the bait. He seemed to forget that, once again, Mao was probably testing him. Besides, Lin had been unhappy for a long time with his designation as Mao's successor. It was an empty title and conveyed very little real political significance. He knew that he was not about to become Chairman of the CCP. That was out of reach. State chairman, however, was a real job, and one that made sense and was within the realm of possibility. Liu Shaoqi had been the second leader to hold the position, and if Lin got the appointment he'd be on a par with the previous heir-apparent. Lin also very likely thought that if he aggressively pursued the post, he'd be able to determine Mao's real attitude toward his official successor, and that with this knowledge he could strengthen and defend his position.

Lin Biao had used the art of concealment to great success as a military leader. Now, in the battle of politics, he placed it at the heart of his strategy. Lin mulled over the various approaches available to him and, on April 11, 1970, he sidestepped the issue of whether or not the post should be retained. Instead, he proposed that Mao should assume the position, and argued that not to do so "would be out of compliance with the psychological state of the people." The post of state vice-chairman, Lin also argued, was not necessary, and he, for one, was unsuitable for the position.

Mao, who saw through Lin's strategy, was displeased with his official successor's aggressive approach. He was even more dismayed to discover that most members of the Politburo, including Zhou Enlai, supported Lin. If anything, Mao had always indicated that he thought someone old and powerless should be appointed to the post. The venerable Dong Biwu, who had served in state positions in the early years of the People's Republic, was one such possibility. The day after Lin aired his proposal, Mao, who at the time was in the central Chinese city of Wuhan, rushed back to Beijing and immediately convened a meeting of the Politburo where he insisted that he had no desire to serve as state chairman and that the post was unnecessary. Zhou Enlai was then in charge of the routine affairs of the Politburo. He was one of the major advocates who supported the post of state chairman, and Mao met privately with Zhou on several occasions. He convinced Zhou to change his position.

Lin, however, refused to budge. Once he saw that Mao had decided to oppose the post of state chairman, Lin realized that, although he had been designated Mao's official successor, he would never be allowed anywhere near the real levers of political power in China. The conflict that simmered between Mao and his "closest comrade-in-arms" now approached a boil.

Zhou once again was caught right smack in the middle of this conflict. Zhou had supported the idea of maintaining the position of state chairman. He wanted to meet the legitimate political needs of Lin Biao, and he also thought it made sense to create a state structure similar to those of other nations that maintained a head of state. Zhou was also aware that Party members had made it clear that they were genuinely in favor of having the position filled. If Mao assumed the post and Lin Biao served as the state vice-chairman, a streamlined allocation of leadership would be allowed. If Mao didn't want the position of state chairman, Zhou saw no reason why it should not be given to Lin Biao. Mao, after all, would remain the paramount leader of the Party, the military, and the nation.

Many in the top Party ranks, including Kang Sheng, one of Mao's most trusted former agents in the security apparatus, agreed with Zhou that there was no need to eliminate the post. Mao's evident position created a real dilemma for Kang, who chaired the group charged with rewriting the state constitution. The whole thing would now have to be resolved at the forthcoming Second Plenary Session to be held on Mt. Lu in Jiangxi Province. There, a life-and-death confrontation would once again play out among the Party's highest leaders that would send the Chinese reeling.

The Politburo Standing Committee (absent Mao, but including Kang Sheng) met in August 1970, just before the Mt. Lu Second Plenary Session. At the meeting, all four members called on Mao to assume the post of state chairman. Zhou Enlai was aware of the broad support for the proposal, but he also knew that Mao did not want to be weighed down with all the demands of protocol that went with this position. He thus proposed that the state chairman could authorize others to perform these duties. When he arrived at the opening of the formal session, Zhou met with Chen Boda and specifically asked him to prepare the necessary wording appropriate to this caveat so that it could be inserted into the constitution once Mao made his position on the matter clear.

Mao, for the moment, was outnumbered on the issue four-to-one on the Standing Committee. As one who exercised extraordinary personal authority, Mao could object to the idea of reinstating the post of state chairman, but as the head of the Party, he was obliged to comply with the fundamental Party principle that the minority must obey the majority. Mao also knew that it was virtually impossible for him to reveal his real reasons for opposing the post. Mao was furious when he found himself in this situation. "If you wish to have a state chairman," he declared, "go right ahead. But I will not serve in the post."

Lin Biao was scheduled to deliver the opening speech to the Second Plenary Session of the Ninth Communist Party Central Committee, which was formally convened on August 23, 1970. Lin still had not decided whether or not he should launch his planned attack on Zhang Chunqiao, whom Mao at their earlier Suzhou meeting had mentioned as a possible successor to Lin. But once he learned that Mao was in distress over the state chairman issue, Lin decided not to push it any further, but to attack Zhang Chunqiao instead. This would force Mao to choose once and for all between Lin and Zhang.

Lin calculated a clear route to victory. In the past, Mao had shed generals He Long and Luo Ruiqing, his longtime followers, in order to win over Lin Biao. Lin couldn't imagine that Mao would now dump him in favor of Zhang Chunqiao, whom Lin considered to be nothing more than a second-rate newspaper "reporter." Lin also felt secure in his treatment of the state chairman post. Lin could not have been more mistaken. On previous occasions, Mao's object had been to purge Liu Shaoqi, and his maneuvering had all been to the benefit of Lin Biao. This time, as it happened, Mao's primary goal was to put Lin in his political place.

Mao convened an enlarged meeting of the Politburo Standing Committee on the afternoon of August 25. In a sudden about-face, Mao gave a repeat performance of the show he'd put on in February

1967, when he had feigned outrage about the criticisms of the Cultural Revolution excesses that his old comrades had voiced in Cherish Benevolence Hall. Mao had declared, "Comrade Lin Biao and I will withdraw from Beijing and go back to Well Ridge Mountain in Jiangxi to fight a guerrilla war." This time, no such declaration rang forth. Instead, Mao telegraphed his disdain for Lin by conspicuously shaking the hands of Xu Shiyou, a general not considered a member of Lin Biao's network, but who had been previously forced to offer his hand to Lin in a show of support for the successor's opening day speech to the conference. "My hands are cold," Mao intoned to General Xu in a dramatic tone of voice. "How can I be state chairman? Just let me live a few more days." Mao then turned his attention to all those present and continued, in the same dramatic fashion, to say: "If you all continue with this, I am going up to the mountains and will leave you here to mess around. And after you finish with your mess," the Chairman went on, "I'll still be up in the mountains and I'll probably stay there for good. Otherwise, remove me as Party Chairman." Mao rounded on those assembled. "Don't mention the question of state chairman anymore," he warned. "If you want me to die soon, then go ahead and have your state chairman. Who is going to serve? Not me. Give me a show of hands those of you who want this post."

All of the assembled Party members were shocked by Mao's remarks, but none more than Lin Biao. In his compromised position, Lin resorted to his traditional role as Mao's top cheerleader and called on everyone to "firmly support Chairman Mao!" Zhou was the only person on hand who was able to mediate the emerging conflict between Mao and Lin. Ever devoted to following Mao, and eager to preserve his own legacy, Zhou had no desire to see the Lin-Mao relationship collapse. A lapse in their relationship would disrupt the central political structure, which, after years of instability and chaos, was at last returning to a workable level of stability.

To prevent Lin from falling further out of favor, Zhou worked long into the night to revise the speech Lin had delivered at the opening day of the plenary session in which he had proposed that

Mao be named state chairman and offered his "theory of genius." Zhou also sent off a minatory note to Kang Sheng. "Please read Vice-Chairman Lin's speech thoroughly a few more times," Zhou wrote. "This is to avoid any unfortunate side-effects that might be produced by the speech. Please mark in pencil anything that needs correction and send it back to me before noon. This precaution is taken purely as a way to afford protection for the vice-chairman. Loyal to the Party, loyal to the leader, this shall be our mantra. Please be advised not to let anyone in on this for now."

Zhou then persuaded Wu Faxian, one of Lin's major cohorts, to make a self-criticism. "The time has come," he told Wu, "to protect the deputy commander from problems that his speech has created. Come out and make a self-criticism, Faxian, and take responsibility because otherwise all these problems will fall on the shoulders of the deputy commander." Wu came forth and took the entire blame for Lin's faux pas.

Zhou, meanwhile, began to put some political distance between himself and Lin Biao. Even as he was moving to shore up the defenses of the official successor, Zhou was mending fences with Zhang Chunqiao, Mao's new favorite. Zhou openly praised Zhang (and Yao Wenyuan, his sidekick), reminding his listeners how gracefully the two leaders had accepted the previous misunderstandings of other people, and how conspicuously they had risen above pettiness. Zhou also made a point of encouraging Lin Biao to make his peace with Zhang. Despite the three separate notes Zhou sent to Lin during a Politburo meeting on August 23, in which he asked Lin to mention Yao and Zhang in his comments as a way of inspiring greater unity among top leaders, Lin completely ignored Zhou's efforts.

Lin and Zhou were entirely different political animals. Lin was generally reluctant to admit to any wrongdoing, and he was also one of the very few people in the Party who dared to defy Mao openly. Lin did not brush off Zhou to put him in an awkward position, but as an outward expression of his defiance. Furious that Mao had set him up, Lin decided to make Chen Boda, his recent ally, his scapegoat. In this way, Chen would be accused of fomenting conflict between Lin and Jiang Qing, and Chen would be made the subject of an investigation.

Lin maintained cordial relations with Zhou Enlai, but toward Kang Sheng he was quite remote and antagonistic. Kang reported to Lin that it was almost unprecedented for conflicts to break out into the open at formal meetings like the plenary session, which were generally so highly orchestrated. He put the blame for the current discord on "Wu Faxian's rumormongering, Wang Dongxing's fire, Chen Boda's whistle-blowing, and the zeal with which Chen Yi jumped at an opportunity to make a comeback." Lin would have none of this. "I know Wu Faxian," he shot back. "In all the years he followed me from the First to the Fourth Field Army, never have I known him to spread rumors." Lin then spoke privately to Wu. "You are not in the wrong," he assured Wu, "so don't make any self-criticism." Lin also sent out word that he fully intended to protect his generals. These old officials in the military were all cannons who liked to explode verbal cannonades, but they had all been through many years of fighting and the country had to rely on them.

Mao turned a deaf ear to Lin's efforts to moderate the situation. Instead, he turned up the heat on Chen Boda. Mao spent three days searching for the right ammunition and finally decided to compose a document of his own that he called "My Views," in which he took aim at Chen Boda's contributions to the theory of genius that had put Mao on a par with Marx and Lenin. Once Mao made this very public attack, the political death penalty had been effectively pronounced on Chen Boda. Chen, lamented Mao, "worked for me for more than thirty years, and not once did he support me on any major issue. This time he showed what he was really made of by engaging in a surprise attack." Mao added, "Fanning the flames of conflict as if we hadn't already had enough chaos, he acted as if he wanted to wipe out Mt. Lu and stop the earth from turning." Mao, however, stopped short of a full indictment of Chen Boda as he summed up his errant political course by describing it as "probably a matter of conscience, not conspiracy." Mao made it clear in his six-hundred word document that he was separating Chen from Lin, but by August

1970, he had already made up his mind, then and there, about the political fate of Lin Biao.

Ye Qun, Lin's wife, according to inside accounts, visited Jiang Qing in the midst of this growing tension between the Chairman and Lin and, in a flash, the Madam rushed back to see Mao to plead on Ye Qun's behalf. "Keep a clear head at critical times," Mao yelled at his ever-exuberant wife. "And be sure your ass doesn't end up sitting on the wrong side." To reinforce his political base, Mao sought out any number of people for talks and vied for support among the old generals, whom years earlier Mao himself had attacked. With Zhou Enlai's help, Mao made amends with Ye Jianying, and offered him the position of overseeing the special investigative group charged with looking into the historical problems connected to Chen Boda's time years earlier in Fujian and Guangdong provinces. Mao even sought out Lin for a talk to make sure that he remained bamboozled by the entire affair. The Chairman used the same method he'd employed when he'd cashiered Lin's predecessor, Liu Shaoqi. "As for Zhang Chunqiao," Mao confided to Lin, in an effort to encourage Lin to let his guard down, "this guy needs two more years of observation. Let's keep him for now. After two years I'll quit and you can take over and handle the work."

STILL SEARCHING FOR THE MIDDLE WAY

Zhou Enlai quickly emerged as the busiest man at the ongoing plenary session as the criticism of Chen Boda intensified. His immediate task was to persuade members who, at the outset of the conference, had committed their positions based on the assumption that Mao would accept the post of state chairman, to reverse themselves and make their self-criticisms. His secondary task was to carefully convey Mao's reasoning for his criticism of Chen Boda, without inspiriting an all-out attack on him. Everyone was compelled to agree that the Cultural Revolution was Chairman Mao's greatest achievement, and Zhou had to make sure that the role that

Chen had played as the head of the Central Cultural Revolution Group remained unblemished.

Zhou had actually spent most of his time in the days and weeks preceding the plenary session planned for Mt. Lu preparing for a full discussion of the national economic situation. Mao's midstream decision to go after Chen Boda had changed the emphasis, but Zhou was determined to steer the meeting as soon as he could back to the real reasons the top leadership had gathered for the conference. Zhou worked day and night to prepare a draft of the upcoming Fourth Five-Year Economic Plan outlining China's economic future. Zhou was under incredible stress and was fatigued by the events that transpired at Mt. Lu, and on the way to a meeting suffered another episode with his heart and had to be revived by oxygen.

The conference passed the draft of a new, modified constitution and also approved the new national economic plan. Mao was all smiles, talking and joking around, on September 6, 1970, the day the Second Plenary Session of the Ninth Central Committee ended. Lin Biao was silent and gloomy. Zhou Enlai, after a quick recovery, could see that a disaster of the highest order was brewing.

It was assumed that once the conference on Mt. Lu had ended, Mao would ease up on Chen Boda. After all, this was the man who had served Mao for years as a senior secretary and ghostwriter. Chen had been dogged and loyal when he joined up with the Chairman to defeat Liu Shaoqi and his supporters during the early stages of the Cultural Revolution. But Mao was not about to modify his attack. In his opinion, Chen had clearly switched his political allegiance to Lin Biao. The Chairman could smell Lin's political ambition. He had made up his mind to crush this threat with one decisive blow. Years earlier, Mao had gone after Liu Shaoqi by first of all targeting Beijing mayor Peng Zhen, Liu Shaoqi's top political ally. Mao decided to use the same plan of attack and target Lin by first dispatching Chen Boda, Lin's new-found political ally.

Mao and Lin both knew that they were reaching a final political showdown. Mao, as undisputed Chairman of the Chinese Communist Party and symbol of the nation, clearly had the upper hand, but

Lin was not about to sit around and wait to be slaughtered. "Better to stand up and fight than sit down and wait for death." Lin, who had spent most of his life on the battlefield, was a stubborn, strong-willed personality. Sensing that all other options had been exhausted, he made his preparations, covertly, for the final battle.

Drawing the Knives

Lin knew that he was embarking on a course of action that threatened not only his own reputation but that of his politically active wife and his children, including his son Lin Liguo, an officer in the Chinese Air Force. Although Lin was prepared to ruin everyone in his family on this high-stakes gamble, he was far less inclined to involve the four golden pillars of steel, his loyal generals, in the "great game" he was playing out with Mao. The Mt. Lu confrontation reportedly had scared the wits out of General Huang Yongsheng, and it had spooked air force Commander Wu Faxian so much that he had attempted to commit suicide by jumping off a building. "If fighting a tiger, rely on your blood brothers," goes the old Chinese adage. "When fighting a war, rely on your father and sons." Lin cast his generals aside in the spirit of this saying and came to rely almost exclusively on Liguo, his own son, nicknamed Tiger. He was Lin's secret weapon in the final showdown with Mao.

Lin had cultivated his son and trained him as his loyal ally since the beginning of the Cultural Revolution. After he accompanied his father to the Mt. Lu Conference in August 1970, Lin Liguo created a secret organization known as the "joint fleet," a reformulation of the research group within the Chinese Air Force that Wu Faxian had formerly chaired that was comprised of Liguo's cronies in the air force. After Lin Biao ordered Liguo to come up with a plan by March 1971, Lin Liguo convened a meeting of the joint fleet in Shanghai, where together they composed the Summary of the 571 Project. In Chinese, "571" (*wuqiyi*) is a homonym for "military uprising."

The Summary of the 571 Project was really a fervent condemnation of Mao, his policies, and his rule over China. The summary listed Mao's various schemes and crimes—"those who are his guests today will be his prisoners tomorrow"—and it denounced Mao as the "biggest tyrant in Chinese history." The article also analyzed the relative power positions of each of the two sides—Mao, on the one hand, Lin on the other—and set a time frame for executing the strategy and achieving the primary goals of the uprising.

No one will ever know whether Lin Biao actually sat down and read the Summary of the 571 Project because there's no first-hand information on the matter, but it is probably accurate to say that the document reflected Lin's views. Young and fearless as Liguo undoubtedly was at this time (he was twenty-one years old), it's unlikely that he could have written such a precise analysis of Mao's crimes and aberrations without having spent years in the inner circles of power. The Summary of the 571 Project, in its entirety, lacked the necessary detail that any coordinated action to actually seize political power would have to possess. It was more like a denunciation of policies and decisions than a plan for a full-scale military coup.

To gloss over political tensions and avoid a political crisis within the top leadership, Zhou Enlai persuaded the reluctant Lin Biao to attend festivities on top of the Gate of Heavenly Peace on May Day, 1971. Lin Biao surprised everyone when he openly displayed his resentment of Mao and sabotaged this carefully orchestrated show of "unity." Lin spoke not a single word to Mao during the evening's traditional display of fireworks and Mao returned the favor by ignoring his successor. Lin sat down for a few minutes with the entourage, which included Prince Sihanouk of Cambodia, before leaving without any of the usual greetings or pleasantries.

Another equally cold encounter occurred the next month when Mao ordered Lin Biao to accompany him to a meeting with Nicolae Ceaușescu, the visiting Romanian leader, and his wife. Lin tried to bow out of the meeting on account of excessive sweating, his persistent malady. When Mao insisted, Lin ignored him. Only after Ye Qun implored her husband to attend did he agree to go. But immediately after he'd greeted the guests, Lin removed himself to a corner outside the hall where he waited until the meeting was over.

Although he made no attempt to conceal his pique and stubbornness, Lin Biao actually wanted to meet with Mao and somehow resolve their discord. These two leaders had survived together more than thirty years of strife and struggle as comrades-in-arms. Mao throughout this long association had been generally pleased that he'd found in Lin someone who seemed to have a true understanding of his character and leadership. Lin had always supported the Chairman unequivocally, and whenever Mao was in a jam Lin had been there to bail him out. Mao, however, refused to budge, even after Lin's wife had made a personal appeal to the Chairman on Lin's behalf. Lin even put his own arrogance aside and asked Jiang Qing to arrange a meeting for him with Mao. But Mao kept the door firmly shut on Lin's several attempts to arrange a meeting. It was obvious that Mao had no intention of trying to repair their irreconcilable differences. Lin beat a quick retreat.

By August 1971, Mao had decided to take some kind of action against Lin. Following his major assault on Chen Boda in the spring at which Lin's supporters—including the four generals Huang, Wu, Li, and Qiu and Lin Biao's wife, Ye Qun—were forced to make public confessions, the Chairman made his first move in the form of a meeting with top officials in the Party and army to discuss how to solve the ongoing "Lin Biao problem." Under the burning hot sun, the Chairman hit the road and headed south from Beijing. He took his time. He stopped along the way to meet and talk with local officials and those in charge. Mao, in these discussions, resorted to the traditional rhetoric of "struggle over the Party line," and then put a label on the August 1970 Mt. Lu Conference, which he called the "tenth" such struggle in the history of the CCP. Mao dropped the name of Lin Biao into his narrative at key points, and characterized the conference in classic Cultural Revolution terms as a "battle between two headquarters," for which Lin would "naturally have to take some responsibility." "Some people consider my advanced age and think I am close to vanishing into the sky," Mao declared at one point, "and so they eagerly think of becoming the state chairman, try to split the Party and seize power. This incident is far from over because the black hand that manipulates this nefarious affair goes far beyond Chen Boda and involves many others." Mao concealed his real purpose with frequent references to the importance of "protecting Lin," but, nevertheless, the Chairman made it clear that when it "comes to changing the leader who committed mistakes in the Party line, the task can be arduous."

Here was an instance of just how shrewd Mao could be. The Chairman was able to kill two birds with one stone when he took his easygoing tour of the south. It allowed him, first of all, to spread the word that he was dissatisfied with the official successor, a way of slowly but surely undermining Lin's base of power. He also knew that his less-than-laudatory comments about Lin would undoubtedly irritate the successor when they reached him through the bureaucratic grapevine, and he would be able to see how Lin would react. Mao was aware that he could not, single-handedly, erase Lin Biao from the new Party constitution passed at the 1969 Ninth Congress that had named Lin his official successor. Try as he might to elevate the conflict at Mt. Lu over the issue of the state chairman to the ultimate political crime of "struggle over Party line," Mao's only real option was to "shake the mountain to flush out the tiger"—as the old Chinese saying goes—and let him react. Mao could use whatever action Lin chose to destroy him. Lin Biao, as it turned out, played right into Mao's hands.

Lin Biao had long prepared for a final showdown with Mao, but as the day of disaster approached he was caught by surprise. Lin, who had been clinging to a shred of hope that Mao had no real reason to destroy him, had never prepared a preemptive strike. When Mao set off on his trip to the south, Lin assumed a calm façade. He telephoned Zhou Enlai and asked him to notify him when Mao got back to Beijing because he wanted to set up a meeting with the Chairman. Lin wasn't monitoring Mao's movements for any ulterior motive. He was just acting on his ongoing fantasy that some sort of reconciliation was still possible. Then, on September 6, 1971, Lin got wind of the conversations that Mao had been holding in the south. He went into a state of shock. Lin had assumed that if Mao did decide to move against him he'd do so after the Fourth National People's Congress, which was supposed to convene sometime after China's National Day on October 1. Lin dispatched Ye Qun, his wife, to summon Huang Yongsheng, Wu Faxian, Li Zuopeng, and Qiu Huizuo, his four generals, back to Beijing for a meeting in late August. Ye Qun detected trouble way ahead of Lin Biao. She believed that Mao would deal with his Lin Biao problem with all deliberate speed once he returned to Beijing and well in advance of the Fourth NPC because the Chairman's greatest wish was to promote Zhang Chunqiao to a top leadership position. If, once again, Mao refused to answer Lin's inquiries, this would be a sign of clear and present danger that Mao had finally decided to dismiss his second in command.

According to official documents, the three alternate plans developed in the Summary of the 571 Project were: to assassinate Mao during his tour of the south; failing that, to set up an alternative government in Guangzhou; and, as a last resort, to flee the country. But Lin never put any such set of plans into action. Instead, his initial response, once he'd learned through a variety of channels the full content of Mao's conversations in the south, was to remain calm, to take no action, and avoid going anywhere. Lin told his wife and son that he "didn't want to live any more," and then proceeded to instruct the builders of his compound in the Beidaihe coastal resort area, where the Lins were holed up, to cease construction. According to his staff members, Lin and his wife stayed closeted in their rooms during those several days discussing possible strategies. Staffers recall seeing Ye Qun coming in and out of the room, often in tears. Liguo, Lin's son, took the clear position that his father should put up a fight before any consideration was given to the idea of flight, but Lin Biao, a man who at one time had decisively commanded tens of thousands of Chinese troops was uncharacteristically indecisive. The only actions that Lin took were purely defensive and involved no real attempt to seize power.

On the afternoon of September 7, 1971, Lin Liguo met with his sister Lin Liheng (Lin Doudou) to go along with his plans. "The critical moment has arrived," he told her.

Last night, the director [read: Ye Qun] suggested that we go abroad. The leader [read: Lin Biao] did not agree, but after repeated arguments by the director he finally conceded to her suggestion. I was asked to arrange for the necessary aircraft using the excuse with the appropriate authorities, in order to circumvent the normal bureaucratic channels for securing airplanes, that time was short. This morning, Zhou Yuchi [general secretary of the joint fleet] was brought here from Beijing for discussions aimed at persuading the leader to stay put for the time being.

The leader then broke down embracing old Zhou and cried out, "I've given over my entire family, old and young, for your protection. You must save them."

The next day, Lin Liguo, armed with Lin Biao's note, secretly entered Beijing and attempted to put into action his own conspiracy to assassinate Mao. But the Chairman, as it so often happened, had already prepared for such an action. Mao had learned of the preparations for a military coup through the establishment of the secret joint fleet before he'd even left on his southern tour in mid-August. For this reason, the Chairman had conveyed his itinerary to only one person: Premier Zhou Enlai. Mao thus began his tour in the utmost secrecy, and then altered his plans by suddenly returning on September 12 to Beijing. Ye Qun and Lin Liguo immediately reported Mao's premature return to Lin Biao. Lin reluctantly decided to take his family and, accompanied by his generals, decamp to Guangzhou, which for years had been the home turf of General Huang Yongsheng. But the plan was dead on arrival. An inside traitor had revealed its every component. The traitor turned out to be none other than Lin Liheng, Lin's beloved daughter.

Lin Liheng had always enjoyed an affectionate relationship with her father, Lin Biao. Her relationship with Ye Qun, however, was quite another matter. Lin Liheng, who wasn't even convinced that Ye Qun was her real biological mother, felt that she had suffered mental abuse at the hands of Ye Qun. Once, when Ye Qun had tried to intrude on her daughter's marriage plans, Liheng had threatened to kill herself. In Liheng's mind the political differences between her father and Chairman Mao were merely a matter of some basic misunderstanding, and that Ye Qun bore responsibility for the deterioration in the bond between the two.

Lin Liheng hoped that her father could resolve his basic problems with Mao through conversation, allowing him to exit the political stage gracefully. Liheng also wanted to teach her mother a lesson. She thought Lin Liguo's three-pronged plan involving assassination, setting up an alternative government in the south, or fleeing the country was pure fantasy.

Lin Liheng's strong-willed brother was far beyond persuasion. She viewed Liguo's plans as something her mother had cooked up in cahoots with her brother while her father, sickly and long isolated from the political arena, was in the dark. Believing that her mother and brother had manipulated her father, Liheng began her own battle to protect her father, beginning with her efforts to keep him sequestered at the coastal resort of Beidaihe while she set out to destroy the political conspiracy that her mother and brother had concocted against Mao. This was the only way, Liheng believed, that her father's legacy and reputation could be protected. Liheng instructed staff in her father's office to keep a watch on every move her mother made. Meanwhile, she decided—if it came to a matter of life and death—to appeal to the Party Central about her actions. Fearing that her father's frail health might suffer under the pressure of this imbroglio, Liheng didn't apprise Lin Biao of her plans.

When Mao returned to Beijing on September 12, Ye Qun flew into a frenzy. Liguo returned during the evening and, according to the account of a servant, joined his mother in informing his father, who was still at Beidaihe, that a Trident aircraft could evacuate them all to a foreign neighbor. Lin Liheng, meanwhile, reported what she knew to the Party Central, via the Central Security Forces. By taking action, Lin Liheng all but ruined her father's plans to decamp to the south and set up an alternative government, which probably would have resulted in a bloody civil war. That this unthinkable tragedy was avoided is to Lin Liheng's credit. Alas, in the aftermath of the entire affair, Liheng did not see it from this perspective. Never had Liheng thought that her actions would result in aiding Mao by bringing Lin Biao to his knees.

At 10 P.M. on the night of September 12, Zhou Enlai received a dispatch from Lin Liheng indicating that Ye Qun and her son planned to kidnap Lin Biao and flee abroad. At the time Zhou was in central Beijing, at the Great Hall of the People, where he was intensely engaged in discussions and preparations around the draft Government Report for the upcoming Fourth National People's Congress. At first, Zhou dismissed Lin Liheng's account as some kind of wild exaggeration. He thought it was a product of the famously tense relationship between Lin Liheng and her mother. Was it possible that the great commander could actually be kidnapped by his own wife and son? Realizing that any carelessness in the matter could be fatal, Zhou dropped everything and put a call in to the Central Security Forces (the 8341 unit responsible for guarding central personnel). He told them to be on their guard. Zhou next placed a call to Liheng and asked her for evidence to back up her dispatch.

Liheng, reluctant to spill all the beans to Zhou, insisted that her father's safety was in question, and pleaded with Party Central to take the appropriate measures to ensure his safety. Zhou, it must be said, was more concerned with what Lin Biao actually wanted to do and whether he really planned to try to flee the country than he was with Lin Biao's well-being. "Do your best to find out what the Leader has in mind and then report back to me immediately," Zhou advised the frantic Liheng.

Zhou acted quickly on Liheng's information about the Lin family's plans to use an airplane to execute their escape. Zhou tracked down the aircraft, which he located at the Mountain Sea Gate (*Shanhaiguan*) airport outside the resort area of Beidaihe. When Wu

Faxian, the commander of the air force, indicated that he was not even aware of the location of this particular aircraft, Zhou realized that something unusual was going on. He immediately ordered Lin's people to fly the plane back to Beijing, but was told that the jet's oil pump had malfunctioned, which the premier knew right away was an obvious lie. Lin Liheng's account, it seemed, was probably true.

ZHOU TAKES COMMAND

According to insider accounts, Zhou performed his usual role and offered to mediate the conflict. Zhou telephoned Mao and offered to travel to Beidaihe to personally intervene in the crisis and talk Lin Biao out of doing anything rash, but Mao vetoed that plan. Mao, who relished the idea that Lin Biao was fighting a fire in his own backyard, saw no reason why Zhou should rush over to mediate his family problems. Instead, Mao ordered Wang Dongxing to monitor the activity of security forces at Beidaihe and to use his outpost in Beijing to keep an eye on how the fire was developing in Lin's back yard.

Zhou immediately picked up the drift of Mao's thinking and withdrew his offer to travel to Beidaihe. Instead, at midnight, in a direct call to Ye Qun, Zhou expressed his concern, and told her that the Trident parked at Mountain Sea Gate airport lacked the proper authorization. In a panic, Ye Qun tried to cover up the situation with the lame excuse that Lin Biao had ordered the jet, in the event that the weather was clement, and Lin wanted "to take a flight in the sky." Warning Ye Qun that flying at night was not safe, Zhou advised her that they should by all means check the weather conditions before taking off. Zhou then repeated his offer to intervene personally in the matter and to come to Beidaihe to talk to Lin Biao.

Zhou was making a genuine offer to mediate, but when Ye Qun heard him say that he was willing to come to Beidaihe, she decided that he had learned about their plan to fly to Guangzhou and that Mao was now completely on top of the situation and was ready to pounce. Now they had no more room for maneuver. This call from

Zhou, evidence later revealed, was the final spark that convinced Lin Biao to board the plane. Almost immediately after her conversation with Zhou had ended, Ye Qun received a call from Zhou Yuchi, commander of the joint fleet, who had been involved in the organization of the Guangzhou flight plan. Zhou Yuchi informed Ye Qun that the premier had just issued an order to ground the plane that waited at Beidaihe. Ye Qun, now desperate, tried to contact Huang Yongsheng in Beijing. As it happened, the general was at that moment at the side of Zhou Enlai, "assisting the premier in this matter," and was thus unable to take any independent action.

Ye Qun's mind was racing. Her thoughts turned at once to the last, desperate option laid out in the Summary of the 571 Project: flight to a foreign land. Lin Biao, however, despite the pressure from his wife and son, hesitated to make this irreversible move. The official successor sat alone weeping, according to the description of a member of Lin's staff, who heard Lin say, "I am a nationalist to the end."

It boggles the mind that a great military commander, who once had directed an army of several million men, exuded such indecision at this critical moment. No one will ever know why Lin Biao allowed his wife to lead him to Mountain Sea Gate airport where he boarded the Trident for that fateful flight. Perhaps he fled out of a desire to live, or out of love for his wife and children, whom he wanted to rescue from the ruin that his own actions had brought upon them. Or, it may have been the case that Lin had taken his usual dose of sleeping pills and was in no shape to think clearly or act decisively so late on that fateful evening of September 12.

As soon as he had spoken to Ye Qun and heard her say that Lin wanted "to take a flight in the sky," Zhou Enlai contacted airport personnel at Mountain Sea Gate with the instruction that the plane was not allowed to be flown at night. He added, "When Lin Biao arrives at the airport, ask him to call the premier." Zhou then dialed Lin Biao's direct line via the Military Affairs Committee of Party Central, but he made his call too late. Lin and his entourage had left the residence and were already on their way to the airport. Zhou still lacked any evidence that Lin had plotted a conspiracy. He took these actions as a precautionary step. The Lins, however, father, wife, and son, were under the distinct impression that Mao had already ordered their arrest.

Zhou was now monitoring the situation very closely and received a report on the movement by the Lins as soon as they had left their residence. Zhou, the experienced hand, known for his deft political skills, fell short on this occasion. He couldn't stop Lin before he boarded the Trident and brought the country to a great political crisis.

Zhou's actions in the Lin Biao incident raise a number of questions, in particular the decision he made not to issue an order that would have prevented Lin from boarding the plane. Was it because Zhou was waiting to see where Lin was heading? Zhou may have thought that he had to act with extreme caution because Lin was the lawful successor to the Chairman of the CCP. Or he may have been following Mao's order to keep a covert watch on Lin Biao and then deliberately let him flee. The drive between Lin's residence and the airport at Mountain Sea Gate took forty minutes—he knew they had plenty of time to place vehicles on the runway to prevent the Trident from taking off. Zhou later acknowledged that this had come up as a possible way to stop Lin, but he had failed to follow through on it. This misstep remains a puzzle. "When Lin Biao was taking flight, I was right by the phone in the Great Hall of the People with General Huang Yongsheng at my side," Zhou Enlai later explained. "At the time, we didn't think that Lin Biao was really going to flee the country, that maybe he really did want to take a flight in the sky and come back. Since that was a possibility, we really didn't think that it would be a good idea to open fire on him."

Once Lin's plane was airborne, Zhou made a call to Mao, and issued an order to Li Desheng, then commander of the Beijing Military Region (and a general in whom Mao had a great deal of trust), and to Ji Dengkui, who had recently been elevated to a high post at the Ninth Party Congress, to take charge of Air Force Headquarters and its branch in the Beijing Military Region and provide all necessary assistance. Zhou then ordered his longtime bodyguard Yang

Dezhong to accompany members of the Central Party Secretariat to the Western Suburbs (*Xijiao*) military airfield outside Beijing to "assist" Wu Faxian. In reality this order was to keep an eye on the man who for many years had been so close to Lin Biao. Zhou then drove to Mao's residence in Central South Lake.

According to insider accounts, Mao was shocked when he first heard about Lin's precipitous actions, realizing the import of his decision to take on Lin in the political arena. When he was informed that the Trident was about to leave Chinese airspace and enter the skies above Mongolia, Mao refused to order any action: "Rain has to fall, women want to marry, these things are immutable," Mao is said to have muttered. "Let him go."

REAFFIRMING LOYALTIES

Lin's betrayal of Mao offered Zhou Enlai an opportunity to once again put his personal loyalty to Mao on display. Observing the profound shock the entire affair was having on the Chairman, Zhou swung into action and shouldered all the major front-line decisions that had to be made. It was crucial to track the course of Lin's plane, but Zhou decided not to monitor the entire country by radar. The premier opted instead to limit the scanning to North China. Messages were sent out for the plane to return, and Zhou made it clear that he planned to be there wherever flight number 256 landed. Zhou Enlai never ordered armed forces to shoot down Lin's plane with ground fire, as rumors claimed. Air Force chief Wu Faxian, who now wanted to draw a very clear line between himself and Lin Biao, actually proposed the idea of intercepting the aircraft before it left Chinese airspace, but Zhou insisted that any decision like that had to be made by Mao. According to Wu Faxian, Zhou tried to calm him down by saying, "No rush, no rush, let's ask the Chairman for his advice." That's when Mao uttered his famous words about "rain has to fall" and "women want to marry." As Zhou later explained when he recalled the occasion, Lin Biao was vice-chairman of the

Communist Party and the deputy commander-in-chief of the military. As a mere member of the Politburo, with no formal role in the military, Zhou was in no position to order the armed forces to shoot down the airplane of the officially designated successor as written into the Party constitution.

Zhou issued an order to ground all aircraft nationwide only when Lin's aircraft crossed the border and entered Mongolian airspace. (No aircraft was allowed to leave the ground or enter Beijing airspace without a joint order issued in the name of five people, namely Mao, Zhou, Huang Yongsheng, Wu Faxian, and Li Zuopeng.) Air force personnel in all military regions and districts were ordered to follow the commands of the top commander-in-chief of their respective military region. Wu Faxian later recalled that he realized the severity of the situation when he saw the expression in Zhou's eyes. "Faxian," the premier warned him gravely, "if one airplane forcibly enters Beijing airspace, your head and mine will both be cut off." Zhou's decision that all military orders had to be issued by Lin's top generals was an act of political shrewdness: it gave the subordinates of these commanders no choice. They had to obey orders.

Zhou had no way of knowing the whereabouts of Lin's airplane once it entered the airspace over Mongolia—radar contact was lost. Zhou's immediate concern then switched from the fate of Lin Biao to the possibility that the Soviets might make a surprise attack on China in response to what they could consider a military move by the Chinese. Zhou persuaded Mao to move to the safer confines of the Great Hall of the People, where underground bunkers and tunnels had been constructed for the leadership in the event of a military crisis. Zhou then called an emergency meeting of the entire Politburo at which he discussed the attempt Lin had made to flee the country. An emergency war directive was drawn up simultaneously to be issued to all military and diplomatic personnel, and to news and propaganda outlets. Calls went out to every province in the country and to all military regions and districts to inform them of the situation and to announce that military units must make immediate preparations for the outbreak of conflict possibly involving the Soviet Union.

By midnight, September 13, Zhou Enlai, who had been making emergency plans all day, was still hard at work. Word had come in that an aircraft had reportedly crashed and was now burning somewhere in Mongolia. In his letter to Mao, Zhou attempted to assuage the Chairman's concerns.

I am sending for your approval the war directive drawn up jointly by the Politburo and the PLA general staff. Participants included Zhang Chunqiao, Yao Wenyuan, Huang Yongsheng, Wu Faxian, Ji Dengkui (Li Desheng was absent because he was at Air Force Headquarters) along with five other deputy chiefs of staff and me.

Have made several calls to every military region (including Shenyang, Nanjing, Guangzhou, Wuhan, Kunming, and Chengdu regions). Plans were conveyed and phone calls made to other military regions as well. Met with Jiang Qing on one occasion and she is now resting. Li Xiannian, Hua Guofeng, and Li Zuopeng have been dispatched to the Jingxi Guest House, Navy Headquarters, and the General Logistics Department, respectively, to carry out their work and maintain phone contacts.

Attached please find two information sheets, both worth reading. It appears that the plane has indeed crashed and is burning, but this could be an attempt by the enemy to confuse us. This morning (September 13) at 6:30 A.M. a helicopter with an additional three of the coconspirators was forced to the ground, and one was shot dead, two committed suicide, and one was left alive. There are plenty of materials explaining these events.

At the moment, security forces from the Beijing Area Air Force Command and the Beijing Military Region are all in position with troops stationed at every airport in the area. Mobile reserve units have been activated for any possible move. All has been taken care of. Sit back and don't worry. Best Wishes to the Chairman!

On the afternoon of September 14, the Chinese embassy in Mongolia sent an urgent cable that Lin and his people had indeed failed to reach their final destination in the Soviet Union. Zhou, suffering total exhaustion, had just taken sleeping pills when the cable reached him. He was so relieved that he lost control and shouted out, "Crashed to death, crashed to death," and then ran to report the good news in person to Mao, who was still cooling his heels in the Great Hall of the People.

The official explanation the Chinese leadership presented of the crash was that the plane had run out of fuel, but so many people afterward refused to believe this that an alternate account gained great credibility: missiles launched on orders from Mao Zedong or Zhou Enlai had brought the aircraft crashing to earth.

The actual unfolding of events was far more complicated than either account would suggest. Soon after the incident, an insider related to this author that following the crash the family of the Trident pilot, Pan Jingyin, was severely persecuted. Driven into the streets, the family became virtually homeless. The family was only rehabilitated years later, when the Chinese Air Force issued a new directive that Pan's family had to be treated with some care. This was a radical policy shift, which came only after analysis of the flight path that the Trident had taken indicated that soon after takeoff it had veered wildly and executed a number of sharp turns. An accomplished pilot, Pan was nonetheless performing bizarrely, perhaps because he wanted to protest the orders he'd been given to head for the Soviet Union. When the plane entered Mongolian airspace and began to approach the border of the Soviet Union, it again veered and turned suddenly back in the direction of China. It was then, heading toward the Chinese border, that the plane crashed. Evidence gathered during an on-site investigation of the crash scene indicated that Pan had been shot. It is not known whether the plane made its 180-degree turn because Pan was protesting the flight path or because Lin Biao had suddenly gotten cold feet. Those in the know within the ranks of the air force who were familiar with Pan's flying skills are convinced that in the event of an onboard emergency, Pan could have carried out a forced landing. If so, the crash must have been the result of something other than mechanical failure.

The conclusion reached by the official investigation that the plane crashed because "it ran out of fuel" is also less than convincing because all the other people on board died of smoke inhalation caused by the explosion of fuel and the fire that ensued. The rumor that a Soviet missile shot down the plane seems equally far-fetched because when the Mongolian government claimed that "a Chinese military aircraft was shot down by missiles after invading Mongolia," the Chinese government uttered not a word.

So ended a battle that began when Lin had been proclaimed Mao's official successor at the April 1969 Ninth Party Congress, and which had deeply divided the revolutionary camp. Mao had survived the ordeal, but he could by no means be considered the winner. Mao was now going to have to make some political compromises to at least stabilize the outcome of the Cultural Revolution. This shift in the Chinese political arena now provided Zhou Enlai with a golden opportunity to put his considerable political skills into practice.

The Lin Biao incident was also a wake-up call to the Chinese people, who for the first time began to express real doubts about the Chairman and his Cultural Revolution. Zhou Enlai's shock over what had happened, however, was beyond what any Chinese could have imagined and in many ways the Lin Biao fiasco had a far greater impact on Zhou Enlai than it did on Mao. Zhou could usually conceal his emotions, but on this particular occasion he broke down and cried, according to Ji Dengkui, who described the emotional scene in an interview with the author: "When the critical moment had finally passed," Ji Dengkui admitted, "everyone breathed a sigh of relief. Over the course of the next few days members of the Politburo remained at the Great Hall of the People, where they could all work together as a team. Li Xiannian, who was in charge of routine affairs at the Foreign Ministry, was assigned the task of providing Zhou with an updated report, and I noticed on entering the premier's makeshift office that he was just sitting there staring off into space with an apparent heavy heart. Unaware of the source of his unhappiness, we both approached the premier and tried to say some comforting words to make him feel better."

"At the beginning," Ji Dengkui recalled, "the premier only listened, without uttering a word. 'Lin Biao has self-destructed,' I noted, 'so we should feel better because from now on the nation can focus on the task of developing the economy.' Zhou was obviously touched by such comments because tears welled up in his eyes and streamed silently down his face and he began to cry louder and louder. He became so choked up at one point that he couldn't speak. Li Xiannian and I saw him crying so badly that we didn't know what to say, and so we just stood there to keep him company. In the end, the premier gradually calmed down, and after a long pause he uttered those few words: 'You don't understand. It's not that simple. It's not finished.' With that he said not one more word."

Ji Dengkui thought that the root of Zhou's sorrow was buried in the profound differences between his and Mao's ideas for managing the country. Mao wanted perpetual class struggle and endless political campaigns, but Zhou wanted to develop the economy. With Lin Biao out of the picture, the question for China was whose view of the country's future would win out as both leaders approached their final days.

14

WHITHER CHINA'S FUTURE?

FOR YEARS, ZHOU ENLAI HAD BEEN FORCED TO GIVE UP ON HIS ambitions to build a strong economy for China to maintain his good political standing. He had assumed, instead, a political posture of endurance and caution following the Chairman closely and promoting the Cultural Revolution. Now that his health was all but ruined by persistent heart problems, Zhou's job was increasingly demanding. The flight of Lin Biao marked the bankruptcy of the Cultural Revolution as a political movement that had imposed severe costs on both the Party and the nation, and had led Zhou Enlai to act against his own conscience. How could he not feel a deep sense of sorrow, knowing that no explanation to History was possible?

Zhou was also intimately aware that the Cultural Revolution was Mao's lifeline and understood that only a fool would try to alter its course. In the days that followed the Lin Biao disaster, Zhou once again devoted himself to the task of protecting Mao's image as he went about the unsavory business of trying to explain the bizarre episode to the Party membership. His logic was inevitably somewhat distorted. "Lin's treason to the Party and nation appears awful,"

Zhou asserted before bemused audiences, "but on second thought, it's a good thing, the biggest achievement of the Cultural Revolution, really. It's also the greatest victory of our twenty-two years of Socialist revolution and construction."

Zhou had a standard reply when in the course of these so-called explanations he was called upon to provide a reason for why the treasonous Lin Biao had been appointed Mao's official successor. "We must look at it from an historical, dialectical and developmental point of view," the premier would reply, and then he'd muddy this ideological nonsense even further by adding, "Lin's position as the successor had its historical reasons that resulted from the Party's overall development at the time."

Mao's entire effort following the Lin fiasco was to scrub himself clean of his official successor as much as possible. Having alienated himself from many high-ranking Party and army officials with whom Zhou still had a relatively cordial relationship, the Chairman set out to improve his relations with the premier, expanding Zhou's administrative influence to include the management of military affairs. In a rare show of his concern, Mao went so far as to offer comfort to top-level officials who had been purged as a consequence of the February 1967 confrontation at Cherish Benevolence Hall. Past acts of wrong were conveniently pinned on Lin Biao. Feigning ignorance of Benevolence Hall, Mao asked Ye Jianying in his usual dramatic way, "Why didn't you come to me at the time? If you had written something to me I could have responded with a few words and corrected the situation."

CHEN YI FINALLY RULES THE DAY

In January 1972, when the fallout from the Lin Biao affair still had not yet settled, Chen Yi, the PLA marshal and foreign minister, died. His death provided Zhou Enlai with yet another opportunity to improve the political tone in China. Chen and Zhou had been close old comrades in arms for several decades, and for Zhou the loss of this friend was a source of great personal pain. Zhou had done whatever he could throughout the Cultural Revolution to protect Chen Yi, and now he made all the arrangements to ensure that a proper memorial service and funeral was organized and that the official media would provide full coverage. Mao had no intention of attending the event, which was scheduled to be held at Eight Treasure Mountain *(Babaoshan)*, the cemetery for revolutionary martyrs. But a groundswell of sympathy for Chen began to develop; Communist Party and military cadres from all around the country gathered outside the hospital where Chen Yi had died. Standing in the freezing cold wind, they insisted on saying farewell to Chen Yi. Because he was making an effort to mend fences with Party and military cadres, Mao decided at the last minute that it was in his best interest to attend the funeral. Once Zhou knew that Mao was coming, he made sure that the internal heating at the site was adequate, reinforced the necessary security, raised the official status of the funeral proceedings, and requested the attendance of all members of the Politburo and other political organizations located in Beijing (including various officials of the National People's Congress, Vice-Chairman Song Qingling among them). Zhou also made sure that all this was conveyed to Zhang Qian, Chen Yi's widow.

Accompanied by Zhou Enlai and Ye Jianying and other old military officers, Mao paid a visit to Chen's family before the beginning of the official proceeding. There, the Chairman placed the blame for Chen's death squarely on Lin Biao. "He reviled all of our old marshals," Mao declared, "didn't want any of them. If the conspiracy by Lin Biao had succeeded, he'd be plotting to get rid of all of us old men."

Even before Chen Yi's funeral, Mao's health hadn't been good. The day of the ceremony was bitterly cold and Mao was seriously underdressed, wearing only a thin coat thrown over his pajamas. His condition immediately took a turn for the worse as his pneumonia quickly degenerated into a pulmonary heart condition. His body suddenly swelled up, and now, at the age of seventy-eight, he fell desperately ill. For days on end following the service for Chen Yi,

Mao fell in and out of consciousness. The Lin Biao incident had delivered a major psychic blow to Mao; he grew increasingly depressed and suspicious, and even as his condition brought him to the brink of death, he refused medical treatment. In an act of desperation, the Chairman's medical staff asked Zhou Enlai to persuade Mao to receive the necessary treatment.

Zhou Enlai had never been on the list of candidates Mao considered to be his successor. Ever modest, Zhou claimed he lacked the talent to serve as a top leader whenever the question of succession was raised. Instead, he always insisted that his role was that of the able assistant. During one of their conversations during his illness, Mao admitted to Zhou, "I don't think I can make it. Everything now depends on you. . . ." Zhou immediately interrupted the Chairman. "No," Zhou replied, "the Chairman's health problem is not serious. We all depend on the Chairman's leadership." Weakly, Mao shook his head. "No," he said. "Cannot make it. You take care of everything after my death. Let's say that this is my will."

Zhou was totally unprepared for the Chairman to execute any transfer of power during his brief illness. Without Mao Zedong, Zhou believed the Chinese revolution would never have succeeded. With the chaos of the Cultural Revolution coming to an end, the Chairman was more important than ever. Under enormous pressure throughout this period of Mao's illness, the premier did all that he possibly could to make sure that Mao survived.

Mao recovered from his illness and overall malaise, thanks to the careful medical treatment administered by his head physician, Dr. Li Zhisui, and as a result, made his decision to invite Richard Nixon to China. The invitation to Nixon was an obvious diplomatic triumph. China stepped into a prominent place on the international stage when the leader of the United States, the "number one imperialist nation," came knocking on China's door in pursuit of peace. This diplomatic coup also had the additional benefit of diverting domestic attention from China's recent troubles and allowed Mao to save face over the losses he'd taken in the Cultural Revolution. Once Mao had cooked up this political stew in his head, he quickly regained his strength and recovered to go out and fight new political battles.

Mao's most immediate task following his recovery was to erase any memory of that comment he'd made to Zhou about his role as successor. Mao still needed Zhou to handle the routine work of the Party Central, and he also wanted to make sure that people did not get the idea that the Chairman was someone who was too quick to change his mind. Mao found an opportunity to make his case when, after Nixon's visit, in May and June 1972, the Party Central held a meeting of leaders from Party, government, and military units throughout the country to summarize their criticisms of Lin Biao. Although the focus was on Lin Biao, Mao used the occasion of these meetings to get Zhou to discuss the mistakes he'd made by siding with the wrong factions in various disputes about Party line. Mao's intention was clear. He wanted to smear Zhou Enlai to prevent him from ever trying to become the successor. Mao also issued an order to once again bring up the Announcement by the Fifth Warrior (*Wu Hao*) affair.

Zhou immediately saw what Mao was trying to do. The demise of Lin Biao had greatly complicated the relationship between Mao and Zhou: Zhou Enlai had now taken the number-two place in the Party that both Liu Shaoqi and Lin Biao had occupied. But Zhou Enlai's ability to thoroughly address these historical questions was impeded by his diagnosis of bladder cancer in May 1972. Nevertheless, in a valiant effort Zhou put his personal problems aside and decided to throw his entire effort into preparing a speech to defend his actions during the 1930s. His primary concern above all others now was to eliminate Mao's suspicions. (His first effort consisted of a rough outline, but the ever-inquisitive Jiang Qing refused to let him off the hook.) Zhou worked late into the night, searching through his files and documents, and ended up spending ten days preparing a speech in which he willingly engaged in a very harsh self-criticism. According to members of his staff, Zhou worked relentlessly; rarely rising from his desk, he went for days without shaving and ate very little. Even though at one point his legs were bloated and his feet had swelled so much that he couldn't fit them into his shoes, he managed to persevere. Once Zhou had completed the basics of his report, he still wasn't sure that it met all the requirements that Mao had set forth. When he sent his self-criticism to Mao, Zhou made it clear in a cover letter that he was more than willing to undergo the kind of scrutiny that he had endured during the period of the Yan'an Rectification in the 1940s when the issue of the Fifth Warrior had first emerged.

"Now that everyone wants to listen to this," Zhou wrote in his cover letter to Mao, "I too have the responsibility to inform people. Twice I have heard the words of the Chairman about the lessons from Party line struggles. Since then I felt that it was even more urgent to write down this draft. Whether it is acceptable or not, at least there is a draft that can be used to pursue any criticisms."

"I am old now and have too many things to handle," the premier continued. "It's possible that one day I will experience a heart attack, and then my ability to pay back any political debts will have been eradicated. Comrades will be disappointed. It will be a life-time regret! Whether this is right, or merely okay, while the Chairman is still healthy, I have at least churned out a draft for the Chairman to look at. For such a long draft (thirty pages) I am really uneasy. If it is usable, it will form the basis of my speech, after which I can make any necessary corrections. Right now, I think it is beneficial for the three hundred plus old, middle-aged and young cadres from the Party, government and military from across the country to hear about all the mistakes of Party line along with other errors in my own personal political history. This way, they can criticize and monitor me, providing a way for me to scrutinize myself and for them a lesson from which to draw. If all this is not possible, at least they will know what kind of Party member I am and how the Chairman has saved and educated me."

Mao, of course, could not have cared less what Zhou Enlai wrote in his draft report as long as the premier knew that the purpose of the meeting was to expose his errant history. With Mao's approval,

Zhou gave a long speech over the course of three consecutive nights at the May–June meetings that had originally been called to summarize the work on criticizing Lin Biao.

Zhou knew that criticizing his own historical mistakes wasn't going to get him over the hump that Mao had set up. He had to utter the very words that Mao wanted to hear: that he, Zhou Enlai, the premier of China, was not qualified to be the successor to the Chairman. Thus it was that, at the end of his long speech, Zhou uttered the following words for all to hear. "It is absolutely necessary and practical for me, a man who has committed serious mistakes in the struggles over Party line, to discuss the six previous such struggles. I always thought, and will always think that I cannot be at the helm and can only be an assistant." Even this comment, however, was insufficient. Zhou went further. "When you are all made aware of my historical mistakes," he declared, "you will be able to break with superstitions—and in this spirit you have the right to make sure that I undergo the necessary reform. And if I fail to carry out this reform and end up committing even bigger mistakes, then you certainly have the right to request that the Party Central engage in a lengthy discussion. A warning is a light punishment," Zhou concluded, "but for more serious transgressions, I should be deprived of all my formal positions. This is normal Party life as established by Chairman Mao." In making this bow to Mao, Zhou effectively deprived Mao of further opportunities to pursue his tricks against the premier, at least for the moment.

But Mao had achieved his goal. He had exposed Zhou as a serial offender who had committed any number of transgressions during the long historical struggle over the correct Party line and this disbarred his chances at succession.

When Zhou Enlai was diagnosed with bladder cancer, his medical team believed that Zhou had an 80 or 90 percent chance of achieving a complete recovery. In line with the rules that governed the top leaders, health care treatment for those leaders whose rank was above that of the average Politburo member had to be approved by Mao Zedong. When Mao received the report on the premier's condition from Zhou's doctors, he issued the following four guidelines to his medical team: 1) Keep it secret from both the premier and "big sister Deng," Zhou's wife; 2) No further examinations; 3) No surgery; and 4) Emphasize care and better nutrition.

In the period that followed Chen Yi's funeral in early 1972, when Mao feared for his own survival, his biggest fear was that Zhou Enlai would reverse the verdicts on the Cultural Revolution. Now, as Zhou Enlai's medical condition took a turn for the worse, Mao could easily mess around with the premier's treatment without even lifting a finger.

15

LONG KNIVES

The Nixon visit of the winter of 1972, and the Shanghai Communiqué with which it had concluded, had made Zhou a star on the world political stage. Although it had never been his intention to do so, Zhou had put his master in the shadows. In doing so, he had broken the ultimate taboo in Chinese politics.

Mao had long resented Zhou Enlai. It's not hard to see how the brilliant Zhou might have troubled the monstrous ego of the Great Helmsman. Zhou knew this, and always, in the past, he'd managed to smooth the ruffled feathers of his master's ego. He was not a real threat to Mao's leadership, as Lin Biao had been. Without Lin, Zhou Enlai had been pushed into the spot of second in command. After Nixon's departure, Mao relied on his grandniece, Miss Wang Hairong, and his personal interpreter, Tang Wensheng (Nancy Tang), to monitor reviews of Zhou in the foreign press. This did not bode well for Zhou.

The situation was particularly sensitive because at the Tenth Party Congress of the Chinese Communist Party, scheduled to convene in August 1973, Mao planned to name his successor. The person Mao had in mind was Wang Hongwen, the ultra-leftist Communist "boy scout" of whom the old guard of the Party had unanimously disapproved. To the old guard, Zhou seemed like the natural candidate. But to Mao, the very idea that Zhou Enlai might become his successor was a form of mental torture that kept him up all night.

The chance to smear Zhou's reputation and to pave the way for Wang Hongwen presented itself in June 1973. The United States and the USSR had signed the Nuclear Nonproliferation Treaty. David K. E. Bruce, the director of the Liaison Office in Beijing, which had been set up as an informal embassy in the aftermath of the Nixon visit, requested to meet with Zhou Enlai to inform him about the particulars of the important treaty and to hand over a personal letter that Nixon had written to Zhou. Foreign Ministry staff drafted a report of the meeting, and Zhou made some corrections and forwarded it to Mao. The Chairman crossed out all of Zhou's editorial comments, with the observation that Zhou was too soft. Then he sent over to the ministry one of his minatory little maxims: "When joining hands with the bourgeoisie, one tends to forget struggle." Zhou Enlai quickly took this reminder to heart.

Before this squall had blown off, however, new storm clouds gathered over the horizon. Commenting on the U.S.-USSR Nonproliferation Treaty, an article in *New Trends* (*Xin qingkuang*), an internal publication of the American/Australian Department of the Chinese Foreign Ministry, opined that the U.S. and the USSR were trying to control the world. Although it had nothing to do with Zhou Enlai's view of the matter, Zhou thought members of his staff could consult the article when they drafted their own document on the subject. This was exactly the opportunity for which Mao had been lying in wait. On July 4, when he was apprised of this situation through a report from Miss Wang and Nancy Tang, Mao decided to ambush Zhou Enlai. Mao allowed it to be known how incensed he was that when drafting its document the Foreign Ministry had not adopted his own view that "the basic trend of the world today was toward revolution." He grumbled that under Zhou's leadership the ministry was heading in the opposite direction. Referring to the document as a "piece of shit" and using words like "revisionism"—the mortal sin in the Chinese Communist liturgy—to refer to Zhou, Mao warned others not to get on board Zhou's "pirate ship."

Zhou Enlai was in the hospital undergoing further treatment for his unchecked bladder cancer when Mao unleashed his crusade, but he immediately sensed that something was seriously wrong when Mao made such a stink over an article that had been intended for internal consumption. He swiftly turned in a self-criticism and ordered a critique of the offending article in *New Trends*. But Mao was not about to let Zhou Enlai slip out of his reach with this kind of standard apologia. He instructed Zhang Chunqiao to incorporate his criticism of Zhou Enlai in the report Zhang was preparing for the Tenth Party Congress, where it would be on permanent record.

This was but a prelude. Four months later, Zhou was the target of those fabricated ideological and political offenses dredged up from the revolutionary days of the Chinese Communist Party underground struggle against the Nationalists in the 1930s. He underwent the violent critique in a series of meetings before the Politburo that all but destroyed him politically and exhausted him physically. This ghastly ritual, among the worst that he'd endured throughout his long life, was set in motion after Henry Kissinger came to China for yet another visit, this time as the newly anointed secretary of state. When Zhou Enlai met with Kissinger on November 11, 1973, he let his eminent guest do all the talking. He was still smarting from Mao's blows.

When Mao met the next day with Kissinger, they discussed "joining hands to oppose the USSR." Kissinger noticed a new development in Mao's discussion of foreign policy. In the past, Mao had sketched the outlines of foreign policy and turned over the details to Zhou, who filled them in with his fine hand above Mao's signature. On this day, Mao discussed the particulars of policy with an unusual attention to detail. Kissinger's observation provides a precious footnote to the events that immediately followed his visit, when Mao unleashed the attack on Zhou that he had long been plotting.

Chinese political historians minimize the role that Mao played in this assault on Zhou, pinning the blame instead on Madame Mao and the Gang of Four. But Mao, with Deng Xiaoping, the recently recalled Party leader who delivered the ultimate coup de théâtre, was at the helm of the initiative to criticize his premier.

In his meeting with Zhou, Kissinger informed his host of Soviet military movements and made suggestions regarding military cooperation between the United States and China. As Mao had instructed him, Zhou told Kissinger to let the matter rest for a while. Kissinger was scheduled to depart on the morning of November 14. On the previous evening, right after the farewell banquet, Kissinger requested another meeting with Zhou to talk again about possible military cooperation. As host, Zhou could not refuse. Nor was there more time to ask Mao for permission to meet with Kissinger. That night, Zhou met with Kissinger and Winston Lord while Nancy Tang served as interpreter. Zhou made no commitments to suggestions that Kissinger proposed for military cooperation—in effect, a tacit alliance—between the United States and the PRC. He merely promised to consult the Party Central and get back to Kissinger with an answer before he was due to depart.

The next morning, without consulting Mao, Zhou proposed to Kissinger that their personnel might stay in contact and maintain a dialogue. It is inexplicable that Zhou Enlai omitted to report to Mao on this important issue when, every step of the way, he had deferred to the Chairman.

According to Qiao Guanhua, his main assistant in U.S. relations, Zhou had rushed out of the late-evening meeting with Kissinger. His staff had every reason to think that he was dashing off to see Mao, but the record shows that he had spent the rest of that night reviewing the videotape of the three-hour meeting between Mao, Kissinger, and Zhou on November 12.

In a memoir, one of Zhou's assistants offers his account of that night's events. Zhou tried to telephone Mao, but whoever answered the phone at the Chairman's residence told him that Mao was sleeping and could not be disturbed. Mao was still recovering from the illness that had sabotaged his health before the Nixon visit, and it was reasonable to suppose that he might resent being awakened from his slumber.

When he got off the phone, Zhou started pacing back and forth in his office. He was faced with a real dilemma. He had to make a decision that night. It's clear in the light of this account by Zhou's aide that he was trying to decide what to do while he watched the videotape of the November 12 meeting. (It was the closest approximation of actually discussing it with Mao.) Finally, on the basis of what Mao told Kissinger in such detail, he decided to give an answer to Kissinger and bear the responsibility.

Mao may have set a trap that night for Zhou, and pretended to be asleep when he really wasn't. (This is exactly what he did, respectively, to PLA marshal Peng Dehuai and State Chairman Liu Shaoqi, both of whom he'd dismissed and beaten to a pulp.) Zhou did not reckon on this possibility. He acted like a true professional. He sent a vaguely worded response to Kissinger in the morning, which was well within the scope of his power as premier.

At the time, Mao was living like a hermit in his villa in Central South Lake, but he was always very well informed about what was going on outside the compound. He asked Nancy Tang and Miss Wang Hairong to give him a clean copy of the transcript of Zhou's final conversation with Kissinger, and went to work pricking little holes in it. He then dispatched the two ladies on a visit to Zhou, ostensibly to check with him on certain technicalities. Suspecting nothing, Zhou cooperated with them completely. Then, on Mao's instructions, the two ladies spread the word that Zhou had badly miscalculated in his talk with Kissinger. They let it be understood that Zhou was frightened of the nuclear threat; that he had committed China to military cooperation with the United States in return for protection under the U.S. nuclear umbrella.

On November 17, Mao called a meeting of diplomatic personnel at which he criticized the Shanghai Communiqué, Zhou's ultimate diplomatic achievement. "Some people," Mao said, "want to lend us an umbrella, but we don't want it." He then ordered a series of meetings, to be held within the Politburo, to "critique the revisionist line of Zhou Enlai and Ye Jianying." The focus was Zhou and his "rightist capitulation" in diplomacy. Ye Jianying, a People's Liberation Army marshal, was the "struggle companion."

Zhou Enlai was caught by surprise not knowing why Mao would suddenly launch such a huge attack. He immediately tried to smooth things over by making yet another self-criticism, at a meeting that Mao declined to attend. Zhou sent his self-criticism to Mao, but this was not what the Chairman wanted. He wanted to wipe out Zhou's star power in international circles and punish him for promoting a critique of ultra-leftism in domestic politics, which Mao construed as an act of subversion directed against himself as Chairman. Madame Mao, who did attend the meeting, pounded the drums for Mao, and made it impossible for Zhou to get a word in edgewise by screaming one epithet after another at him whenever he tried to speak. From "rightist capitulation," Madame Mao went on to accuse Zhou of "selling out the national autonomy," "trying to hoodwink the Chairman," "getting down on your hands and knees to the Americans," and ranting so furiously that finally Zhou hammered his fist on the table and shouted: "I, Zhou Enlai, have made many mistakes in my life, but I cannot be accused of rightist capitulation."

Zhou's attitude gave Mao the perfect excuse to intensify his attack. He expanded the series of meetings to include people who were not members of the Politburo, the top executive organization of the CCP. He wrote out a list of the names of people he wanted to be there, and included on it the name of Deng Xiaoping.

Enter Deng Xiaoping

The so-called struggle meetings were not unlike a kangaroo court. They were now moved to the Great Hall of the People, evidently to accommodate more participants, and the "boy scout," Wang Hongwen, Mao's new chosen successor who presided over the convocation. Those managing the meetings appointed Miss Wang and Miss Tang to act as Mao's official, personal liaison to keep the Chairman informed of the day-to-day progress.

For ten days, from November 25 to December 5, Zhou Enlai underwent intense scrutiny. Nancy Tang conducted an eight-hour session for those participants who had recently joined the meetings, to bring their zeal up to speed. In her pep talk, Miss Tang introduced these new arrivals to some of the political jargon from the early years of the Cultural Revolution that Mao had dusted off for the occasion, when he'd used them to topple Liu Shaoqi and others, potted phrases like "running an independent kingdom" and "ready to be a puppet of the Soviet invader," which he now directed at Zhou Enlai. Mao, Miss Tang informed her listeners in the course of her briefing, had even asserted that Zhou Enlai was so frightened of the Soviet Union that in the event of an invasion "he is willing to be their puppet." Maligning Zhou in this way, Mao hoped to make associations between Zhou and past Chinese leaders who had allowed themselves to be used as puppet rulers by the Japanese and, in the process, disgraced China.

This was war, and everything pointed to Zhou Enlai's political defeat. It finally dawned on Zhou Enlai that he was not just dealing with one of Madame Mao's periodic rampages. Chairman Mao Zedong himself was out to get him. If all the accusations held water, he'd be toppled, just like all the others before him. Finally, Mao would wipe out a lifetime of service, just the way he'd finished off Liu Shaoqi and the others. To preserve his credentials to the end, Zhou Enlai bowed to the critique/struggle at these meetings and performed the necessary self-criticism, pouring filthy water all over himself.

Most of the people in attendance disagreed with the initiative and actually sympathized with Zhou Enlai. But to protect themselves, they poured ideological sewage on Zhou, and made fast and loose with terms of their own like "national betrayal," "going down on your knees to capitulate," "overlooking the Party Central," and "hoodwinking the Chairman." Some used the occasion to overturn past verdicts on themselves or to settle personal scores. After decades of political experience within the Party, Zhou was no stranger to this kind of mass stampede. Still, it was more than he could bear. He was shattered, mentally and physically. He could no longer eat or sleep. And yet he understood what was at stake. In times past, he too had sat through similar meetings in which he'd had to compromise his own character as a witness in the sham vilification of tried-and-true Party workhorses. When Zhou lay on his deathbed two years later, and Qiao Guanhua, his trusted lieutenant in foreign affairs, came to apologize and beg Zhou's forgiveness, Zhou confided, "The situation was beyond your control. Everyone spoke up. You had been working with me for several decades, especially on the American issue. How could you have gotten off the hook without speaking up? Besides, no one is perfect. Why should I be above criticism?"

Throughout the course of these gatherings, no one talked to Zhou. He was a pariah. In the corridor, people turned to one side when they saw him coming their way, to avoid an encounter. After Mao raised the bar on Zhou at the struggle sessions, Madame Mao grew ever more strident. She dubbed the meetings "the eleventh struggle between two lines within the Party" (standard terminology in the CCP when announcing a major division among top leaders), and openly accused Zhou of "trying to supplant the Chairman," screaming that Zhou "couldn't wait to take over."

Jiang Qing, Wang Hongwen, Zhang Chunqiao, and the leftist polemicist Yao Wenyuan joined others to form a "help group" that met regularly to discuss tactics with which to deal with Zhou. Soon, people began to drop out, until only the original four, above named, remained. And so began the Gang of Four.

Mao didn't want to actually destroy Zhou Enlai. He only wanted to give him a real beating, and bloody his self-esteem. It would have been too politically risky to altogether ruin Zhou Enlai. The nation was still reeling from Lin Biao's defection, and besides, without Zhou Enlai, how could he possibly run the nation on a daily basis? This was a question that Mao had been pondering ever since he'd begun to entertain doubts about the loyalty of Zhou Enlai, and it explains why he decided to retrieve Deng Xiaoping from political disgrace during the Cultural Revolution and bring him back into the arena of national politics.

Historians perpetuate the misconception that Deng Xiaoping was somehow Zhou Enlai's protégé, but Deng had always been Mao's man. Mao had groomed Deng and set him on his career course from the beginning. That's why, during the Cultural Revolution, when so many veterans were irrevocably ruined, Mao decided to let Deng hang on to his Party membership. Deng was always loyal to this relationship, and, years later, during the de-Maoification that followed upon the central leadership's denunciation of the Cultural Revolution, when Hu Yaobang, the organization chief of the Party, tried to conduct an open criticism of the then deceased Mao, Deng blocked it. He owed so much to Mao that he did not want to appear to bite the hand that had fed him. He did not want people to remember him later as "China's Khrushchev."

It's true that Zhou Enlai and Deng Xiaoping knew each other, but inside the Party they were never close. In the 1920s, when they were both in France, Deng was running a mimeograph machine while Zhou was already a recognized leader. In the early 1930s, Zhou ran the Party Central, based at that time in Shanghai, while Deng was still trying to find his footing in the Soviet bases in the rural south. By the 1940s, however, when Mao was settled in the Yan'an revolutionary base, Deng had become Mao's star, and Zhou, now the representative of the "dogmatists," was a target of the Rectification Movement. When the Communists seized state power in 1949, Zhou immediately became premier and Party head of the government system, and Deng was a vice-premier. After the 1956 Eighth Party Congress, when Liu Shaoqi was installed as the new state chairman, Mao made Deng Xiaoping general secretary of the Party in addition to his position as vice-premier, to rein in Zhou Enlai and Liu Shaoqi.

After Lin Biao's defection, Mao realized that Deng Xiaoping was the only possible candidate to rival Zhou Enlai, and so he brought

Deng back to Beijing from a remote area of Jiangxi Province, to attend the meetings to "struggle against" Zhou. This way, he'd drive a breach between Deng and Zhou, and test Deng.

Next, Mao changed his tune. He was not about to let the ranting of his wife betray him. He had taken care of Zhou. He sent word through the two ladies, Miss Wang and Miss Tang, that the meetings should now encourage "unity." He also mentioned, in a manner that was deliberately offhand, that this was not, as Jiang Qing had been insisting, the "eleventh struggle between two lines within the Party." Quite the contrary. It was normal to conduct criticisms against even Zhou Enlai, who, unlike Lin Biao, was untouchable, to the disadvantage of everyone. It was wrong, Mao went on to suggest, to say that Zhou "couldn't wait" to supplant him, adding that the speaker herself was the one hungry for power.

Deng Xiaoping was well aware of why Mao had brought him back to participate in these struggle sessions. He took the situation in with one glance. Mao expected him to say the very words that Mao wanted to hear without having to speak them himself. So far, throughout the meetings, Deng had kept his silence, but his political future depended on what he said. He answered the challenge by offering a piece of advice to Zhou Enlai.

"Your position is just one step away from Chairman," Deng said. "To others, the Chairmanship is within sight, but beyond reach. To you, however, it is within sight and within reach. I hope you will always keep this in mind."

The message was brief, but the words were laden with meaning. Deng implied that Zhou Enlai had committed the offense of which Mao had wanted to accuse him. Each word bore a drop of poison that Zhou Enlai was forced to sip, even though both he who administered this advice and he who had to swallow it knew that Zhou, the loyal servant, had never harbored any such ambitions. This was Deng's chance to reclaim Mao's confidence. He had to speak out. He had no choice. He knew how to leave well enough alone, though, and limited himself to these few words.

They were enough for Mao, who, in his retreat, was constantly in touch with Nancy Tang and Wang Hairong. When they reported what Deng had said, Mao was pleased. "I knew he would speak up," he said. "No need to give him a nudge."

Two weeks later, Mao personally presided over a meeting of the commanders and political commissars of China's military regions, an occasion that provided him with the opportunity to announce that Deng Xiaoping would thenceforth be a member of both the Central Military Affairs Committee that oversees the PLA and a full member of the Politburo.

Deng had pulled off his political comeback—all at Zhou's considerable expense.

But this was hardly the end of the story. It was merely another twist in the torturous and often hair-raising relations between Mao Zedong and Zhou Enlai. Once again, Mao had shoved Zhou Enlai to the edge of the political precipice. But the Chairman couldn't quite bring himself to send his loyal minister hurtling into the abyss. Many of Mao's accomplishments would not have been possible without Zhou Enlai's orchestration. He needed the quick-witted Zhou, who had helped him win the Communist revolution, and who, more recently, had guided China onto the world stage. To neutralize Zhou Enlai, Mao brought Deng Xiaoping onto the scene. Deng and Zhou seemingly saw eye-to-eye on many issues, and they were, moreover, tough men, who understood the political maneuvering they had to do to survive in Mao's game. Zhou and Deng made peace with one another. Their rapport gave birth to Mao's worst living nightmare as they joined together to push China toward economic and political modernization.

16

FROM DUET TO DUEL

IN EARLY 1974, AN IDEOLOGICAL CAMPAIGN ENGINEERED BY THE left wing of the Chinese Communist Party once again swept across China. This time it took the form of a movement to "Criticize Lin Biao and Confucius" and it was nothing less than a second Cultural Revolution. Mao Zedong and Jiang Qing staged this campaign as the second installment of an effort in which they had joined forces to transform Chinese politics along radical leftist lines and failed to focus on China's economy.

The target of this political and ideological campaign was far from clear to the Chinese people, who had grown weary of mass movements. Party elders and the political elite, however, understood quite clearly why the Chairman had launched yet another such assault. Months earlier, in November 1973, at a key meeting of the ruling Politburo, Zhou Enlai had come under attack from Jiang Qing and her crew. The leftist faction had accused Zhou of serious "miscalculations in foreign affairs," which amounted to one more Party line struggle that could only be resolved by total, unequivocal political defeat. These meetings had taken place behind locked doors, their closely guarded secrets revealed only to a small elect within the top tiers of the highly insular CCP, so the campaign to "Criticize Lin Biao and Confucius" was a public revelation that deep splits had riven the entire upper reaches of the Chinese Communist Party.

Everyone knew that while Mao wanted to settle ancient grudges with a host of political leaders, Zhou blocked him from taking revenge. China's longtime premier had spent his entire career carefully skirting direct confrontation with the Chairman, and, because Zhou had survived, and acted as a protector, an entire coterie of political leaders had weathered Mao's primordial wrath. Zhou's reputation, in and outside the CCP, had insured this. Zhou's political influence also checked Mao's desire to sweep clean the political slate. Furthermore, Zhou represented something much more fundamentally enraging to Mao that drove the Chairman in his final years to finally try to destroy his putative ally. He embodied two political postures in Chinese life that Mao wanted to eradicate forever from the society: Zhou did his best to oppose the entire enterprise known as the Cultural Revolution, that absurd distraction to the country that had left China poor and underdeveloped; and he perpetuated, within the framework of inner-Party politics, the kind of political maneuvering that Mao, the romantic revolutionary, had opposed all his life. This was the Confucian Way that Mao had detested.

Mao pursued every means available to disassociate himself from the turncoat Lin Biao, but everyone knew that Lin Biao was the second big boss of the "leftist shop" that had constructed the Cultural Revolution. Mao's initial effort to put the official successor on a political par with Liu Shaoqi and other purged leaders of the CCP by branding Lin and those who had backed him as nothing other than "rightist elements" was simply too far-fetched. Absolutely no one would buy it. Zhou Enlai, meanwhile, orchestrated a parallel campaign to promote widespread criticism of ultraleftism in China. This only further frustrated Mao's plans to save the legacy of the Cultural Revolution. Mao moved quickly to squash Zhou's campaign against ultraleftism. The Chairman was acutely aware, however, that the Party and the country gave extensive support to Zhou's effort. Political forces were quickly forming an all-out assault on Mao for taking his country down the high-minded road to the disaster of the Cultural Revolution.

So it was that, in his final years, Mao decided to launch a political holy war against History to defend the Cultural Revolution to the end. The original goal of the Cultural Revolution's struggle would remain the same, but this time Mao planned to unleash his attack from a fundamentally different angle.

Mao came from a peasant family in a poor mountain village. Few in his long line of ancestors could read or write, and the prospect of anyone from the Mao clan during the imperial era passing the civil service examinations to become a Confucian scholar-official at all times had been exceedingly remote. Mao himself had received only a few years of private schooling. He had displayed little, if any, interest in the classical canon of Chinese philosophy. Mao was drawn to China's rich variety of folk tales extolling the virtues of legendary heroes: rebels against the established Confucian order who came from the bottom of society, idealized in such Chinese literary works as *All Men Are Brothers* (*Shuihu chuan*). Confucian principles represented something radically opposed to this colorful adventurism. They revered eternal "harmony between heaven and humankind." Mao was ever the loner and extreme individualist. His contempt for Chinese tradition relentlessly drove him to challenge authority throughout his political life.

If Zhou Enlai occupied the center of the Chinese Communist revolution, the question arises: Why did Zhou become the target of Mao's final rant against Confucian doctrine, the last villain in Mao's campaign to save the Cultural Revolution?

The first answer is that Mao wanted to forestall what had happened in the Soviet Union in the 1950s. He wanted to abort the birth of a Chinese Khrushchev who might quickly turn the country away from its revolutionary goals and reduce the entire enterprise to economic development. Liu Shaoqi and Lin Biao, the two men most likely to take China down the post-Stalinist road, had been driven to an early grave by the Chairman. This did not, however, bury the fear that had led Mao to "create great chaos under heaven" that would take China to the brink of anarchy in 1966. Eight years later, it continued to torment the Chairman, who had come to believe that it might be impossible to save the Cultural Revolution. Zhou Enlai, in Mao's eyes, was the latest Khrushchev-like figure.

Mao had always felt Zhou's loyalty to the Chairman's radical political goals was superficial, a purely political calculation. That Zhou never once openly opposed him did not recommend Zhou as a loyal servant. Furthermore, Mao had long considered the premier a symbol of Confucian virtue, which, despite its revolutionary purposes, was a kind of virus that infected the Chinese Communist Party. Although they could cooperate for political purposes, in their private lives, Mao and Zhou rarely interacted. Not once in all the years they spent together in Beijing did Mao Zedong ever set foot in Zhou's personal residence at Western Flower Pavilion, in the leadership compound of Central South Lake, in central Beijing.

Always the humble gentleman, practicing tolerance and personal endurance, always considerate and balanced, but profoundly smooth and sophisticated, Zhou, in Mao's view, was really a phony, someone without an ounce of political principle. He swung back and forth like a pendulum, depending on the prevailing political winds. Mao, whose revolutionary career had begun with the assault on the "Confucian shop" in the 1919 May Fourth Movement, simply could no longer stomach Zhou's political ethos.

Nor was the Chairman altogether relaxed, either, about the enormous personal affection Zhou Enlai had won over the years, in and outside the Communist Party in China, or the immense reputation he commanded in the polite world of international diplomacy and general world opinion. Mao's resentment toward Zhou intensified dramatically, especially after the Lin Biao incident in 1971, which seriously deflated the Chairman's reputation in the eyes of the Chinese people, and escalated Zhou's status both at home and abroad. Never had Mao met his match in political struggles against rivals like Zhang Guotao, Wang Ming, Peng Dehuai, Liu Shaoqi, and Lin Biao, or Chiang Kai-shek, or even Joseph Stalin, and it hadn't once crossed his mind that, near the end of his life, the premier would turn out to be the toughest nut to crack.

The two men had worked pretty much in tandem during the CCP's struggle for power that culminated in the establishment of the PRC in 1949. The thought of purging Zhou had occasionally crossed Mao's mind, but Zhou had always somehow very skillfully maneuvered the Chairman in ways that persuaded him to hold off from taking any action. This was something that the Chairman now found particularly hard to swallow. Mao was a master political gamesman, never short of tricks with which to sunder his opponents, but he knew after all these years that besting the shrewd Zhou would be no easy matter. Compared to Zhou, Liu Shaoqi, and even Lin Biao, had been relatively easy prey. Zhou always seemed to be one step ahead of the Chairman's maneuvers. In the early 1970s, direct confrontation was out of the question. Zhou's star was on the rise. Any attack on him by Mao could provoke a storm of protest, within the CCP, and even in the People's Liberation Army, that might cause the entire political situation to spin out of control. Mao searched far and wide for just the right subject with which to finally nail the premier to the wall.

BRINGING IN JIANG QING

Mao put Jiang Qing in charge of the campaign to Criticize Lin Biao and Confucius. The Madam would test the waters for him while the Chairman played his usual role and stayed behind the curtains to observe each move. Mao also wanted Jiang and the leaders of the Cultural Revolution faction to earn their political stars and stripes within the Party by creating a foundation for their future control of the apparatus. No one was more aware than Mao that Jiang Qing combined high ambition with minimal talent. She treated everyone with the same condescension and disrespect. But not once had the Chairman doubted Jiang's absolute loyalty. This had been on full display in the battles to bring down Liu Shaoqi and Lin Biao. He knew she'd bring the same degree of fealty to the Chairman's every wish in the attack on Zhou. Mao's criticism of Jiang had always reflected his disappointment when she failed to turn into the kind of political leader he had hoped to forge. Yet with all her flaws, Jiang had been protected by Mao and trained for this task. Jiang Qing would lead the vanguard as it aimed its critical fire at the venerable Zhou Enlai.

Mao's basic strategy was simple. Getting rid of Zhou would relieve the Chairman of the greatest threat to his political legacy and buttress the political reputation of Jiang Qing, thereby strengthening the political forces in the CCP that were still devoted to the ideals of the Cultural Revolution. Should this maneuver fail, should Zhou survive the onslaught, Mao figured he could beat a fast retreat and blame the entire affair on his rabid wife. At a minimum, the campaign to Criticize Lin Biao and Confucius would deal at least a temporary blow to the political forces that had been gathering to reverse the verdicts on the Cultural Revolution, and prevent any radical swing to the conservative wing in Chinese politics. And so it was that the campaign against Lin and Confucius bought Mao just a little more time to hang on to the political reins and abort a full-scale assault on his brand of radical politics.

In March 1975, the campaign to Criticize Lin Biao and Confucius shifted its focus to foreign affairs. The initial criticism that Jiang Qing and her cohort had leveled, in November 1973, against the way Zhou handled foreign affairs had not yet dissipated, which told the premier that he should remain on guard. Mao still had a number of political tricks up his sleeve, although just how far Mao planned to take this line of attack was a matter the shrewd Zhou himself could not divine.

Zhou had briefly entertained the thought that he could finally breathe a sigh of relief. In July 1974, Mao had explicitly warned Jiang Qing and her supporters—Zhang Chunqiao, Yao Wenyuan, and Wang Hongwen—not to form a Gang of Four. In October, Mao had given the political upstart and Gang of Four figure Wang Hongwen a dressing down; simultaneously, Mao supported a policy of pushing the national economy forward. This moment of reprieve, however, was woefully short. Quickly, Zhou had to assemble his political forces on all fronts to prepare yet another protracted effort to maneuver and muddle through a political crisis of which he might end up the victim.

This time around, Zhou prepared for the worst outcome. He believed that the ideological witch hunters had at last singled him out as their primary target, just as they had organized attacks on "capitalist roaders" that had ended in the purge, at the height of the Cultural Revolution, of Liu Shaoqi. But Zhou was a different breed of cat. He swung into action at once, relying on his "soft *taiqi*" maneuvers to dissolve the political fix in which he found himself. He displayed little overt awareness that he was the target of the campaign. Scrupulously he also avoided all confrontations with his antagonists, staying on the political sidelines without abandoning his critical administrative role. He interacted with Jiang Qing while avoiding the slightest possible misstep.

In the midst of the ensuing struggle, Zhou Enlai came to the assistance of many of his old comrades. Geng Biao, who at that time headed the crucial International Liaison Department of the Chinese Communist Party, was the first beneficiary of Zhou's political wisdom. The soft-hearted Geng expressed an immediate desire to resign the moment Jiang Qing blasted him with one of her polemical harangues. Zhou took Geng aside to arm him with his own cardinal rules for political survival. Above all, stick to your guns and absolutely refuse to give up your post.

As Mao's wife fired volley after volley at him, Zhou was acutely aware that the Chairman was hiding behind the scenes. She ranted against the historical role played by the twelfth-century B.C. Duke of Zhou, whose book on political rituals Confucius had canonized. Zhou decided that Mao had allowed paranoia to engulf him. As Zhou saw it, he could only assuage Mao at every opportunity, and avoid any direct confrontation with Jiang Qing, and do his best to convince the Chairman that he had no plans to reverse the verdicts on the Cultural Revolution and resort to revisionism.

After Zhou Enlai's diagnosis of bladder cancer in 1972, Mao's thoughts had turned to finding someone who could manage the premier's enormous workload, and whose elevation in the political hierarchy would lead to a fundamental change in the central power structure of the CCP. The opening of the campaign to Criticize Lin Biao and Confucius accelerated the Chairman's efforts to finally achieve his objective: to push Zhou aside and neuter his vast influence over the Party and the military apparatus.

But Mao's options were limited. Mao was acutely aware that Jiang Qing had ambitions to fill Zhou's shoes, but he offered little support for the idea. He could rest assured that his perennially loyal wife and political handmaiden would have at Zhou with a vengeance no less savage than that with which she'd attacked Liu Shaoqi. She was rock solid. The problem was that she was a pathological gossip with the air of someone powerful, but she was fundamentally unequipped to operate the machinery of Party and state. The Chairman's only option was to settle for a reconfiguration of the power structure at the center, so that leftist forces would assume the role of "managing revolutionary achievements" by defending the political and ideological accomplishments of the Cultural Revolution, while the forces of the right "pushed the task of production," handling economic affairs and insuring that the country moved forward, while he, the Chairman, maintained the balance between the two sides.

In this reconfiguration, the Chairman concluded that Jiang Qing should lead the leftist forces, while the recently promoted Deng Xiaoping should step in to oversee the rightist camp.

Zhou was deft at winning his own political allies, and he remained supremely confident that he would ultimately unite with Deng, and win him over to his side, in what would become a titanic political struggle at the top of the CCP. Zhou's formula, simple but surefire, was to endure the grievances thrown his way, but emerge, finally, with the big victory while never appearing, even superficially, to disobey the Chairman. Arms did sometimes find themselves being forcibly twisted as, perhaps, the original intent of the Chairman's "highest instructions" were modified to maintain the political balance. Zhou had achieved one victory after another over the years by sticking to this procedure, and he was not about to change his formula. Zhou quickly realized that Deng Xiaoping, the venerable old cadre, and the leftist forces defending the Cultural Revolution, were like fire and water. Given half a chance they would slit each other's throats. Zhou knew that once Deng revealed his true self and asserted his political position he would possess an ally, one who would assist the premier to right all the wrongs perpetuated by the infamous Cultural Revolution of which Deng Xiaoping had also been a victim.

In March 1974, Mao decided to send Deng Xiaoping to head the Chinese delegation to the Sixth Special Session of the United Nations, scheduled to be held that year from April to June. Zhou Enlai was China's most astute actor on the international stage and would have been the natural spokesman. Mao's decision not to send the premier could have been explained by Zhou's disturbing medical condition. But Mao was utterly indifferent to such a consideration. He wanted to use the UN meeting as yet another way to puncture Zhou's reputation and bring about his planned redistribution of power at the Party Central. Mao enormously resented what in China had been celebrated as "the diplomatic achievements of Zhou En-lai," and even if Zhou had been in the best of health the Chairman would have taken every effort to ensure that all opportunities to shine on the international stage would be denied him. By robbing Zhou of the chance to make an appearance at the UN, Mao also signaled to the world that the aging premier was not long for his position of power and would be replaced.

Still on the periphery, Zhou appeared oblivious to the sleight of hand performed by Mao when he promoted Deng. Zhou also knew the foreign affairs administration of the Chinese government well enough to know that no one would dare propose Deng as the head of China's UN delegation without first consulting him. Zhou Enlai had been the front man and real founder of China's diplomatic posture for decades. He'd devoted himself to promoting China's interests in the international arena, often against great odds. One of the premier's fondest hopes in his final years was to appear in an international setting like the UN, where he could speak on behalf of the Chinese people to the rest of the world. But it was not to be.

Zhou felt personal disappointment about this lost opportunity, undoubtedly his last, to represent the Chinese people to the world community at the UN, but he was even more concerned about the political message that Mao's decision to send Deng in his stead conveyed to the Chinese nation. Once again, however, Zhou knew that to speak out would be suicidal, and so the premier uttered not a word to protest his hurt pride, and avoided any investigation into why the Foreign Ministry had bypassed him. Instead, he wasted no time in approving the report to send Deng to the UN. Just as Zhou was calculating how to keep Mao at bay, Jiang Qing stepped in to block the decision to send Deng to the UN. (Deng's appearance at the UN offered him an obvious advantage as Zhou's natural successor.) Although it decidedly was not the Madam's intention, the ruckus she provided at the Politburo meeting provided some cover for Zhou.

Mao was embarrassed and annoyed as he watched Jiang Qing in action. All along he had hoped that the leftist forces his mercurial wife represented, eager as they were to prosecute political movements and ideological witch hunts, could establish some basis of cooperation with the rightist forces represented by Deng, which were committed to economic advancement, so that the achievements of the Cultural Revolution would become self-sustaining. But Jiang Qing became an absolutely disruptive figure in Politburo meetings. In an unprecedented act, the Chairman spoke out forcibly and directly to ensure that his decision to send Deng to the UN would go forward despite the fulminations of his wife.

"It was my idea to send Comrade Deng Xiaoping abroad," Mao made clear to everyone. "Jiang Qing, you'd better not protest. Be careful, and, above all, be cautious."

Mao's message was more than clear to Jiang Qing and the entire Communist Party. Following this episode, as the Chairman became increasingly dubious about the Madam's political skills, Mao's attitude toward Jiang Qing shifted somewhat, and he began to distance himself from her.

"MEDICAL TREATMENT MUST SERVE POLITICS"
(*YILIAO WEI ZHENGZHI FUWU*)

In March 1974, just when the decision was rendered that Deng Xiaoping would represent China at the Special Session of the United Nations, blood was found in Zhou Enlai's urine. The tumor in Zhou's bladder had reappeared. Before long his overall physical condition bordered on collapse. Extremely weak, Zhou suffered enormous pain.

Mao was totally unprepared for Zhou's rapid physical decline. For years, as China's political housekeeper, Zhou had managed routine affairs of domestic and foreign policy, and this had liberated Mao to fend off all challenges and consolidate his power. The entire country could easily grind to a halt without the necessary direction that Zhou had provided from the all-important Party Central, especially since Deng Xiaoping, newly rehabilitated, was not yet altogether familiar with the basic tasks of routine administration. Despite Zhou's condition, Mao refused to authorize any long-term stay in the hospital for the premier until after a series of high-profile visits scheduled by foreign dignitaries to the People's Republic that demanded Zhou's presence.

When told to withhold treatment, Zhou's medical team reacted with anxiety. The tumor in Zhou's bladder now provoked nonstop heavy bleeding. Warning the Party Central that the premier might faint or suffer heart failure in reaction to the persistent bleeding at virtually any moment, they appealed for permission to perform the necessary surgery. Their constant pleas fell on deaf ears.

Numerous articles published in China following Zhou's death in January 1976, and the subsequent purge of the Gang of Four in the aftermath of Mao's own demise in September of the same year, placed the blame for the hesitant treatment of Zhou's medical condition squarely on Jiang Qing and her radical supporters. It was a case, the mainstream media claimed, of "an intentional purge that entailed killing without bloodshed." The fact is that Jiang and her friends had no say in a matter so critical, one that was the exclusive preserve of the central leadership. The central Politburo, which took orders directly from Chairman Mao Zedong, made the final decision involving Zhou's medical treatment. The Chairman alone ruled on the treatment of the premier.

From the moment cancer was first detected in the premier, Mao began to intervene directly in decisions involving Zhou's health. Informed by Zhou's medical team of the diagnosis, Mao had issued instructions to Wang Dongxing, the chief of security services for the central leadership, from behind the scenes as was his custom. He had told Wang that the situation involving Zhou's condition must be treated with the utmost secrecy. When it was initially diagnosed, Zhou's cancer was in an early stage, and the outlook for successful medical intervention was good. His medical team agreed that the premier's condition would only worsen if left untreated. Alas, in China, the words of the Chairman of the Communist Party carried considerably more weight than those of mere doctors. "This is Chairman Mao's instruction," Wang Dongxing snapped at the unsuspecting medical team, which had thought naïvely that Zhou's medical condition was of the highest priority. "The Chairman has considered Zhou's condition in terms of the overall political situation and he's given priority to the premier's condition," Wang told the medical team. "We must listen to the Chairman's advice and follow his wise pronouncements on this matter."

And so it was that, from 1972 onward, the premier of China went without any significant medical treatment for what everyone knew was a potentially fatal disease.

Zhou's medical team never ceased to appeal for a reversal of the decision through a variety of channels to the Party Central. On one occasion, the chief of Zhou's security detail became so desperate that he personally provided Wang Dongxing with a small, bottled sample of the premier's bloody urine in the vain hope that seeing would be believing. But Wang was unmoved by the obvious evidence that Zhou's condition was getting worse.

Finally, the venerable Marshal Ye Jianying broke the logjam. When the senior leader, who carried great political weight, joined the Chairman for a meeting with foreign guests, he told Mao in no uncertain terms that Zhou needed treatment, and fast. Mao agreed to allow doctors to make a complete examination of the premier's bladder, but he combined this with explicit instructions that the treatment had to stop there. The medical team resisted Mao's order. Covertly, to stabilize Zhou's condition, his doctors removed the cancerous sections during their surgical examination in March 1973. But it was too little, too late.

On May 9, 1974, as his cancer spread to other parts of his body, Zhou's medical condition took a turn for the worse. The medical chief of staff for the central leadership pleaded with Party Central to grant Zhou Enlai an extended hospital stay for major surgery. "Operations are ruled out for now," intoned Zhang Chunqiao, a close associate of Jiang Qing, who spoke on behalf of the Party. "Absolutely no room for debate." Zhou Enlai, the argument went, was "so central to the administration of all government and Party policies, including the military and internal political matters, that no one can take his place." Even Marshal Ye Jianying, who had convinced Mao to allow a measure of medical intervention and generally sided with Zhou, concurred. Zhang Chunqiao had expressed "the opinion of the Party Central and overall this was a positive suggestion," Marshal Ye told Zhou's medical team. "Major surgery to remove the cancer must be temporarily put aside," Ye declared, "and must not be pursued at this juncture." Zhang Chunqiao took the whole matter one step further. He tried to alter the opinion contained in the official medical report on Zhou's condition, to engage in a cover-up, but the medical team refused to comply.

Zhou continued to work under conditions of severe and persistent weakness that stemmed from his massive loss of blood on virtually a daily basis. His medical team knew that he could pass out at any moment, but as long as the Party Central refused surgery, the medical team resorted to blood transfusions to avoid a medical catastrophe. Whenever Zhou was called upon to meet with foreign dignitaries, or to attend a major event that involved China's foreign affairs, his medical team would gather on the sidelines, just beyond the sight of the various dignitaries. Zhou Enlai finally had his first proper operation at the People's Liberation Army Hospital Number 305, just outside the Central South Lake compound, on June 1, 1974. Two months later, blood reappeared in his urine, and all signs pointed to a metastasis of the cancer into other major organs. On August 10, 1974, after a second round of major surgery, Zhou came to the quick realization that his days were numbered.

17

SICK-BED POLITICS

Zhou made his last major public appearance on September 30, 1974, on the eve of China's twenty-fifth celebration of its liberation by the Chinese Communist Party on October 1, 1949. In retrospect, this turned out to be one of the most important days of his long political career. Zhou realized that this was probably his last chance, as the premier of China, to put his personal mark on the country's political future. He went out of his way to create an atmosphere of political unity that was entirely contrary to the long, tumultuous years of the Cultural Revolution, which thrived on ravaging internal strife. Zhou had no sooner recovered, somewhat, in August, from his second surgery, when, in his typical meticulous style of work, he reviewed more than two thousand names on a list of possible celebration guests. Invitations to the event went out to many of the surviving victims of the purges both inside and outside the CCP whose lives had been severely disrupted over the last decade by the rabid leftist forces orchestrated by Mao Zedong and his wife. This was an obvious slap at the divisive politics of Jiang Qing and her crew. Zhou also contacted Wang Hongwen, another of Jiang Qing's allies, who, at the time, was in charge of handling the routine business of the Politburo. Zhou asked Wang for an even longer list of people to invite from all walks of life.

Thanks to Zhou's extraordinary effort, the National Day celebrations were a great success. After decades of political turmoil and conflict, people representing a vast range of personal and political experience greeted and blessed one another. This was a sign that real political change was in the air. To the apparent consternation of his political foes, Zhou was the talk of the town. As the Cultural Revolution wound down, a common feeling had begun to emerge among the Chinese people that the mere political existence of Zhou Enlai provided a major counterbalance to all the ultra-leftist forces that had arisen in the CCP over the course of the last several years. The appearance of yet another, leftist-inspired, mass movement, in the form of the campaign to Criticize Lin Biao and Confucius that Zhou had been unable to forestall was, indeed, cause of concern to many, especially once it became public knowledge that the premier had been hospitalized. People everywhere looked to express the anxiety they felt, while offering Zhou their personal respect and blessings. Much of this general anxiety quickly dissipated, however, on that fateful day in late September when, frail and thin, Premier Zhou Enlai made his appearance at the official National Day reception. Everyone stood up throughout the hall and applauded with heartfelt enthusiasm, and then began to chant in unison, "Premier Zhou! Premier Zhou!" The entire hall roared with thunderous applause. People in the front row rose to personally shake hands with the premier, while people in the back stood on chairs, ignoring all formality, to wave their hands.

A scene of such wild and uncontrolled public adulation was, for Zhou Enlai, a rare thing. This overt expression of affection for Zhou while the Cultural Revolution was still playing out was undoubtedly a great comfort to the premier after the political turbulence he'd experienced in the elite political whirlpool. It also set a precedent. Zhou now belonged to the Chinese people.

While Zhou's National Day appearance was a personal triumph, he worried about the potential repercussions from Mao. Zhou thus moved immediately to make the national broadcast of the event over Central China Television decidedly low key, instructing the media to delete phrases of personal praise for him. Although, at the time, Mao was far away from Beijing, nothing in the capital city ever escaped his watchful eyes, and he was, indeed, displeased by the public display of affection for Zhou. Yet, at every turn during his short presentation to the audience, Zhou had larded his comments with unequivocal praise for the Chairman, coating almost every comment about China with "under the leadership of Chairman Mao."

The enormous public affection displayed for the premier caused the Chairman to fundamentally reorient his approach for finally bringing Zhou down. Initially, Mao had left Beijing in the name of recovering from an illness, while the real purpose of his sojourn was to cook up a scheme to attack Zhou. But watching the public reaction to Zhou at the National Day reception drenched Mao and his plans with cold water from head to toe. To go ahead with his scheme to oust the premier would obviously invoke enormous opposition from within the Party and the general public. Now aged and increasingly fatigued, Mao felt he could no longer follow his every whim. The confidence that had led the Chairman to launch the Cultural Revolution was now largely spent.

Reluctantly, Mao took the long-term view and decided that the plan to attack Zhou publicly would have to be put on the back burner, at least for the time being. Instead, Mao rapidly shifted gears and ordered Zhou to begin making preparations for the long overdue Fourth National People's Congress (NPC). The largely powerless but highly symbolic national conclave of people's representatives had last met in 1964 before the outbreak of the Cultural Revolution. The Chairman hoped that the huge meeting would ease pressure on the Party and also provide an escape valve for people who had suffered from years of struggle, people obviously tired of one political campaign after another. Mao also hoped that the gathering would forestall any further deterioration in the dynamic of the Cultural Revolution. A conviction about the necessity of ongoing struggle had formed the most basic belief of Mao's life, but at this critical juncture the Chairman showed his more benevolent side and issued very non-Maoist instructions "for the benefit of peace and unity." The social tension and anxiety that had accompanied the campaign to Criticize Lin Biao and Confucius suddenly subsided. People felt a glimmer of hope now that finally, perhaps, they could get on with their lives.

But the entire People's Congress was a subterfuge, a charade that Mao had contrived to appease the appetite of the people, while he continued to plot the ruin of Zhou by the more circuitous means of designing a reorganization of the central leadership that the congress would rubber stamp. This would "hang up" the premier as Deng Xiaoping gradually pushed him aside. The personnel arrangements that preceded all such formal gatherings in China involved meticulous planning from the outset. Despite his central role in preparing for the congress, these plans all but ignored Zhou, leaving him to wonder whether he would continue as premier. Mao relied on his personal assistant, and favorite attendant, Zhang Yufeng, to convey to Wang Hongwen, Jiang Qing's ally, that it was his intention to make Deng Xiaoping a vice-premier, which everyone would interpret as a clear signal that the Chairman considered Deng the counterweight to Zhou. Mao's actions, so clearly set forth, intensified the political struggle throughout the highest ranks of the CCP. Jiang Qing was furious that her attacks on Zhou in the campaign to Criticize Lin Biao and Confucius had not brought her the reward she thought she deserved. She was also keenly aware that Deng Xiaoping's political style was most unlike that of Zhou Enlai. Deng was straightforward and unyielding.

Deng, meanwhile, entertained complex and contradictory feelings toward the Chairman. He was grateful to Mao for giving him the opportunity to return to work, and he certainly wanted to do a first-rate job. Deng's great desire was to live up to the Chairman's expectations, and he was happy to carry the burden for Mao. Deng couldn't possibly work with Jiang Qing and her Cultural Revolution supporters, however, after the mess they'd created in the past several years, which he had been assigned to clean up. So Deng decided at the outset to all but ignore the Madam. He absolutely refused to be drawn to her side of the political spectrum. "My mind is made up," Deng is said to have remarked, "and if it brings about another purge of me, well, then, so be it."

Mao had hoped that Deng Xiaoping and Jiang Qing could manage to work together in his newly arranged power structure, carrying on the Cultural Revolution in both political and economic terms. But Jiang Qing virtually sabotaged this plan. In cahoots with her Politburo pal, Zhang Chunqiao, she made constant trouble that irritated the entire membership of this critical decision-making body. Mao threw his support behind Deng as a counterweight to Jiang, and reversed himself on preparations for the First Session of the Fourth NPC by bringing Zhou directly into the planning process for the new makeup of the central leadership. Now the two sides could fight it out, and the whole time Mao could watch discreetly from behind the scenes.

Mao also made it abundantly clear by conveying through Wang Hairong, and his personal interpreter, Nancy Tang, that "the premier is still the premier," and that Zhou Enlai and Wang Hongwen, who currently performed the crucial task of managing the routine affairs for the Politburo, would jointly manage the preparation work for the Fourth Congress. Mao attempted to act as an arbiter and emphasized that all matters had to be handled jointly. Then, just to make his stand on Jiang Qing crystal clear, which for the usually opaque Mao was an unusual move, the Chairman added that "Comrade Xiaoping was right that Jiang Qing must be dealt with from a position of strength," and at the same time reiterated that he supported the promotion of Deng Xiaoping to vice-premier and army chief of staff.

Mao went even further. He drew a clear line between himself and his wife. He conveyed his wishes through Wang Hairong and Nancy Tang, and instructed Zhou to work on achieving some element of stability and unity in the country. He noted that Jiang Qing was not someone who could listen to other people. All she wanted to do, he realized, was to create her own ostensible steel and hat factories, where she could continue to manufacture political inquisitions against real and imaginary political enemies. Mao now made it known that he was fully aware of the widespread unhappiness that this tendency to do nothing but pick fights with everyone the Madam had aroused. "I asked her not to form her 'Shanghai Gang' with the likes of Zhang Chunqiao and Yao Wenyuan," Mao lamented openly. "Her words cannot be fully trusted. She only represents herself. I've had one meal with her in three or four years," Mao admitted.

Zhou's Political Recovery

Zhou Enlai once again emerged in the last months of his life as the central figure on the stage, just when he thought he was ready for the political Dumpster of Chinese politics. Even when he was sequestered in the hospital, Zhou never really shut himself off from the outside world. Zhou' s position had been precarious ever since the extended Politburo meeting in November 1973, when his management of foreign affairs had been harshly criticized, so even as he endured an increasingly dire condition, he was content to be given work that provided him with an element of relief. Zhou didn't miss a beat. He organized meetings day and night from the hospital to make sure that the Fourth Congress proceeded like clock work.

Zhou decided to write a personal progress report to Mao as preparations for the critical congress neared completion:

Chairman: Comrades Hairong and Wensheng conveyed to me the Chairman's precise instructions, and I have reviewed the comments in the report Comrade Hongwen prepared and presented to the Chairman on October 20. All the instructions will be followed without delay and with no objections. The final list of those attending the congress will be completed by late November and sent immediately to the Chairman for your approval. It's critically important to bring on board middle-level and young cadres.

I most actively support the Chairman's proposal to appoint Comrade Xiaoping vice-premier and army chief of staff. This move will have an extra benefit by providing comrade Yang Chengwu [a PLA general] with sufficient time to learn the ropes, which will gradually allow Comrade Xiaoping to give up his position as army chief of staff, so that he can go about training new cadres to take on leadership positions. If war breaks out, the positions of vice-premier and chief of staff will thus be split, and both will be able to assist the Chairman in all his tasks.

Comrades Hongwen, Chunqiao, and Xiaoping each agrees that the crucial documents necessary for the Fourth Congress to proceed—the name list of those attending, the draft of the new state constitution, and the Government Report—will all be ready for your perusal by November.

My condition and spirit have greatly improved since July 17, when I last saw the Chairman, although I'm a bit weaker, I must admit. Assuming the People's Congress convenes sometime in December 1974, I have no doubt that I'll be able to shoulder the task of making the necessary appearances at the beginning and the closing session of the convocation. (Here Zhou's written script is unclear to the author, evidence of Zhou's uncontrollably trembling hand.) Comrades Hairong and Wensheng will report my treatment to you in person. If the attempt to burn the tumor off my bladder is unsuccessful, I will undergo additional surgery. About this the Chairman must not be concerned. Comrade Dongxing attends all my physical examinations, and you should forward any questions you have about the details of these to him.

My greatest wish is for the Chairman's good health. The Chairman's health is of the utmost importance if good leadership is going to be assured.

Comrades Hairong and Wensheng will convey to you any other matters.

Zhou Enlai, 4:30 A.M., November 6, 1974.

Zhou knew that Mao was using him to maintain a balance of power within the central leadership so that no one faction—right or left—would gain absolute control over the country's affairs and the direction it took. Zhou also knew that Mao continued to regard him with suspicion, and he had written the letter in a way that would soften the Chairman's grudges against him, which was a tactic that Zhou had refined over the years.

It was the first time that Zhou had communicated formally with Mao since his surgery in June. The very words that Zhou chose to express in his scrawled hand indicate that he was too ill to think clearly. The premier's writing had never been so shaky.

Deng Xiaoping had assembled and Zhou had reviewed a draft Government Report that was the featured presentation at such formal gatherings of the Chinese state and, by December 1974, preparations for the First Session of the Fourth NPC were nearly complete. The personnel arrangements were also finalized and three options had been presented to the Chairman for his decision. Then, at the most critical moment in the entire deliberative process, when blood was once again detected in his discharge, Zhou's physical condition took a decided turn for the worse. The premier's medical team called for immediate treatment. Suddenly, plans elaborately developed that called for Zhou to visit Mao with Wang Hongwen in the city of Changsha were put on hold.

None of this was good news to Marshal Ye Jianying, who had monitored Zhou's medical condition on a consistent basis. Ye well knew that if Wang Hongwen, Jiang Qing's ally, was the only representative who made the trip to Changsha, the leftist view of the current political situation would have an inordinate influence on the Chairman. Ye Jianying consulted with his coterie of old cadres and, his great concern for the premier's health notwithstanding, advised Zhou's medical team that the premier had to make the trip.

Zhou readily agreed. He always put work above his personal welfare. "Thrown onto the stage of History, I must complete every task" was his working mantra. Zhou was well aware that the Chairman, now in his early eighties, had started to focus his attention on the assignment of power to ensure that it was properly distributed among the central leadership; he knew that the personnel arrangements that the Fourth Congress was going to ratify were vital to the entire country's future. He could allow nothing to go wrong on this essential matter. Zhou was not long for the tumult of Chinese politics. His days definitively numbered, the premier felt a sudden surge of freedom to persuade Mao to pursue the proper path.

Zhou fought off his weakened medical condition and flew with his entire medical team to Changsha on December 23, 1974, to meet with Chairman Mao Zedong. Zhou's weakness had so progressed, according to the subsequent accounts of his medical staff, that when, ever so slowly, and shaking with every step, he boarded the plane, he was literally wrapped in a heavy overcoat, complete with hat, scarf, and a surgical mask.

Mao's political calculations proceeded apace. He followed his commitment to install Deng Xiaoping as first vice-premier with the decision to make Zhang Chunqiao, the leftist leader, second vice-premier. To Zhou, it was more than obvious that it was Mao's tactic to achieve a balance of power at Party Central. Zhou was also aware that Deng was only a member of the Politburo, while Zhang had a rank superior to Deng's as a member of the Standing Committee of that executive body, and so Zhou went out of his way when he met with Mao at Changsha to make sure that Deng's position would equal Zhang's. "Pleading for approval" by the Chairman, Zhou made an explicit suggestion that "Comrade Xiaoping ought to become a member of the Standing Committee, or, at the least, a vice-chairman of the CCP." By proposing this promotion in such a way that put membership on the Standing Committee ahead of the position of Party vice-chairman, Zhou promoted Deng, but also protected himself against any possible recriminations that he was covertly suggesting Deng as Mao's successor. As Zhou gave his backing to Deng Xiaoping, he also threw a few blows the way of Zhang Chunqiao. Zhou had gleaned a number of important, and perhaps damning, pieces of information about Zhang from Mao's speech writer Chen Boda back when the Cultural Revolution began, but Jiang Qing had conveniently covered up all of this information. At the height of the campaign to Criticize Lin Biao and Confucius, none other than Kang Sheng, the former police chief of the CCP, had expressed his serious concerns about Zhang Chunqiao's background, which Kang urged Zhou to report directly to Mao.

This was, Zhou realized, the most sensitive of issues. Zhang Chunqiao was, as everyone knew, the brains behind Jiang Qing's clique of leftist radicals. Zhang was also one of Mao's favorites. Mao looked upon the Shanghai leader as someone who stood by him. Mao had considered handing the mantle of supreme power to Zhang on many occasions. Zhang had managed to out-maneuver Lin Biao, and Zhou Enlai was not about to challenge him directly. Zhou relied instead on those obedient conduits Wang Hairong and Nancy Tang to convey his doubts about Zhang Chunqiao's historical record to Mao. In typical Zhou fashion, he soon followed this hint of concern at a private meeting with the Chairman on December 26 when he conveyed further, damning information all in the name of Kang Sheng. After this, he said no more because Zhang Yufeng, Mao's assistant and longtime favorite attendant, was also present.

Mao's reaction to this reflected his longtime view that the importance of any "historical problem" surrounding a political figure depended on the current political situation. At the moment, Mao needed Zhang Chunqiao, so not much more became of this matter. At the same time, Mao issued his declaration of "two to one" on the matter of Jiang Qing. He criticized her for forming the Gang of Four with Zhang Chunqiao, Yao Wenyuan, and Wang Hongwen, but he also praised the Madam for the role she had played as a critic of Liu Shaoqi and Lin Biao. Mao also added his own two cents by asserting that the campaign to Criticize Lin Biao and Confucius was nowhere near a second Cultural Revolution.

Mao withheld his response to the various comments that Zhou made at their private meetings in Changsha. Instead, the Chairman invoked Deng Xiaoping's observation that "too much attention is paid to details." Repeating his mantra that "the premier is still the premier," Mao now advised Zhou to "seek out the best medical treatment," and to get out as often as he could instead of staying in the hospital for long periods. Mao also counseled Zhou to turn matters of government and state administration over to Deng Xiaoping. Right away Zhou understood Mao's criticism of his tendency to get weighed down in the details, and willingly offered up a self-criticism.

The trip to Changsha was a highlight for Zhou. Despite his illness, his spirits were so high that in his spare time he played cards with his staff, and, on December 26, he commemorated Mao's birthday with a dinner that he paid for out of his own pocket.

The First Session of the Fourth National People's Congress convened on January 13, 1975. Zhou Enlai delivered the official Government Report on behalf of the state administration. Zhou had given these official reports on many such occasions, but everyone knew that this time Zhou was delivering a farewell address to the nation. It was his last political speech. The Fourth Congress had provided a reprieve for the entire population. The campaign to Criticize Lin Biao and Confucius had lost steam, and Zhou Enlai had managed to survive yet another political crisis. A new battle loomed on the horizon, however. For soon, Zhou Enlai would have to confront the cancer raging within him.

18

THE FINAL BATTLE

TIME WAS RUNNING OUT ON ZHOU ENLAI. FACED WITH HIS imminent demise, Zhou's goal was nothing less than that of putting the Chinese nation and its future on a stable footing after the Cultural Revolution that had all but sundered the Chinese revolution at the hands of Chairman Mao and Jiang Qing. To help him achieve this enormous task was the estimable Deng Xiaoping.

Zhou Enlai had more or less taken up official residence in the People's Liberation Army Hospital Number 305 in central Beijing. In January 1975, Zhou left his bed to attend the First Session of the Fourth National People's Congress in the company of Deng Xiaoping. In a decisive speech to the congress, Zhou Enlai outlined a dramatic new direction that with Deng's assistance he had charted for Chinese policy. For an entire decade, a political and ideological struggle had consumed the nation. Zhou now called for China to shift its focus to the difficult, but necessary, tasks of modernizing its agriculture, its industry, its national defense, and its fields of science and technology, all of which were lagging behind the rest of the world. Zhou Enlai called this new directive the "Four Modernizations."

After the conference, Zhou returned to the hospital. He thought this was a good strategy anyway, to let Deng Xiaoping take over and get the job done that he had plotted, quite convinced as he now was that he understood Mao's ultimate intention, which was to turn the job of running China over to Deng. But Zhou was also very sick. Cancer now reappeared in his bladder. Tests also revealed a tumor the size of a walnut in Zhou's large intestine. His medical team immediately sought permission to perform the necessary operations to remove the cancerous growths and stabilize Zhou's condition.

Doctors in China could not conduct major medical procedures on top leaders without the approval of the Politburo Standing Committee. Such was the long-standing rule. Thus, in 1975, Deng Xiaoping and Marshal Ye Jianying, leaders among the old CCP cadres who had generally despised the Cultural Revolution and had shown little enthusiasm for the political style of the mercurial Jiang Qing, now had to negotiate emergency surgery for Zhou Enlai with her allies Wang Hongwen and Zhang Chunqiao. For once, these tough political adversaries managed to see eye-to-eye. They all gave their consent to surgery and sent their decision to Mao, who always had the final say. This was something no one better understood than Zhou Enlai. Weak though he was, the premier wrote his own letter to Mao, just to make sure he got the treatment he needed. He provided the Chairman, in quite specific detail, a description of his condition, and, in so doing, made an artful appeal to Mao's enormous vanity. "The position of this tumor," he wrote, "is in the general area where, forty years ago, I suffered from that abscess on my liver, of which I was cured only as you, the Chairman, led us northward through the swamp lands of western China. I survived," Zhou added, "to live another day." This brilliant little move cornered Mao on the chess board. What could he do? Essentially, Zhou Enlai was telling him: "Oh Great Savior, forty years ago you brought me back to life. Will you not save me yet again, this time?" Within a few days, Mao, too, gave his consent to surgery.

Zhou made room for Deng Xiaoping to do his work. He stayed in the hospital while Deng charged ahead. Burning with zeal, Deng launched a major rectification of personnel and policies in the political sphere. Deng's work style was entirely different from that of Zhou Enlai, who pursued his ends with quiet attentiveness, ever careful not to offend anyone along the way. Deng, in contrast, was decisive and tenacious. He was sweeping in his approach to all issues. During the Cultural Revolution he had been rusticated to a May 7 cadre school in a remote corner of Jiangxi Province near the provincial capital of Nanchang, where he had suffered rough treatment. The experience left him unfazed. When Mao purged an entire generation of old Party and military cadres, he pushed Deng out of a top leadership post along with everyone else. Deng performed manual labor, read the works of Mao and Karl Marx, and used the opportunity to observe the grassroots political situation. While other top leaders resorted to suicide in the midst of the frenzy, Deng kept a cool head. Now, after years of exile and silence, Deng's turn had come to offer a remedy for the chaos and disorder that the Cultural Revolution had left in its wake in the form of all-out rectification.

Mao's concept of rectification was limited to the army, whose loyalty he wanted to ensure. But Deng seized on Mao's language as the premise to jump-start widespread changes that would affect virtually every aspect of Chinese life. He used the minatory note from the emperor as the authority he needed to cut through the chaos that had infected China. Deng Xiaoping wasted no time in applying his new political muscle to tackle the transportation system. Once China's railways were running again, every sector of the economy—in particular coal mining, steel production, and defense—began to recover. Mao was impressed. Deng had created improvements across the board in rather short order. The Chairman looked upon the diminutive, but tough vice-premier with a more approving eye.

Mao was not, however, primarily interested in the Chinese economy. He had allowed Zhou Enlai to propose the Four Modernizations, and he'd given the green light to Deng Xiaoping to launch his clean-up of Chinese industries, but his primary motive was political. In addition to keeping the army in line, Mao wanted to calm the country, and provide a distraction that would allow him to finalize the Cultural Revolution and put it on a permanent footing.

He had a similar ulterior motive when he instructed Zhou and Deng to reorganize the inner circle of top leaders at the Fourth National People's Congress. Zhou had masterminded this reshuffling, which triggered the radical shift in focus to economic growth and technological modernization, and which fell at the expense of Jiang Qing and the Gang of Four. It was all part of Mao's ultimate goal, along with his plan to launch a movement to study the writings of Marx and Lenin on "the dictatorship of the proletariat," which, he hoped, would yield further justification for his Cultural Revolution among the founding fathers of Communism. Even as Mao appeared to put his support behind Deng's economic reforms, the press, with Mao's tacit approval, launched a criticism against "empiricism," which could be understood as a stab at Zhou Enlai and his plans for a radical shift in focus to economic growth and technological modernization.

The sudden shift in the political winds caught Jiang Qing by surprise. But soon, she deduced Mao's true motive: a chance to get back at Zhou Enlai for the political whipping they had suffered at his hands during the First Session of the Fourth National People's Congress. They would use the attack on "empiricism" to regain their power. It was a classic opportunity, as the old Chinese adage goes, to "nail the king by killing his horse." For even though Zhou was gravely ill, he was still the heart and soul of the old base in the Party that Jiang knew had to be pushed off the political stage if she wanted to perpetuate the Cultural Revolution. Jiang Qing was astute enough, finally, to understand the difference between the approach Mao was taking to Zhou Enlai and the one he took when it came to Deng Xiaoping. Deng had won Mao's favor. Not so Zhou Enlai. Mao's deep-rooted suspicion of Zhou went back to those early conflicts of the revolutionary era in the Jiangxi Soviet. Jiang Qing concluded that it probably wouldn't much upset Mao if she and her gang unleashed an attack on Zhou. Moreover, a fusillade aimed at Zhou would send a warning to Deng Xiaoping that his position was far from secure. But Jiang Qing underestimated Deng's political savvy.

Deng understood Mao's underlying strategic design. He knew that Mao had hired him to be the little gun to keep Zhou Enlai in line, and prevent the premier from reversing the verdicts on the Cultural Revolution. He had no intention of playing this role, however. He was, first of all, utterly in agreement with Zhou Enlai when it came to the chaos created by the ill-considered Cultural Revolution. Both men shared a conviction about rebuilding China's economy and were committed to stabilizing the country to create a foundation for economic growth. Deng was also grateful to Zhou, who, in his own covert way, provided him cover to address his labors without major interference. Good-natured, easy to work with, Zhou was someone Deng could count on to protect him. Deng responded by quickly taking the side of the premier on all political matters.

Deng also saw right through the campaign against empiricism that Jiang Qing had concocted against Zhou Enlai. The "*Fengqing* ship incident" tipped him off. On this occasion Jiang Qing berated both Zhou and Deng, who had concluded, together, that instead of constructing ships in its own yards, China should buy or lease oceangoing vessels from foreign shipbuilders. Although a minor episode, it opened Deng's eyes to Jiang Qing's motives. Her ultimate purpose, Deng further surmised, was to undermine the large number of old Party cadres who had emerged from the obscurity and exile they had suffered in the Cultural Revolution and were now poised to reclaim control of the country's affairs. Deng was a card-carrying member of this group. He realized that if he gave the Madam even the slightest opening, she would attack him and destroy his hard-fought efforts to modernize China.

Zhou Enlai never confronted his opponents; he always made a strategic retreat. Deng Xiaoping, in contrast, never withdrew. He fought back. He was never afraid to alienate his opponents and take the consequences. Much to the surprise of Jiang Qing and her cohort, the combative Deng answered the opening salvo of her campaign against empiricism by standing up to her and blocking the move, noting that in private conversation with individual members of the Politburo Jiang had made it clear that her ultimate goal was to "bring about the downfall of the premier."

ALL IN THE FAMILY

After the First Session of the Fourth National People's Congress, Mao had been quite pleased because it seemed to him that Zhou had reshuffled the top leadership in a way that would prevent an all-out assault on the Cultural Revolution. Yet he was also irritated that Jiang Qing, so petty-minded, so partisan, had failed to comprehend the catastrophe that the nation confronted. Mao's strategic plan was clear: The leftists led by Jiang would handle political and ideological matters, while the rightists headed by Deng would concentrate their efforts on the economy. But Jiang Qing wasn't up to the job. She alienated people on the left and on the right, notably Deng Xiaoping. Jiang systematically sabotaged Deng's best-laid plans for the country, one after another. She never gave Deng a single day of peace.

But Jiang Qing was the only person Mao could trust to protect the fruits of the Cultural Revolution. In his opinion, the time had come to harvest the benefits of the massive intra-Party purge that he had engineered before the political advantages this had created were reversed and even suppressed. Wildly aggravating though she was to almost everyone, Jiang Qing was the only person capable of doing the job. Mao decided to launch a counterattack of his own against Deng, even as Jiang Qing and company were in a somewhat enfeebled position thanks to Deng's feisty response to their attack on empiricism. This was classic Mao. He could see where things were heading. Even though Deng Xiaoping had promised to "never reopen the case" and reverse the verdicts, Mao had never really trusted Deng's attitude toward the Cultural Revolution. Zhou was fading fast. The old Party cadres, led by Deng Xiaoping, were poised to lay waste to Mao's treasured field of achievement. The intricate balance that the Chairman had masterminded between the revolutionary ideologues and economic advocates threatened to topple.

Mao took his time. He was an old hand at political gamesmanship. He restrained Jiang Qing, which prevented her from initiating any full-scale attacks, and all the while he continued to shower praise and flattery on Deng Xiaoping. Coming out in full support of the move in the Politburo to subject Jiang Qing to "criticism and self-criticism," Mao further antagonized the Madam by elevating Deng into the Politburo. He quickly assigned Deng to a post in which he replaced Jiang loyalist Wang Hongwen, the young firebrand, and also put Deng in a position to oversee the struggle meetings against the Madam that the Chairman himself had authorized. This gave Mao an opportunity to covertly monitor every move that Deng made as he took center stage.

To dismember the emerging coalition of Deng and Zhou and to disarm the vast number of old cadres in the CCP and PLA who had detested the Cultural Revolution, Mao decided to play down the importance of the premier while he took every opportunity to lavish praise on the new vice-premier. As once he had done with Zhou now, so too, with Deng, Mao would recall "the good old days" of the Central Soviet in Jiangxi Province when, the Chairman now claimed, he and Deng had together fallen into disgrace at the hands of the pro-Stalin faction. He went even further than that when he asserted that Deng, in those crucial hours, "served as the representative of Mao Zedong." He wanted Deng to expose his true colors and to separate Zhou from Deng by appealing to his vanity. Crafty though Deng was, he was also quite vain.

When Mao heaped praise on Deng by calling him his longtime personal representative, Zhou knew where the political winds were blowing. He might not have been able just yet to grasp the entire situation, but he knew, instinctively, that he would have to be a fool to draw any optimistic illusions from the apparent implications of Mao's behavior as he lashed out at Jiang Qing. Mao's occasional attacks on his wife were pure theater. He staged them for show, as a seemingly positive sign, to silence critics of the Madam within and outside the Party. Jiang and her crew always responded to Mao's fireworks by improving their comportment, but they remained, as ever, rooted in their positions of power and influence under the protection of the all-powerful Chairman. Zhou knew how dreadful the consequences could be when others misread Mao's attacks on Jiang Qing. Sometimes Mao invited others to criticize his wife, but woe to those who answered the invitation. Zhou was present at the Cherish Benevolence Hall incident, in early 1967, during the height of the Cultural Revolution. He had chaired a series of meetings of the Standing Committee of the Politburo when a sharp and acrimonious debate had broken out. This was the so-called February Adverse Current of the same year. Mao had actually encouraged veteran comrades, led by the agricultural specialist Tan Zhenlin, to lash out at their mistreatment by leftist forces led by Jiang Qing. The Madam hit the roof. It was all but impossible to rein her in. Mao came to his wife's defense and rebuked the very critics he'd authorized to speak up against her. Utterly ignorant of the special relationship between Mao and his wife, they had overplayed their hand. Zhou was left standing alone to defend the fort against the leftist wave.

This was exactly the situation that Zhou confronted eight years later. Once again, he realized that he'd have to reinforce his defenses against yet another leftist wave. Meetings of the Politburo had been scheduled to unleash criticisms and struggle against Jiang Qing. Despite his illness, Zhou Enlai personally oversaw the preliminary arrangements. He wanted to make sure that no one miscalculated; that the attacks remained within the range authorized by Mao. (After each meeting, Zhou consulted closely with Deng Xiaoping, making it clear that the criticisms had to stay within the confines of the Standing Committee of the Politburo, and strictly adhere to the intent of Mao's May 3, 1975, speech, in which he'd once again warned Jiang and her cohort against forming a Gang of Four.) For two days, Zhou prepared a draft report that outlined in great detail a work plan for the study and the implementation of Mao's instructions on various theoretical issues and problems related to the Politburo discussion.

Jiang Qing did not respond kindly to this assault by the Chairman and the Party leadership. The criticisms were supposed to "help" the selected target, but to the Madam the whole business was a big blow, restrained though it was compared to the countless struggle meetings over which she had personally presided at the height of the Cultural Revolution. As one who customarily launched struggle meetings against other people, the Madam found it hard to be on the receiving end. How unfair it seemed to her, how unjust the criticism, when she had consistently acted on Mao's personal instructions when it came to the major issues. Criticism at the hands of Deng Xiaoping and Marshal Ye Jianying—both of whom despised the Cultural Revolution—would forever taint her revolutionary credentials. Once the meetings had concluded, she made a beeline for Mao. She claimed that Deng had launched a surprise attack, inspired purely by the desire for political revenge. She told the Chairman that she'd only agreed to these meetings for tactical reasons, to buy time. She begged her husband to provide her with the necessary political cover.

The Chairman didn't budge. "Write your own self-criticism," he told his wife. For to win this high-stakes game in the circumstances that now prevailed, Mao knew he would have to keep his purposes utterly concealed. The Shanghai leader Zhang Chunqiao, alone among Jiang Qing's many supporters, seemed to discern some aspect of Mao's design. "Chairman Mao's instructions on not forming a Gang of Four must be firmly carried out," said Zhang in his own self-criticism. "We must try to unite with other people. At a minimum, this will reduce burdens on the Chairman." Not even the cagey Zhang, however, realized that Mao was luring Deng Xiaoping's true self out into the public glare. For Deng posed a greater threat to Mao than Zhou Enlai. Deng had the political will to negate what Mao considered to be his greatest achievement.

Mao was the card shark par excellence, and he played his hand with a poker face. He promoted Deng and handed to him the responsibility of managing the day-to-day business of the Politburo away from Jiang Qing's confidant, Wang Hongwen. He urged Jiang Qing to follow up her self-criticism at the formal Politburo meeting with a personal visit to Deng Xiaoping. The Chairman actually set a model for cooperation and staged a meeting with Deng Xiaoping himself, acknowledging the necessity of his wife's self-criticism. He had, he suggested, awakened to the current situation after he had examined all the problems that the Madam's actions had created. Jiang and her supporters indeed deserved credit for having fought against Liu Shaoqi and Lin Biao, but things were different now.

Deng Xiaoping, never a political fool, was fully aware of the risks that came with his high-profile position. He was once heard to utter, "The Chairman put me on a razor blade." Even so, Deng's political instincts, on this occasion, seem to have let him down. He was not altogether sensitive to the prevailing political climate. Mao had convinced Deng that he was genuinely annoyed by Jiang Qing, that he had entrusted to Deng's charge, after a decade of chaos and ruin, the recovery of the nation. Finally, Deng fell victim, as so many CCP leaders had, to the sometimes ambiguous relationship of Mao and Jiang Qing. Deng moreover failed to perceive that his ambition attracted Mao's suspicions and prematurely revealed his ultimate goal of reversing the verdicts on the Cultural Revolution.

By the summer of 1975, it was clear to all who saw him that life was running out on Zhou Enlai. Cancer had gutted his body. His weight had dropped to sixty-seven pounds. Even so, Zhou's political life remained his chief obsession, and now a new concern arose. On May 3, when the Chairman leveled his charges against Jiang Qing and her cohort, warning them not to form a Gang of Four, he had also brought up the old, historic grudges that had long divided the two leaders. Zhou never found it easy to recall the history of his on-again, off-again relationship with Mao. He had hoped that Mao would allow him to make a graceful exit from the political scene in his last days. The conflict between the two leaders that erupted at the 1932 Ningdu Conference may have seemed like ancient history, but Zhou realized at the time of Mao's May 3 talk that Mao would never let him off the hook. As he approached the end of his life, a profound fear began to trouble Zhou Enlai that Mao would puncture his integrity when he was least able to defend it. To block this move while he still could, despite his persistent physical decline, Zhou took matters into his own hands and, on June 16, 1975, he composed a letter to Chairman Mao. He had no choice. He began with a detailed description of his worsening condition before shifting to the touchy matter of their old conflicts:

> In the forty years that have elapsed between the Zunyi Conference and today, I have been instructed by the Chairman, and yet I continue to make mistakes and indeed have even committed crimes. For this I am extremely ashamed. Although my illness has led me to reflect on the past, I would like to age gracefully. This should be written up in a report.

He closed his letter by wishing Mao good health.

Once he'd written his letter to Mao, Zhou wrote Mao's confidential secretary and favorite attendant, Zhang Yufeng, entreating her to read his letter to Mao only when the Chairman was in the best of spirits. But Zhou's letter to Mao invoked no response. Instead, Mao leaked the contents of the letter to a confidant who was clearly on the leftist, pro-Cultural Revolution wing. "He is trying to buy face from me," Mao slyly commented to his leftist confidant, "he doesn't support my thoughts. He opposes the Cultural Revolution in his own clever way. He's relying on his base in the Party, the government, and the army, where respect for him is considerable. He's no different from Liu Shaoqi and Deng Xiaoping."

Ever sensitive to Mao, Zhou understood the lack of a response to his letter. To relieve Zhou's terrible apprehension, the Chairman had merely to trouble himself to pass a word or two to the people who hovered within earshot to let Zhou know that he would hold no grudge. Instead, the Chairman informed Zhou Enlai with his silence that when it came to dealing with Mao Zedong his luck had dried up. At death's door, Zhou now had to engage Mao in one final battle in order to age gracefully.

Reconciling With the Past

As he agonized over his physical condition and the future of his country, Zhou also concluded that in his remaining time, no matter how limited, he would have to come to terms with past political acts he had committed against former comrades in the name of political convenience. He could not go to his grave without making amends for these inexcusable deeds, and yet any attempt that Zhou made to seek reconciliation with old cadres was fraught with difficulty because he had to remain keenly alert to any negative reaction by Mao. The first such opportunity arose in 1974 on Army Day, when, on August 1, the revolutionary exploits of the People's Liberation Army are commemorated. Mao was in the central Chinese city of Wuhan, where he ordered the immediate release of General Yang Chengwu and other military officials, whom the Chairman now decided had been wrongly purged for supposedly "listening to Lin Biao" during the height of the Cultural Revolution. The Chairman, after years of siding with Jiang Qing and political upstarts like Wang Hongwen, had struck upon this obvious tactic to improve his relationship with the old cadres in the Party and army. On August 1, when Mao decreed that Yang and his military cadres should attend the Army Day celebrations, Zhou seized the chance to make amends for his own previous political actions.

Yang Chengwu assisted Zhou in the summer of 1967 when, as political conflicts spiraled out of control, they forced the Chairman to expose two of Jiang Qing's political favorites, the radical leftists and wild polemicists Wang Li and Guan Feng. For the role they played in driving China to the brink of civil war and damaging China's international reputation by engineering the sack of the British mission in Beijing, Wang and Guan became the scapegoats of the moment. It was a symbolic turning point in the Cultural Revolution. Mao seemed to be announcing a strategic retreat. He also appeared to be offering the premier a convenient escape route out of the dead end that the increasingly powerful leftist forces had constructed for Zhou's career.

Yang Chengwu turned out to be the loser in this situation. Jiang Qing and Lin Biao engaged in a concerted counterattack so powerful that even Zhou Enlai had to fall in line to protect himself. Despite his personal reservations, he added his voice to the chorus of attacks on Yang at various struggle meetings. Yang subsequently spent several years in internal political exile. For his part in this episode, Zhou suffered remorse and guilt. "Eternal loyalty to the Cultural Revolution Group," Zhou shouted in 1967 at a March 24 struggle meeting directed at the now isolated Yang. "Defend Jiang Qing to the end."

Following the 1971 Lin Biao incident, Zhou moved quickly to have Yang reinstated. It took three separate reports to Mao but, in 1974, after some hesitation, the Chairman finally permitted Yang to return to work. This provided Zhou with the opportunity to issue a personal apology to Yang. Zhou left the hospital so that he could attend the crucial meeting at which Yang and a number of recently rehabilitated cadres were formally received, but he did not speak personally to Yang until weeks later, after the August 1 Army Day reception. Yang later recalled the scene for his biographer:

1974 was the year of my liberation, when, after years of exile, I was permitted to attend the August 1 Army Day celebration and reception. The premier asked me to stay behind after the formal festivities, and immediately engaged me in a heart-to-heart conversation, in which he showed unusual emotions as he expressed his deepest apologies. "Chengwu, ah I am so sorry," he told me. "During your purge, I made many statements that were incorrect, and I uttered a number of words that in my heart I knew were quite untrue. I apologize to you and openly acknowledge my mistakes."

Tears welled up in my eyes and I shouted back, "Premier, this was all the work of Lin Biao and his men. I know in my heart that all along you wanted to protect me."

But the premier would have none of that. He dismissed my pleas with a wave of his hand. "I am acknowledging my mistakes to you," Zhou continued, mouthing what had become a popular slogan in the advent of Lin Biao's demise. "Put all the hatred on Lin; praise Mao as the source of all happiness."

Then Zhou's demeanor became very sober. "Chengwu, ah, I have some very bad news to tell you," he said. "I had hoped to hold off on this, but, after mulling it over, I decided to tell you. Your eldest daughter, Yang Yi, was murdered during the midst of the political struggles."

I was in shock. It was as though I had been struck unconscious by a heavy blow. When I finally came to my senses, all I could hear was the premier's sorrowful voice. "This was a failure on my part," he was telling me. "I knew Yang Yi and considered her to be a good child. During the various battles, she was in the midst of putting together some materials on Lin Biao and his radical sidekick, Wu Faxian, but before she could finish, class struggle was launched against her. Unfortunately, my full attention, at the time, was devoted to the visits by Nixon and Kissinger, and so before I could intervene, the tragedy had already occurred. I immediately issued instructions not to cremate her body, to apply no makeup to the corpse, and to bury her in a simple wooden coffin, in a grave with a marked tombstone. Once your release was secured, the matter would be handled by Ye Jianying and the Party Committee of the Air Force. I will not live to see another August 1 celebration, but in my remaining days I am going to make sure a full investigation is carried out. Today, I advise you to hold off on telling your wife. Revolutions always come at a cost."

Zhou was also haunted by his failure to halt the persecution of many veteran comrades during the Cultural Revolution at whose side he had fought during the long struggle for liberation. He had stood by and watched while his old revolutionary comrades, victims of unjust persecution, died in grief. Guilt ate away at Zhou by day as he reflected on the early days of revolutionary struggle they'd experienced together; by night, images of these veteran brothers-at-arms returned to haunt his dreams.

Chen Yi was one such example. Zhou shared with Chen Yi a good working relationship that was buttressed by their profound friendship. When Chen Yi was made a target of the Cultural Revolution, Zhou personally put himself between Chen Yi and the Red Guards by going at Chen's side to mass struggle meetings. In the end, Zhou failed to save Chen, and his old friend was finally purged. Someone on Zhou's medical team recalled that one night, during his final days of life, the premier suddenly woke up from a terrible dream, and his staff rushed to the side of his bed. "Chen and I were half way up a hill," he told them. "Chen slipped and fell, and I couldn't grab him in time. Then both of us tumbled together over a cliff."

Marshal He Long was yet another old warrior from the revolutionary era about whom Zhou now felt great remorse. Zhou's ally and protector during the 1927 Nanchang Uprising, He Long became a marshal in the People's Liberation Army (one of only ten officers to achieve the supreme military title), only to plummet at the hands of the Red Guards, before he died under suspect circumstances. On June 9, 1975, China's top military organ, the Central Military Commission, decided to hold a ceremony to formally inter the old marshal's ashes. The CCP dropped any formal investigation of the charges against He Long to protect the Cultural Revolution, which He Long had detested. It was a very sensitive matter for the Politburo, especially for Jiang Qing and her crew. Notice of the ceremony was strictly limited to internal Party channels and the Politburo issued detailed regulations that called upon the Military Commission to keep the ceremony low key and completely confidential, with "no formal funeral committee, no eulogy, no wreaths, no reporting."

He Long's family went berserk. Miss He Jiesheng, He Long's eldest daughter, wrote a letter to Mao Zedong in which she formally asked him to follow the modest June 9 events with a more elaborate, formal ceremony to repair the bad impression left by the Politburo's actions. "The dead are unconscious," she wrote. "It is the living who will restore his virtue." He Jiesheng then approached Zhou Enlai. The He family resolutely refused to attend the June 9 ceremony unless other actions were authorized that would compensate for the insulting disrespect shown by the Politburo, and He Jiesheng hoped that Zhou could offer his help.

Zhou reacted swiftly to this golden opportunity. He dispatched Deng Yingchao to explain to the family that it was necessary to be sensitive to the overall political situation. Meanwhile, Zhou approached Mao on the family's behalf. Mao signed off on Zhou's requests. Acting quickly, as he always did in situations like this, the premier, despite his weakened condition, upgraded the ceremony. He moved it to a more appropriate site, gave his assent so that wreaths could be placed, and he appointed Marshal Ye Jianying to head the ceremonial committee. Now that Mao had agreed to a eulogy, Zhou Enlai decided to deliver it himself. Zhou's medical team advised him not to attend the ceremony. He had to summon every ounce of strength in his body just to take a few steps. It was a tough decision, but he was determined to go, and when the staff tried to change his mind, Zhou lost his temper. Deng Yingchao knew that any attempt to dissuade her husband would be futile. Instead, she telephoned Xue Ming, He Long's widow, and begged her to control her emotions. At the ceremony, held at the Eight Treasure Mountain cemetery for revolutionary martyrs outside Beijing, Zhou was the model of rectitude and condolence. In his weakened state, he nevertheless managed to make a sincere and deep bow to the urn that contained He Long's ashes, three more bows to He Long's portrait, and three additional bows to He Long in the company of the members of He Long's family. Those seven bows gave some comfort to his conscience, but he knew that it was all too little, too late.

Zhou's personal intervention had remedied an unjust Politburo decision, but it hardly eased the guilt he felt about He Long's fate.

By the summer of 1975, although his medical staff withheld his fate from Zhou, he showed all the signs that he had entered the terminal phase of his illness. No treatment could save him now. Still able to walk, Zhou paid one last visit to places burned into his memory. He returned to his personal residence of Western Flower Pavilion in the central leadership compound of Central South Lake, where he had lived for some twenty years, and he went to the Great Hall of the People, the massive structure completed during the Great Leap Forward and the scene of so many of his major political triumphs, including the Nixon visit. He met with his secretary, and together they prepared for his death by putting his documents in order. He gave some thought to the idea of ending his medical treatment, and even considered requesting a release from the hospital so that he could go home and spend his final days with his family. But all this was out of the question—the permission to do so would never have been granted.

With death waiting just outside the door, Zhou kept a close eye on day-to-day developments and paid particular attention to the Chairman's attitude. In mid-1975, the political climate in China was probably as clement as it had been since the Cultural Revolution had begun a decade earlier, but Zhou was not about to give himself up to excessive optimism. He was too familiar with Mao's highly unpredictable nature. Zhou limited himself to those measures he needed to retain stability. Mao, too, was suffering from a variety of illnesses including Parkinson's disease. His days were also numbered. China's political future was at stake. Deng Xiaoping now controlled the levers of real power, an authority that his promotion to CCP vice-chairman and army chief of staff and membership on the Politburo Standing Committee had only reinforced. There was no reason to pick a fight with the leftists. Zhou's tactic was to fight one battle at a time. The Chairman was in his own room, aware of every step that anyone made. Zhou counseled caution, to sidestep any of the many political traps that Mao had set.

Zhou and Marshal Ye Jianying both warned Deng Xiaoping not to push his policy initiatives too far. (Economic, military, and education reform were now in high gear.) As Deng began his speedy repair after the chaos of the Cultural Revolution, Mao refused to interfere. Mao needed Deng to restore order to China, just as he had needed Deng and Liu Shaoqi when he had called upon them to clean up the mess after the disastrous 1958–1960 Great Leap Forward. The Chairman knew perfectly well that Deng had not discarded his fundamentally pragmatic approach that Mao deplored. Deng clothed his political strategy in the left-wing ideological language of the "three instructions." When making a toast at the October 1 National Day reception, he called upon people of the whole country to continue to carry through Mao's instructions to study the theory of the dictatorship of the proletariat and combat revisionism, to promote stability and unity, and to boost the national economy. Even so, everyone knew Deng was intensely opposed to the ideals of the Cultural Revolution. Overflowing with the confidence that Mao was his champion, and so determined was he to advance his own agenda, Deng turned aside the warnings of Zhou and Ye Jianying. He belittled fears of persecution and instead asserted the power of his own sense of personal bravery.

Zhou Enlai appreciated the enormous risks that Deng Xiaoping was willing to take, but, as time passed, Deng's approach to reform concerned Zhou deeply. Zhou completely agreed with Deng's commitment to repair the damage the Cultural Revolution had wreaked on China, and he was also a force behind Deng's plans to modernize the country, but the premier opposed the incredible haste with which Deng advanced his agenda. The way Deng went about initiating these plans put both of them in jeopardy together, isolated and denounced by leftist critics as "capitulationists." Deng was the point man on reform. In the absence of political support, Deng would have to defend the fortress all by himself. His position was very vulnerable. Shots were coming at him from every direction. If Deng fell, the entire impetus of economic and political reform that, following Mao's death would catapult China to a world power, would collapse with him.

Zhou decided that he had to make a move in Deng's defense before it was too late. After careful consideration, Zhou made a formal recommendation. In it, he offered to resign his role in the Party and government so that the vice-premier could take over as premier. He realized that his own position in the political leadership was the major target of the incessant political intrigue in which the defenders and advocates of the Cultural Revolution were engaged. He was also convinced that the entire nation would confront disaster if either Jiang Qing or one of her Gang were to take over as premier. Mao, too, evidently harbored similar concerns, and so, although Zhou knew that recommending Deng for his own job could have adverse results, he cast all caution aside. Besides, Mao had no choice. Because Zhou wrote a personal letter from his sick bed to formally recommend Deng's promotion, he forced the Chairman to give it his serious consideration.

Originally Mao had considered replacing the ailing Zhou Enlai with Deng, but, by mid-1975, political conditions had completely changed the Chairman's calculations. Mao was now deeply annoyed with Zhou because Zhou knew exactly what button to push when he wanted to get the Chairman off his bed at Central South Lake. Mao's response was to fire a blast of criticisms at Deng and meanwhile make a point of ignoring Zhou's recommendation. The canny premier persevered. He continued to get the word out to friendly ears that Deng should be his officially anointed successor. Zhou hated being called a capitulationist. That was not the way he planned to let the world remember him, and he was determined, even on his death bed, to win this final round with Mao. For the first time in his long dalliance with Mao, Zhou Enlai took the offensive.

ZHOU VERSUS MAO: THE LAST ROUND

On September 7, 1975, Zhou met with a delegation of visiting Communist Party officials from Romania. His medical staff objected strongly to this meeting, but Zhou insisted on it. Zhou informed his guests that he had received an "invitation" to join Marx. He then quickly shifted the conversation to the topic uppermost on his mind. He told his Romanian guests that Vice-Premier Deng Xiaoping had already assumed Zhou's various and important roles in the Party and the government managing routine affairs of the Party Central, and that Deng would continue to pursue the policy of Four Modernizations in line with developments since the First Session of the Fourth NPC. His meeting with the Romanian delegation was

Zhou's ultimate move. He expected his guests to reveal his comments to the outside world, a tactic, he believed, that would prevent Mao from unleashing an all-out assault against Deng.

Two weeks later, Zhou Enlai went under the knife for the fourth time. This time, he knew he might not come out of the operation alive. While his doctors and the rest of his medical staff awaited his arrival in the operating room, Zhou organized his final political defense. He called for a transcript of his 1972 report to a CCP convocation, a document entitled "True Story of the Incident Involving the Fifth Warrior (*Wu Hao*) Cooked up by the Kuomintang." In this report, Zhou had answered accusations Jiang Qing had leveled against him during the Cultural Revolution that concerned an event that took place in 1931, when Zhou worked in the Shanghai underground. This was the basis of the claim made during the Cultural Revolution by Red Guards, with the backing of Jiang Qing, that Zhou Enlai was a capitulationist. Now, forty years after the original event, while awaiting surgery to save his life, Zhou locked himself in a small room and reviewed and revised the entire transcript of his report on this seemingly obscure episode. Yet again, Zhou Enlai wrote a letter to Mao in which he requested the Chairman to give his okay so the report could be sent to every Party, government, and military leader in all of China's provinces so that Jiang Qing would not exploit this episode after he died. For although Mao had warned Party leaders at a May–June 1972 meeting not to make any false allegations against Zhou in the future, Zhou was worried that in the course of the inevitable political struggle that would follow his death, this obscure case from the ancient revolutionary past would be revived at the expense of Deng Xiaoping, his chosen successor.

Zhou remained alone, locked in the small room, fighting off the effect of drugs the doctors had administered to calm him down and reduce his pain before they gave him anesthetics. He ignored his wife, Deng Yingchao, and Party leaders Ye Jianying, Deng Xiaoping, Zhang Chunqiao, and Wang Dongxing, all of whom remained outside, trying to coax Zhou forth so that he could undergo the surgery. For a solid hour Zhou stayed in the room, tying up loose ends. Once he had signed his name to his newly revised report on the "Incident Involving the Fifth Warrior," and noted the time and place of its completion, Zhou was ready. He handed the report to his wife and instructed her to send it to Mao with the request he had composed, in which he asked Mao to give his permission so that it could be transmitted throughout the uppermost levels of the Party, the government, and the military leadership.

Zhou, utterly exhausted, was ready to confront his fate on the operating table. His mind was clear. He had settled all outstanding matters. One last act remained for him to perform, however. He had to say something on behalf of Deng Xiaoping, who, when Zhou departed the scene, would be left hanging by a political thread. He had to get the message to Mao, clearly and unequivocally, that the time had come to stop his usual game of Ping-Pong—favoring one side, then reversing and favoring another—and to take a stand once and for all behind Deng Xiaoping. Zhang Zuoliang, Zhou's personal physician, witnessed the scene, and recounts it in his memoir:

> Wheeled up to the operating room, Zhou suddenly turned his head to the right and said in a heavy, but low, hushed voice, "Where is Comrade Xiaoping? Please ask him to come here." I immediately passed the word back: "Comrade Xiaoping, the premier has requested your presence." Deng hurried to be next to the premier, who took his trembling hand and, voice shaking with emotion, shouted out for all to hear: "Comrade Xiaoping, your work over the years has shown that you are truly tougher than I am." Deng was overwhelmed with emotion when he heard this accolade from the premier, and with great solemnity he shook Zhou's hand as firmly as he could, standing there without saying a word. Deng then waved his hands in a salute, sending Zhou off to the operating room, wishing the premier a safe journey as he wiped away his tears.

Zhou was so emotionally riled that his medical staff thought it would have a detrimental effect on his surgery. They rushed him into the operating room. Even then, as Zhou entered the operating theater, he called out, one last time: "I am loyal to the Communist Party, loyal to the people! I am not a capitulationist." Everyone on the scene was shocked. Dumbstruck all those present wondered what the premier was getting at. In such a situation, a man's wife understands the situation better than anyone else. Deng Yingchao, Zhou's wife of fifty years, instructed the security chief, Wang Dongxing, to report the entire episode to Mao. Perhaps she and her husband had agreed in advance on this tactic, to make sure that Zhou's message to Mao came through crystal clear, to give final political clearance to his longtime protégé. Zhou's intent was obvious. He wanted to make sure in his waning days that his revolutionary reputation wasn't going to be contaminated by some unknown, obscure crime of which few were even aware. In this respect, the hospital scene was not some uncontrolled, hysterical outburst or a spontaneous expression of sorrow. It was a superb professional performance enacted for its maximum political effect.

Surgery revealed the worst. Zhou's bladder was coated with malignant tumors, which had spread to other parts of his body. His condition was so bad that the doctors concluded that any additional surgery would only further the spread of the disease. Deng Xiaoping kept his request to Zhou's medical team simple: "Reduce the pain and extend his life as long as possible."

Mao was taken aback by Zhou's uncharacteristically strong reaction to the charge that he was somehow a capitulationist. Mao assumed that Zhou would simply tolerate any such elliptical attacks on him, as he had done over the decades, without provoking the slightest confrontation. This time around, the attack on Zhou was by implication only, but the target was obvious to everyone. Now that Zhou had started cutting loose, letting the world in on his pent-up political sorrows, he'd put Mao on the defensive, faced with the embarrassing possibility that, in the final stages of the premier's life, the Chairman of the Chinese Communist Party could appear to be so ornery to a dying man. Mao's emotions boiled up inside, but he could not explode. Fear and trembling now infected the inner circles of the top elite; not a word could be uttered against Deng Xiaoping in public. Zhou's influence inside and outside the CCP was something that not even Mao could dismiss, especially since the premier had given his personal recommendation that Deng should be the man to officially succeed him. Any thought that Mao might have entertained of stabbing Deng in the back was, for the moment, inconceivable.

Now that the political situation was at a stalemate, the number-one topic of conversation throughout the Party was Zhou Enlai's medical condition. Everyone knew that Zhou's influence would not diminish as long as he was able to hang on, and that he could prevent the situation on the political scene from going from bad to worse. Zhou's top priority was now to protect Deng Xiaoping, and so, now that he had successfully stifled Mao's open opposition to Deng, he went about securing the deal with his customary aplomb.

But Zhou's bladder was hemorrhaging one hundred cubic centimeters of blood a day, and the tumor in Zhou's large intestine was also growing inexorably. His medical team, having run out of options, was keeping the premier alive with constant blood transfusions. On October 24, Zhou's doctors performed a futile series of surgeries intended to prolong Zhou's life, but Zhou visibly deteriorated within a few days of the operation. Zhou Enlai, the premier of China, would never again rise from his bed. Suffering nearly unbearable pain, he was now unable to mount any political defense for Deng, who had conveyed to the premier his impression that Mao had finally decided to strip him of all his newly granted powers to pave the way so that those who advocated perpetuating the Cultural Revolution could be installed in every position of power.

"Imperial Intransigence"

Just at the moment Zhou's medical condition was declared critical, Mao Zedong had decided to unleash his attack on Deng Xiaoping. At first, the Chairman moved slowly, in a way that would give Deng an opportunity, like Zhou, to admit his mistakes and survive. To set up this particular move on the chess board, the Chairman offered

Deng the opportunity to supervise a campaign to acknowledge the "great accomplishments of the Cultural Revolution under the formula of 'three demerits to seven advantages.'" Deng's countermove, however, avoided the classic Maoist trap, when the vice-premier pointedly refused the offer to perform the task, and indicated he was not "qualified" to lead such a review. Mao quickly concluded that Deng Xiaoping would never "alter his colors." That's when he decided to purge Deng.

Without revealing his intentions, Mao had a talk with Deng, encouraging him to carry on the good work and informing Deng that he had ordered Wang Hongwen, a close ally of Jiang Qing, to listen to Deng. Then, at the end of their little chat, Mao dropped one of his clever remarks: "The wind always knocks down the tallest tree." Deng immediately made a beeline to the PLA hospital to see Zhou and informed the premier of Mao's comments. Zhou just lay there and stared at Deng and finally let him know his reaction. "Why can't you just be a little tolerant?" Zhou said. He then turned his face with a bitter look of sadness to the wall. Another campaign denouncing all efforts of the "right deviationist attempt to reverse the correct verdicts" on the Cultural Revolution swept the country. Deng Xiaoping was the number-one target. Zhou's ability to determine the future of China was now exceedingly limited; Zhou might escape this world in death, but he could no longer defend his political standing, or that of Deng Xiaoping. A few months later, Mao acted on his words and cashiered Deng, knocking down what had become the tallest tree. And so it was that for the third time in his political career, Deng Xiaoping was purged, as he was stripped of all his positions in the immediate aftermath of Zhou's death in January 1976.

With little room to maneuver, Zhou did what he could to make sure that nothing in the historical record could be employed against him following his death. Confiding, as he often did, in his wife, Zhou warned her to be mentally prepared for the assaults on his character from the likes of Jiang Qing and her crew, who had secretly retained all the records of the struggle meetings launched against Zhou during the months of October and December 1973, when his handling of foreign affairs had been pilloried by the Madam. Zhou also made it clear to Deng Yingchao that he wanted to dispense with the usual elaborate funeral ceremony in which guards would maintain a vigil over his coffin. He reminded his wife of an agreement that they had made in the early 1950s. He did not want his ashes to be interred; instead, they were to be scattered at sea. Zhou made a point to his wife's secretary that, above all else, "great care must be shown for big sister Deng."

The evolving political situation provided Zhou a final source of great sorrow. The premier, who had followed the Chairman dutifully throughout his long career without skipping a beat, had never hesitated in his loyalty and enduring service to Chairman Mao. At the end of his life, Zhou could not attract the slightest glimmer of recognition or understanding from Mao, who seemed determined only to reexamine ancient grudges.

Zhou, deeply rooted as he was in Chinese philosophy, was inherently unable to discard the Tao of "loyalty," which held that "even when the emperor is errant, the minister must be loyal." The indifference that Mao exhibited toward his loyalty deeply depressed Zhou Enlai, but it did not anger him. He responded to Mao's assault with yet another self-criticism, and dispatched one memo after another inquiring after the Chairman's health, to check on the Chairman's eating and sleeping habits, and his security arrangements.

Among the leaders in the top coterie at this time, Ye Jianying probably had the greatest insight into Zhou's character. Marshal Ye visited the premier on a daily basis and sat at his bedside, where they engaged in seemingly endless discussions, yet not once did Zhou mention his own sorrow to his comrade. But Ye Jianying could not fail to register his friend's suppressed frustrations. On every occasion he reminded Zhou's secretaries to keep pen and paper within reach. "The premier has high principles," he advised them on one occasion. "He has buried away in his mind many thoughts and grievances, especially toward many individuals high in the Party Central, so if at any moment he happens to reveal some inner thoughts, make sure you write them down." Not a word fell from the lips of the premier, however. He directed his only comments to Deng Yingchao. "I still have a lot to say," he once told her, but he never disclosed what was on his mind.

By late October 1975, all Zhou could do was lie in his bed and stare at the ceiling and protest, not with words, but with subtle sighs. Zhou did what he could, for posterity, by repeatedly instructing Ye Jianying how to conduct the battle so that the ultimate power would never fall into the hands of Jiang Qing. Zhou also issued a not-so-subtle warning to Wang Hongwen, one of Jiang Qing's closest associates, reminding him of Mao's admonition: "Jiang Qing has ambitions."

Zhou's greatest concern in these waning days was Deng Xiaoping. Did Deng have the internal fortitude to stave off the political change that Mao had ordered? And would the driving force with which Deng Xiaoping pursued his every goal win out in the end? The instructions that Zhou sent to Deng through Ye Jianying were perfectly clear: "Do not go head-to-head with Mao; seek him out and have a heart-to-heart talk with the Chairman." But Deng Xiaoping had no use for this kind of negotiated style. "Never give up on principal issues," Deng declared in a pronunciamento that left Zhou with little to do but invite Deng to the hospital for a man-to-man talk. On this occasion, according to a memoir written by Deng Rong, the daughter of Deng Xiaoping, when Zhou asked the vice-premier whether he would ever "change his attitude," Deng's response was an unequivocal "never." Zhou's response, according to Deng Rong, was just as unequivocal. "I am relieved," he said. The defiance of Zhou's response, as Deng Rong reports it, strikes an odd chord, contrary as it was to his usual disinclination to challenge Mao's authority behind his back. With Mao, Zhou Enlai had a history of avoiding even the slightest hint of confrontation; his style was purposely elliptical to parry Mao's decisions. Zhou's admission of relief suggests that in his last days the premier had finally washed his hands of the affair altogether and that he had nothing more to say on the matter of how Deng Xiaoping should deal with Mao.

Unconcerned with Zhou's reaction to his planned attacks on Deng Xiaoping and his reputedly "right deviationists," Mao went ahead with his plan, while Zhou, in typical fashion, uttered not a word in protest. With his wife at his bedside, the premier kept his silence and simply held hands with his lifelong companion, conspicuously avoiding any sensitive political subjects. Their unspoken compact of many years remained intact.

Zhou also fought his battle with depression and sorrow by listening to "Dai Yu's Flower Burial" and "Bao Yu's Weeping Soul" from *Dream of the Red Chamber*, his favorite Shanghai opera. Sung in the Yue style, generally by a chorus of female singers, the opera follows the story of a man living in a world full of women, with whom he seeks a warm place for dishonest feelings: "Spring fades, young looks age, followers fall, people die, no one knows." Zhou's medical staff had a hard time listening to such depressing melodies as the music wafted through the hospital room. Often they would switch to more relaxing music, only to be rebuked by Zhou. It could be that Zhou, near the end of his life, finally identified with Bao Yu, the protagonist of the famous novel on which the opera is based, whose major goal is to retreat from the every day of family life (read Communist Party) and become a monk. No one will ever know. The official media in China covered up this and many other aspects of Zhou's final days in an effort to avoid damaging his political image. And yet it seems true that, at the end, Zhou was trying to let the world inside his bitter mind, and reveal to all the depths of his feeling, to provide some dimension to his conventional worldly image.

Even as he fully cooperated with his doctors in an all-out battle against his cancer, Zhou Enlai remained in the dark about the full extent of his deterioration. Mao had issued instructions to Zhou's medical team to withhold the results of his final two operations, while Zhou entertained the illusion that the surgeons had removed the tumors from his bladder. Even Mao's "highest instructions," though, could not hide from Zhou the meaning of this severe deterioration. He could feel the lump that protruded from his lower abdomen. He could see for himself the chunks of blood that his bladder spewed forth, that sent him into paroxysms of pain. Mao had instructed the medical teams not to use radiation treatment to control the bleeding, on the assumption that such a move would surely reveal to Zhou how far gone he was.

Once his bleeding could no longer be stanched, Zhou grew increasingly aware of his rapid deterioration. He realized that his two previous surgeries had "had no strategic goals." He suggested that his entire bladder be removed once and for all. The medical team, which operated under all sorts of political constraints, had no idea how to respond. "Gain back your strength," they cautiously advised him, at first, in the belief that Zhou's weakened condition would prevent him from sustaining a major operation. But Zhou, dissatisfied with this tepid response, thought that continued postponement would only worsen his condition. Increasingly desperate, Zhou, in one dramatic act, yanked all the tubes out of his body and announced that he would "survive on my own." This sent the members of his team scurrying into such a state of high tension that they finally began radiation treatments to bring the bleeding under temporary control.

By late November, Zhou's basic bodily functions started to slip away. Although his hope of defeating the disease was now exceedingly dim, Zhou was not about to give up. He thought that if he could survive another six months, surgeons could remove his bladder and recovery would begin. Zhou remained defiant. "I must eat a little more," he kept saying, even as the simple act of eating became extremely difficult, as every swallow induced nausea and made him break out in a cold sweat. He was determined to regain his strength for another operation. This made every meal into a battle, one that he was devoted to winning with the assistance of his staff. By mid-December, however, any such victories became increasingly rare, as his intestinal system became blocked. His medical team began to feed Zhou intravenously, and administer frequent blood transfusions to sustain his life. Riddled with infection, he required massive doses of antibiotics and experienced frequent high fevers. Like all cancer patients, Zhou suffered unbelievable pain and continuous torment in his last days as his organs became virtually glued together, as a subsequent autopsy revealed, by the ubiquitous cancer cells. But Zhou Enlai was no ordinary man, and his physical endurance mimicked his enormous psychical tolerance. Pain would sweep over his body, causing him to tremble uncontrollably, and drive him in and out of consciousness. His body was bathed in a cold sweat. And yet while he was awake, he wouldn't make the slightest sound. Only during his sleep could one detect a light moan. When the pain finally became unendurable for him, Zhou's staff administered pain killers that in the beginning lasted for four to five hours, but eventually wore off in a mere two or three hours. At times, Zhou would unconsciously grab the hand of his wife or that of a nearby doctor, and on occasion he'd request that the Communist *Internationale* be played (he thought it would revive his strength). To the end, Zhou Enlai was devoted to the CCP. "Make a telephone call to the Party Central headquarters," he once directed his doctor, "and tell them that however long the Party wants me to live, I will live." In this effort, he was assisted by his wife. "Communist Party members must be strong, must be enduring," she exhorted the staff. Privately, though, even Deng Yingchao found the suffering too much to bear.

Somehow, Zhou managed to make it into the New Year of 1976. By this time he was falling into a coma, from which he would periodically emerge for short intervals. Deng Yingchao arrived at Zhou's bedside with a new issue of the journal *Poetry*, in which there appeared two poems written by Mao Zedong in the mid-1960s: "Reascending Well Ridge Mountain" and "Two Birds: A Dialogue." Two days into the New Year, Zhou emerged from his coma and appeared to be in better spirits. A "glimmer of life returned," as, several times, he invited his staff to read and reread Mao's poems, listening quietly and uttering a mere word or two of reaction. Upon hearing the lines "Don't fart any more! Look the world is being turned upside down," uttered by a wayward sparrow in "Two Birds," Zhou broke into a smile, and was heard to murmur, probably sardonically, "China produced a Mao Zedong!"

Six days later, on January 8, 1976, Zhou Enlai, the Premier of China, died.

Epilogue
More Power in Death than Life

The death of Zhou Enlai had an enormous impact on the political situation in China: the entire nation sank into a sea of deep sorrow, and markets nationwide sold out of black mourning clothes. Everyone felt a tremendous sense of loss when their longtime premier died: old cadres in the Party and military; members of the largely powerless Democratic parties, retained as political cover by the CCP since 1949; intellectuals; and the common folk. People were overwhelmed with a growing anxiety about the current political situation. Even as the national press, including *People's Daily*, played down Zhou's passing, while Mao issued directives prohibiting people from mourning the premier openly, Beijing residents gathered in Tiananmen Square in the center of the city to commemorate Zhou with wreaths laid in his honor at the foot of the Monument to Revolutionary Martyrs. Everywhere, people wept for the death of the premier. But they wept with anxiety, too, about what might now befall them in this uncertain political environment. The emotional level quickly intensified when people realized that Zhou had decided before he died not to have his ashes interred with other CCP notables at Eight Treasure Mountain cemetery. Suddenly, discontent and resentment toward the Cultural Revolution, long suppressed, gathered unstoppable momentum, so that mourning the loss of Zhou Enlai served as a pretext to "support Deng Xiaoping, punish Jiang Qing, and cast insinuations at Mao Zedong."

Thus it was, on the day that the hearse bearing Zhou's body traversed the streets of Beijing, millions of people spilled out of their homes, factories, and schools, and stood in freezing weather openly sobbing. Here, in one spontaneous demonstration, the true political mood in all of China found expression.

When the Chairman heard the news of the death of Zhou Enlai he was both delighted and worried. He was delighted because in the brutal mafia-like battle that is Chinese politics, the departure of a rival as difficult as Zhou Enlai eased Mao's own sense of dread of how he might have been treated following his own demise, had Zhou outlived him. But he was worried—Zhou's political soul was everywhere to be found, deeply rooted in the guts of the Party and the military, where, from the central to the local level, the premier had attracted a host of followers and supporters, most notably Deng Xiaoping and Marshal Ye Jianying. Old and respected cadres all, they had been very open about expressing their profound discontent with the Cultural Revolution. They had also made it clear that they would seize any available opportunity to turn the political tables on those who had prosecuted this madness, including Mao. Ever willing to use the dead to suppress the living, these tough old fighters now operated under the banner of Zhou Enlai's memory to pressure the Central Party leadership into diverting the attacks on Deng Xiaoping that Mao had personally inaugurated.

Mao was not naïve enough to misinterpret the events transpiring in the aftermath of Zhou's demise. In death, Zhou's had become the rallying point for the forces of revisionism both inside and outside the Communist Party. When the remaining members of the Politburo confronted the issue of whether or not Mao should attend the funeral, they left it to Mao's medical staff to render the final decision. Seeing no real problem if the Chairman chose to attend the services for a period of an hour or so, Mao's doctors arranged for a wheelchair to be made available for him during the proceedings. At the scheduled opening of the ceremony, all eyes were on the entrance. In the end, the Chairman never showed his face. (He relied on an official cover story that claimed he was too sick to even walk.) If the Chairman's plan to carry out intense criticism against Deng Xiaoping was to proceed, Zhou, even in death, would have to be included. It was for this reason that Mao refused to attend the premier's funeral. The Chairman of the Chinese Communist Party expressed no condolences for Zhou Enlai other than the perfunctory official wreath he sent over in his honor.

A general consensus emerged among members of the Politburo that Mao should have attended the funeral. By doing so he would have laid to rest the many rumors of internecine political struggle and supported overall work within the Party. But the Chairman had refused to play along. Every detail needed careful consideration in strategizing his attack on Zhou. In the words of people who were in a position to know, Mao made it clear that "I was free not to attend," as he once again accused the premier of opposing the Cultural Revolution. "All these old cadres," Mao muttered, "had listened to me, supported me, and shouted 'long live,' but none of it came from their hearts. Of this I was fully aware, and so the huge gap separating the premier and me can never be closed."

Three weeks after Zhou's passing, on January 30, 1976, the eve of the Chinese New Year, the political climate was as cold as the chilling winter temperature as Jiang Qing led her cohorts in another assault on Deng Xiaoping, Zhou's purported successor. Still mourning Zhou's death, most Chinese were both fed up with mass movements directed at Deng and worried over the future of the country. But aware of the terrible power of the Communist Party, none dared express their anger openly. That night near Mao's residence in Central South Lake the thunderous booms and bright lights of fireworks filled the air. Alarmed and confused, the security staff at the compound reacted immediately as there were strict prohibitions against fireworks anywhere in Central South Lake, especially around Mao's ultra-secure living quarters. When people in the capital realized what had transpired, rumors spread like wildfire among political circles that Mao had shot off the fireworks that, in Chinese tradition, are an expression of celebration. To have fired fireworks so soon after Zhou's funeral was considered the highest disrespect for the dead. The population, which had suffocated so long under Mao's imperious system of personal totalitarianism, reacted in fury. Mourning for the death of Zhou Enlai now served as the trigger for the greatest political crisis since the Cultural Revolution.

On April 5, 1976, the day that Chinese *saomu*, or "sweep the graves," of their deceased ancestors, once again throngs of Beijing residents gathered in Tiananmen Square to mourn Premier Zhou, while also expressing their open and defiant contempt for Jiang Qing and the Gang of Four. A flurry of speeches, poems, and big character posters inveighed against the Madam and her supporters, but also directed ire at the Chairman. "The era of the modern Qin Shihuang," they announced, broadcasting an obvious comparison between the third century B.C. unifier of China and Chairman Mao, "is over."

For decades, Mao had considered himself the virtual embodiment of the Chinese people's will and so the scene on Tiananmen Square on April 5 was more than distressing. Never in his wildest dreams had the Chairman imagined the possibility that at the very site where millions of young Red Guards had shouted "long live" to him at the apex of the Cultural Revolution frenzy, the same multitudes would now be roaring in protest against his rule. As an expert at mobilizing the masses in his earlier efforts to seize power and destroy his rivals, Mao did not take long to grasp the essence of what was transpiring on the Square, where his authority was now being directly challenged. The "heroic" life he had led was now thrown by this one incident into a shambles. The judgment of History, he knew, would be exceedingly harsh.

Now the great Chairman of the Chinese Communist Party was suddenly overwhelmed by fear and depression. Zhou Enlai was dead, but his soul had managed to bring great trouble to Mao, who, in desperation, revised the nine polemical articles from the days of the Yan'an purges that he had intended to use in his final assault on

Zhou. Considering how unpopular were Jiang Qing and the Cultural Revolution Group, Mao launched a double trick: On the one hand, he attacked anti-Cultural Revolution forces in and outside the Party and tried to repress the masses from organizing spontaneous memorial activities, acquiescing to the decision to deploy force against the April 5 demonstrations on Tiananmen Square. On the other, Mao had to readjust his original plan of allowing the Central Cultural Revolution Group to control all the levers of power and instead chose as his new successor the political lightweight Hua Guofeng to be acting premier.

While both Deng Xiaoping and Ye Jianying were pushed aside and relieved of their posts, Hua Guofeng was brought in as a transitional figure, a man to represent—at least on the surface—symbolic change. But the real goal was to firmly establish Jiang Qing and her cohort, whose job it would be to implement the Cultural Revolution legacy after Mao's death. Following the 1971 Lin Biao incident, Mao no longer trusted anyone but his family, which is why he had ordered his nephew, Mao Yuanxin, back from the Xinjiang region to coordinate the ongoing campaign against Deng Xiaoping. Just as the Cultural Revolution had been launched to transform China from the impersonal rule by the Communist Party to the personal rule by Mao Zedong, so too did Mao now want power to devolve gradually into the hands of his wife and nephew, creating permanent rule by the Mao clan.

It had long been Mao's plan when years earlier he had cultivated his son, Mao Anying, to assume the mantle of authority. (A plan that was short-circuited by his son's death in the Korean War.) Now it was up to Jiang Qing and Mao Yuanxin to achieve the goal of true patriarchic rule over the Middle Kingdom. For that reason, in his letter to Hua Guofeng whom Mao hoped would unite with the Cultural Revolution Group, the Chairman assured Hua that "With you in charge, I'm at ease," while also instructing the unsuspecting Hua that "if you have any questions, consult Jiang Qing."

Before the last political attack on Zhou Enlai could be unleashed, Mao Zedong, Chairman of the Chinese Communist Party, died.

Within a few weeks, Hua Guofeng would throw in his lot with the old cadres, acquiescing to the arrest of Jiang Qing and her support- ers, who in subsequent years would be put on trial and imprisoned. (It was in a hospital under house arrest that Jiang Qing eventually took her life in 1991.) Hua was gradually replaced by the resilient, no-nonsense Deng Xiaoping who as China's paramount leader from 1978 to his death in 1993 would do exactly what Mao had feared: de- nounce the Cultural Revolution as a "disaster" and move China to- ward the goals of wealth and power that all along had been the goal of Zhou Enlai and most Communist Party leaders.

The death of Mao Zedong on September 9, 1976—a mere eight months after the demise of Zhou Enlai—brought a close, at last, to an era of chaos and terror in modern Chinese history. It is true that the soul of Mao Zedong still floats over the political terrain of main- land China, but it is also true that China is finally on its way to real modernization.

For years, Zhou had been a follower of Mao Zedong, careful never to utter a word of opposition. In this sense, Zhou had assisted in the creation of the very totalitarian system of which he became the victim. Yet in terms of historical legacy, it is Zhou Enlai who has emerged the victor over Mao. Zhou's death not only struck the death knell of the Cultural Revolution, but also announced the bankruptcy of the Communist myth. If someone so devoted and loyal as Zhou ended up suffering such pathetic treatment at the hands of the Chairman of the Chinese Communist Party, how could anyone trust in the aims of the revolution? With the close of the Maoist era, a new chapter of economic growth and social stability has begun for the People's Republic of China. But with these re- markable changes have also come profiteering, embezzlement, and abuse of authority by Communist Party officials whose power re- mains unchecked. Is this the ideal Zhou had from the very begin- ning of his commitment to bringing revolution to his motherland? Will China once again return to the blood and storm of revolution or will it become a society of freedom, democracy, and wealth?

Author's Note

Zhou Enlai: The Last Perfect Revolutionary is based largely on the Chinese edition *Wannian Zhou Enlai* (*Zhou Enlai's Later Years*), published by Mirror Books in Hong Kong in 2003. I accumulated most of the documentation for this work, much of it classified and translated in the List of Sources, over the decade during which I worked at the Chinese Communist Party Central Research Office for Documentation (*Zhonggong zhongyang wenxian yanjiushi*) in Beijing, where I researched the history of Zhou Enlai and the Cultural Revolution. (I was the official biographer of Zhou Enlai at the Research Office.) In preparing the official biography of Zhou Enlai, I had access to the highly classified archives of the Chinese Communist Party, and interviewed hundreds of high-ranking Party officials and former employees and colleagues of Zhou Enlai. The English edition includes additional material on the early life of Zhou Enlai and his career as a revolutionary in the Chinese Communist Party (CCP) during its struggle to win power in twentieth-century China.

My reasons for writing this volume have to do, first, with Zhou Enlai's importance in modern Chinese history. It is my belief that Zhou intended to be a good person, but failed. In this sense, his life story conveys the tragedy of the Chinese Communist political system, from which he ultimately emerged, at the end of his life, as a victim. Zhou Enlai was neither the god current Chinese officials have put on a pedestal, nor the unequivocally evil person whom anti-CCP types have portrayed. As I hope to convey in this book, Zhou Enlai was an enormously complex man, hard to define and even harder to understand without a full appreciation of the difficulties described in this volume that beset China during his lifetime.

The second impetus for writing this book reflects my own personal experiences after I decided to defy government orders to stay away from Tiananmen Square when on June 4, 1989, elements of the People's Liberation Army crushed the Tiananmen Square pro-democracy movement. Immediately, I was struck by the stench of blood and death. Later, my wife insisted on taking me home, where, as I stood on the balcony of my apartment, I could hear the roaring of tanks and the ripping of machine-gun fire. "Use your pen to record history," she implored me. Right then and there I decided to tell the truth to the Chinese people about the CCP, the Cultural Revolution, and the role in all of this of the "beloved" former premier of China, Zhou Enlai.

Mine was an act of betrayal. But then I had always regarded myself as somewhat of a rebel. From my early childhood, I had experienced the residual effects of Communist China. Both my parents had been students at Yanjing University (later Peking University). They had joined the CCP during the anti-Japanese War (1937–1945) in hopes of driving away the invaders and building a new, free, democratic China. But soon after the establishment of the People's Republic in 1949, my father—a victim of the purges that swept the CCP following the conflict between Mao Zedong and Marshal Peng Dehuai at the 1959 Mt. Lu Conference—was exiled to Tibet. A similar fate later befell my mother, who, during the height of the Cultural Revolution, was denounced as a counterrevolutionary for some intemperate remarks she had uttered about Mao's wife, Jiang Qing, and the powerful Police Chief Kang Sheng. While my mother was incarcerated in the notorious Qincheng Prison outside Beijing where she was relegated to seven years in solitary confinement in deplorable conditions, I lived the life of a son of a counterrevolutionary, a political outcast deprived of any right to attend university or even join the military. Barred from living in urban areas, my only option was to reside in the remote and poor countryside where we did hard labor (farm work, and later working in the boiler room of a paper mill) more than ten hours a day, and at night read every book I could get my hands on.

Following the fall of the Gang of Four in 1976, my mother was released from prison and I was able to pursue a relatively normal life. I secured a position at the Central Research Office for Documentation. This had been established in 1979 as a ministerial-level center for the study of CCP history with prime responsibility to edit and publish the collected works of Party leaders. After years working in the very inhumane system that had doomed my parents, following the events of June 1989 I faced the same dilemma that had determined the fate of my parents. Writing this book meant confronting a system that, despite boasts of political reform (*gaige*) that had filled the airwaves since the reemergence of Deng Xiaoping in 1978, remained essentially the same crushing, totalitarian apparatus that Mao Zedong had created during his tenure from 1949 to 1976. Indeed, when the tanks rolled into Tiananmen Square on the night of June 3, 1989, all the Cultural Revolution language and "logic" rolled in even faster than the tanks. The political system in China is like a pot of traditional herbal medicine to which water may be added even as the herbs stay in the pot, never to be thrown out.

Fortunately, my wife had been born in the United States, and, after returning to America to reinstate her legal status, she began to make arrangements for my visit. This was dicey. During the 1989 student demonstrations I had organized members of my work unit at the Research Office to express our support for the students. Following the military crackdown, I was labeled as someone who had committed serious political mistakes. A protective superior had enabled me to hang on to my job at the Research Office, although I had seen too many classified documents, and top authorities were afraid that I would reveal inner-Party secrets to the outside world (a fact that, paradoxically, may have provided me with job protection).

My plans to travel to the United States went nowhere. But in 1992, when Deng Xiaoping made a tour of the vibrant special economic zones in the south to indicate his continued support for economic reform in China, the political climate loosened up a bit, and I was finally allowed to emigrate to the United States. I realized it would be a feat to transport the details of my research on Zhou Enlai to the United States, given my somewhat tarnished reputation. And so it was that, little by little, on index cards carried to American soil by friends and colleagues, documentation for this biography made its way safely out of China. Thanks to the assistance of individuals such as Li Shenzhi, former vice-president of the Chinese Academy of Social Sciences, who recommended me to the John King Fairbank Center for East Asian Research at Harvard University, I was able to begin my initial writing. My troubles, however, were far from over. Once word reached the Chinese government that I was writing a book, Party officials tried every trick at their disposal to prevent publication. The government even offered to pay me a high price to acquire the rights, and, at the same time, reminded me that my mother, who was still alive, had suffered a great deal during the Cultural Revolution. Fortunately, through the efforts of my wife and friends, notably Professor Ezra Vogel of Harvard University, we managed to survive, and five years later I completed work on the Chinese manuscript.

Zhou Enlai's Later Years was banned in mainland China immediately upon its release in 2003. The Chinese government is acutely aware that the collapse of the former Soviet Union and Eastern European Communist countries began with the demystification of official history and the reevaluation of major historical events and people. The government remains committed to covering up the truth and preserving the memory of Zhou Enlai as the last remaining untarnished icon of the first generation of CCP leaders. Despite its advances in the economic arena and the loosening up of Chinese society, the CCP wants to retain its long-held grip on how Chinese history is told. In its way, the government continues to promote national amnesia by imposing taboos on many subjects, particularly the life and times of Zhou Enlai. Although the Chinese government brought enormous pressure to bear on her, my mother nevertheless provided spiritual support as I wrote this book of betrayal. "It's a task from heaven," she once told me, "to tell the Chinese people the truth of the Cultural Revolution." And when Chinese government officials confronted my mother, the answer she gave to their tactics was simple. "My son," she told them, "has grown up and it's not up to me anymore." During her last days, I was a pariah in China. It was impossible for me to return for one last visit, and my mother, to my unending regret, never got to see the Chinese edition. "Heaven and earth separated forever," as the Chinese say. The Chinese and now the English edition are dedicated to her.

Translators'
Note

In this translation of *Zhou Enlai: The Last Perfect Revolutionary*, by Gao Wenqian, the translators have undertaken to render with great care the original version of the book, which is of indispensable value as a historical work. Thanks to his position that gave him privileged security clearance, Mr. Gao spent a decade studying classified Chinese Communist Party documents that are considered to be so highly sensitive that they remain inaccessible to all but a few people close to the source of power in China today. These documents form the essence of the author's source material from which, over a matter of years (during which time he lived in exile), Mr. Gao has fashioned a profoundly revealing portrait of Zhou Enlai and his relationship to the Chinese Communist Party and its leadership—in particular to Chairman Mao Zedong. The Chinese version of Mr. Gao's book is somewhat longer than the present volume. For the English edition, the translators have eliminated material that is of interest primarily to scholars of twentieth-century China and Chinese readers well versed in the details of Chinese political issues. The translators, however, have used their license to shape the current version of Mr. Gao's book advisedly, for the immense and specific details that the author has marshaled to create his work make it a fascinating account, and provide the quality of an

eyewitness experience, which this book delivers. Because this book re-
lies heavily on archival material, the translators and author have applied source identification in a List of Sources. The translators wish to
thank Ruth Li and Joanne Wang for their invaluable assistance.

Acknowledgments

I would like to take this opportunity to thank PublicAffairs for its wise decision to publish my biography *Zhou Enlai: The Last Perfect Revolutionary*. Thanks to Susan Weinberg, my publisher, Clive Priddle and Morgen Van Vorst, my editors. Through this book, the Western readers will learn the true history of the Chinese Communist revolution.

I would also like to thank professors Peter Rand (Boston University) and Lawrence R. Sullivan (Adelphi University) for their enormous efforts in undertaking the translation and editing work. My gratitude also goes to Joanne Wang, my literary agent, for her persistent and diligent work. Without their hard work, this book would not have the chance to meet with Western readers.

I am grateful to the late Mr. Li Shenzhi and to professors Ezra Vogel and Roderick MacFarquhar of Harvard University and Professor Andrew J. Nathan at Columbia University for their support while I was writing the Chinese edition.

Finally, my greatest gratitude is for my wife, who has been sustaining me through all these difficult years, providing a safe haven from wind and rain. Without her support, I would not have completed this book.

List of Sources

Chinese language sources listed below in English translation constitute the main source material that Gao Wenqian accessed while working as the head of the Research Group on Zhou Enlai at the Chinese Communist Party Central Research Office for Documentation (*Zhonggong zhongyang wenxian yanjiushi*) in Beijing. Scholars interested in complete citations should consult the Chinese-language version of the book entitled *Wannian Zhou Enlai (Zhou Enlai's Later Years)*, published by Mirror Books, Hong Kong, in 2003. The English-language sources noted at the end of this list were consulted by the author and translators.

CHINESE LANGUAGE: INTERNAL INTERVIEWS

Ji Dengkui, Fall 1987 and Spring 1988.

Qiao Guanhua [Foreign Minister 1974–1976 and 1983], September 23, 1981; October 6, 1981.

Qiao Guanhua and Ms. Zhang Hanzhi [Director, Department of American and Oceanic Affairs, Chinese Foreign Ministry], October 6, 1981; August 26, 1981; November 11 and 25, 1981; January 11, 1981.

Wang Li, July–August, 1983 (Recorded).

Wu Faxian, November 18 and 25, 1983.

Xiang Xun, Secretary to Peng Zhen, January 6, 1984 (Recorded).

Xu Xiangqian (PLA Marshal), Fall 1986.

Yang Chengwu, Fall 1987.

Zhang Hanzhi, June 30, 1980, quoted in *Two-Case Materials from the Central Party Archives.*

LETTERS, DIARY ENTRIES, AND DIRECTIVES

Central Committee, *Directive to the Front Committee of the Fourth Army*, September 28, 1929.

Kang Sheng, *Letter to Mao Zedong on Several Problems Involving Confessions by the Traitors An Ziwen, Bo Yibo, and Others*, September 16, 1966.

Lin Biao, *Letter to Zhou Enlai and the Central Cultural Revolution Group*, June 16, 1967.

Mao Zedong, *Letter to the Front Committee of the Fourth Army*, Late September, 1929.

_____. *Letter to the Red Guards of the Middle School Subordinate to Tsinghua University*, August 1, 1966.

_____. *Written Instructions on a Letter from Wang Hairong and Tang Wensheng*, May 29, 1967.

_____. *Letter to Jiang Qing*, March 27, 1974.

Zhou Enlai, *Diary Entries in Japan*, January 8, 9, 11, 29, February 4, 6, 17, March 10, April 23, and October 20, 1918.

_____. *Letter to Feng Wenqian*, April 3, 1918.

_____. *Letter to Chen Songyan*, December 22, 1918.

_____. *Letter to Chen Shizhou*, January 30, 1921, in *Selected Works of Zhou Enlai's Correspondence* (Beijing: Central Research Office Press, 1988).

_____. *Letter to Yan Xiu*, January 25 and February 21, 1921.

_____. *Letter to Li Xijin and Zheng Jiqing* (n.d.), in *Selected Works of Zhou Enlai's Correspondence* (Beijing: Central Research Office Press, 1988).

_____. *Letters to Mao Zedong and Lin Biao*, March 18, 1967; March 22, 1969; September 13, 1969; February 13, 1970; April 3, 1970; May 17, 1970; May 27, 1970; August 22, 1970.

_____. *Letters (handwritten) to Mao Zedong*, April 2, 1966; September 9, 1966; December 6, 1966; March 13, 1967; December 12, 1969; March 24, 1970; March 15, 1971; September 13, 1971; January 8, 1972; January 25, 1972; May 30, 1972; June 7, 1972; March 30, 1973; June 26, 1973; November 18, 1973; December 14, 1973; February 6, 1974; March 26, 1974; November 6, 1974; February 2, 1975; March 30, 1975; June 16, 1975; July 5, 1975; July 15, 1975.

_____. *Letter (handwritten) to Mao Zedong on Problems of the Supplementary List of Personnel for the Eleventh Plenum of the Eighth Central Committee*, August 6, 1966.

_____. *Letter (handwritten) to Jiang Qing*, September 20, 1966.

_____. *Letter to Mao Zedong on the Issue of Releasing Liu Lantao from Prison*, October 24, 1966.

_____. *Letter to Lin Biao*, February 24, 1967.

_____. *Handwritten Copy of Corrections to the Record of the "February 26 Meeting at Cherish Benevolence Hall,"* February 1967.

_____. *Telegram Drafted on Behalf of the Party Central Ordering the Restoration of the Guangzhou Military Region*, March 10, 1967.

_____. *Letter (handwritten) to Chen Yi*, May 5, 1967.

_____. *Letter (handwritten) to Mao Zedong Regarding "Incident of the Fifth Warrior,"* May 19, 1967.

_____. *Comments (handwritten) on Jiang Qing's Letter Regarding "Incident of the Fifth Warrior,"* May 19, 1967.

_____. *Letter (handwritten) to Mao Zedong Regarding the Case of Liu Shaoqi*, September 25, 1968.

_____. *Letter (handwritten) to Jiang Qing on Various Issues Involving the Arrests of Liu Shaoqi*, September 25, 1968.

_____. *Corrections to Ye Qun Speech to a Group at the Second Plenum of the Eighth Party Congress*, October, 1968.

_____. *Letter to Kang Sheng*, February 13, 1970.

_____. *Letter (handwritten) to Kang Sheng*, August 26, 1970.

_____. *Letter to Various Comrades of the CCP Small and Large Group on American Affairs in the Ministry of Foreign Affairs*, July 3, 1973.

_____. *Joint Letters (handwritten) with Wang Hongwen to Mao Zedong*, January 1 and February 1, 1974.

_____. *Letter (handwritten) to Members of the Politburo Located in the Capital*, January 25, 1974.

_____. *Draft Note (handwritten) to be Distributed to Party Central on "Brief Report on the Middle School of Ma Zhenfu Commune, Tanghe County, Henan Province,"* January 29, 1974.

_____. *Outline for Distribution to Members of the Standing Committee of the CCP Politburo*, December 28, 1974.

_____. *Letter (handwritten) to Members of the CCP Politburo*, May 21, 1975.

_____. *Letter to Mao Zedong Regarding the Memorial Ceremony for Marshal He Long*, June 7, 1975.

_____. *Letter to Zhang Yufeng*, June 16, 1975.

_____. *Joint Letter with Deng Xiaoping and Peng Zhen to Mao Zedong*, April 12, 1966.

_____. *Joint Letter with Jiang Qing and Chen Boda to Mao Zedong*, January 11, 1967.

RECORDED CONVERSATIONS, REPORTS, SPEECHES, AND OTHER DOCUMENTS

Central Committee (ad interim) of the Chinese Communist Party, *Telegram to the Soviet Central Bureau*, November 1932.

Central Committee of the Chinese Communist Party, *Draft of Ten Regulations on Grasping Revolution and Promoting Production*, December 9, 1966.

Central Party Archives, *Selected Materials*.

Chen Boda, *Speech when Meeting with Rebels from the Foreign Ministry*, early morning, August 23, 1967.

Chen Yun, *Outline Report (handwritten) of the Enlarged Meeting of the Politburo at the Zunyi Conference*, February (or March) 1935.

Conversation with Tang Wensheng and Wang Hairong, June 20 and 21, 1980, quoted in *Two-Case Materials from the Central Party Archives*.

Criticism of Talks by Zhang Hanzhi with Mao Zedong on the "Gang of Four," July 21, 1980, quoted in *Two-Case Materials from the Central Party Archives*.

Deng Xiaoping, *Speech to the Enlarged Meeting of the Central Politburo*, May 25, 1966.

Deng Yingchao, *Talk on the Fiftieth Anniversary of the Long March*, 1985.

_____. *Conversation with Zhou Enlai Biography Group. Discussion Meeting with Zhou Enlai Staff Members*, November 26, 1980.

Executive Committee, European Youth League, *Report to the Central Youth League*, August 20, 1924.

Exposé Materials on Wang Li: Discussing the Accusations Against Zhou Enlai with Lin Biao and Jiang Qing, October 13, 1967 and October 3, 1979, in *Two-Case Materials from the Central Party Archives*.

Foreign Ministry of the People's Republic of China, *Archives Supplied by Central Party Archives*.

_____. *Cable to Chargé d'Affaires Lei Yang in Poland*, January 15, 1970.

_____. *Cable to Ambassador Wang Youpin, Vietnam*, March 19, 1970.

_____. *Telegrams*.

_____. *Instructions Regarding Issues for Discussion by Representatives of the People's Republic of China and the United States*, June 17, 1970.

List of Sources

Hu Qiaomu, *Talks on Various Conditions Surrounding the Issue of "Opposing Rash Advance,"* November 4, 1982.

Jiang Qing, *Comments on the Liu Shaoqi Case,* September 16, 1968.

_____. *Instructions on "Liu Shaoqi's Criminal Records of His Three Arrests" Compiled and Submitted by the Special Investigative Group on Liu Shaoqi and Wang Guangmei,* September 16, 1968.

Kang Sheng, *Speech to the Opening Session of the Second Plenum of the Ninth Party Congress,* August 23, 1970.

Lin Biao, *Speech to the Central Work Conference,* August 13, 1966.

_____. *Telephone Conversation with Mao Zedong,* April 11, 1970.

Lin Liheng, *On Exposing the Crimes,* in *Two-Case Materials from the Central Party Archives.*

Liu Shaoqi, *Outline of Self-Criticism at the Eleventh Plenum of the Eighth Central Committee,* August 1966.

_____. *Speech at the Eleventh Plenum of the Eighth Central Committee,* August 4, 1966.

Mao Yuanxin, *Notes,* November 2, 1975, in *Two-Case Materials from the Central Party Archives.*

Mao Zedong, *Speech to the Enlarged Meeting of the Central Politburo,* July 13 and September 7, 1943.

_____. *Speech to the Central Politburo,* November 13, 1943.

_____. *Talk at the Enlarged Second Preparatory Meeting for the Eighth Party Congress,* September 10, 1956, reproduced in *Party Documents,* no. 3, 1991.

_____. *Comments to the Chinese Ambassador to the Soviet Union on the Question of Attending the Twenty-Third CPSU Congress,* March 13, 1966.

_____. *Speech at the Enlarged Meeting of the Central Politburo Standing Committee in Hangzhou,* March 18, 1966.

_____. *Talk with Kang Sheng, Jiang Qing, Zhang Chunqiao and Others,* March 28–30, 1966.

_____. *Talk with Kang Sheng and Others,* March 30, 1966.

_____. *Response to the Telephone Request for Instructions by Zhou Enlai on his Planned Trip to Romania* (conveyed by Mao's secretary, Xu Yefu), June 6, 1966.

_____. *Comments to Zhou Enlai on Receiving the "Notice of the Central Committee and State Council on Several Concrete Problems of the Cultural Revolution,"* September 1, 1966.

_____. *Comments on Letter Requesting Instructions from Zhou Enlai,* September 14, 1966.

_____. *Speech at the Debriefing Session of the Central Work Conference,* October 24, 1966.

_____. *Speech at the Central Work Conference,* October 24 and 25, 1966.

_____. *Comments on the "Report on the Cultural Revolution" Submitted for Examination by the Central Cultural Revolution Group,* October 29, 1966.

_____. *Talk With Select Personnel of the Central Cultural Revolution Group,* January 8, 1967.

_____. *Speech to the Central Briefing,* January 16, 1967.

_____. *Talk at a Briefing for the Enlarged Meeting of the Military Affairs Committee of the Central Committee of the Chinese Communist Party,* January 22, 1967.

_____. *Comments on a Telegram to the Shenyang Military Region,* March 3, 1967.

_____. *Comments on the Report to Establish a Beijing Revolutionary Committee,* March 10, 1967.

_____. *Comments on Essay Submitted by Qi Benyu on "Patriotism Is Still Betrayal,"* March 23, 1967.

_____. *Comments and Corrections on the Report of the Party Central on Problems in Anhui Province.* April 1, 1967.

_____. *Comments on the Letter from Zhou Enlai,* May 1967.

List of Sources

_____. *Comments on the Letter from Fan Haiquan*, student, History Department, Peking University, January 16, 1968.

_____. *Talks at Meeting with the Central Cultural Revolution Group*, June 3, 1968.

_____. *Comments on Report from the Foreign Ministry*, June 17, 1970.

_____. *Joint Comments with Lin Biao, Zhou Enlai, Jiang Qing and Others on the Report of the Special Investigative Group on Liu Shaoqi and Wang Guangmei*, July 1970.

_____. *Talk With Edgar Snow*, December 18, 1970.

_____. *Comments on the Eulogy for Chen Yi Submitted by Zhou Enlai*, January 9, 1972.

_____. *Comments on the Letter From Zhou Enlai*, March 15, 1971, and July 5, 1973.

_____. *Speech to Staff Members of the Military Affairs Committee*, October 4, 1971.

_____. *Speech at a Meeting Held in Chengdu Prefecture*, November 14, 1971.

_____. *Talks at Meeting of the Central Party Politburo and at Gatherings of Responsible Personnel from the Major Military Regions of the Central Military Affairs Committee*, June 12, 14, 15, and 21, 1973.

_____. *Meeting with Henry Kissinger*, February 17, 1973.

_____. *Talks with Zhang Chunqiao and Wang Hongwen*, July 4, 1973.

_____. *Talk with Zhou Enlai in Changsha*, Late December, 1974.

Ni Zhifu, *Comments on the Counterrevolutionary Activities of the "Gang of Four,"* August 26, 1980, in *Two-Case Materials from the Central Party Archives*.

Notes of Talks by Deng Xiaoping and other Central Party Leaders when Meeting with Zhou Enlai's Medical Team, October 16, 1975; November 16, 1975; and November 27, 1975.

Notice Issued by the CCP and Government Departments Regarding Organizing Revolutionary Teachers and Students from Across the Country to Come to Beijing to Observe the Cultural Revolution, September 5, 1966.

Records of Meetings of Zhou Enlai Staff, November 26, 1980.

Ren Bishi et al., *Telegram to the (ad interim) Central Committee on the Experience and Disputes at the Ningdu Conference*, November 12, 1932.

Selected Records of the "July 20th Incident," in *Two-Case Materials from the Central Party Archives*.

Soviet Central Bureau, *Telegram to Zhou Enlai, Mao Zedong, Zhu De, and Wang Jiaxiang*, September 30, 1932.

_____. *Brief Report on the Proceedings of the Ningdu Conference*, October 21, 1932.

Special Investigative Group on Liu Shaoqi and Wang Guangmei, *"Investigative Report on Criminal Spying by Wang Guangmei" Submitted to Party Central*, July 1970.

Wang Dongxing, *Talk on the Framing of Charges Against Liu Shaoqi by Jiang Qing, Kang Sheng, Xie Fuzhi, and Others*, July 2, 1980, in *Two-Case Materials from the Central Party Archives*.

_____. *Talk on Crimes by the Gang of Four*, August 13 and 15, 1980.

Wang Hongwen, *Briefing Documents*, in *Two-Case Materials from the Central Party Archives*.

Wang Jiaxiang, *Speech to the Enlarged Meeting of the Central Politburo*, September 14, 1938.

Wang Ming, *Speech to the Meeting of the Central Politburo*, December 9, 1937.

Wu De [Beijing mayor], *On the Counterrevolutionary Activities of the "Gang of Four,"* August 11 and 12, 1980, in *Two-Case Materials from the Central Party Archives*.

Xie Fuzhi, *Instructions on "Comprehensive Report on Liu Shaoqi's Crimes of Betrayal after Three Arrests" Compiled and Submitted by Special Investigative Group on Wang Guangmei*, February 26, 1968.

Yao Wenyuan, *Talk on Various Matters Regarding the Drafting of the Political Report to the Tenth Party Congress*, n.d.

Ye Jianying, *Speech at the Meeting to Criticize Luo Ruiqing*, April 24, 1966.

Zhang Chunqiao and Qi Benyu, *Talk with Representatives of the "Beijing Aviation Red Flag,"* November 8, 1966.

_____. *Critical Comments on Zhou Enlai's Draft of a Central Notice*, n.d.

Zhou Enlai, *Speech to Meeting of the Central Politburo*, August 13, 1929.

_____. *Report to the Third Plenum of the Sixth Central Committee Promulgating the Decisions of the Comintern*, September 1930.

_____. *Speech to the Standing Committee of the (ad interim) Central Politburo*, December 28, 1927.

_____. *Telegram to Soviet Central Bureau and the (ad interim) Central Committee*, November 12, 1932.

_____. *Speech at the Meeting of the Central Politburo*, November 27, 1943.

_____. *Telegram to Mao Zedong, Zhu De, and Wang Jiaxiang*, June 19, 1932.

_____. *Joint Telegram with Mao Zedong, Zhu De, and Wang Jiaxiang, to the Central Soviet Bureau*, July 25, 1932.

_____. *Telegram to the Soviet Central Bureau*, July 29, 1932.

_____. *Telegram to the Soviet Central Bureau*, September 24, 1932.

_____. *Statement to the Enlarged Meeting of the Central Politburo*, August 22, 1937.

_____. *Summary (handwritten) of Speech to the Central Politburo*, November 15, 1943.

_____. *Speech to the Fujian Group at the Enlarged Meeting of the Central Work Conference*, February 3, 1962.

_____. *Speech on Intellectuals*, March 2, 1962, in *Collection of Zhou Enlai's Works* (Beijing: People's Publishing House, 1984).

_____. *Speech to the Enlarged Meeting of the Central Politburo*, May 21, 1966.

_____. *Speech to Small Group of Enlarged Meeting of the Central Politburo*, May 23, 1966.

_____. *Speech to Enlarged Meeting of the Central Politburo*, May 26, 1966.

_____. *Speech to a Meeting of Cultural Revolution Activists from the Middle School of Beijing Normal University*, July 29, 1966.

_____. *Speech to the Eleventh Plenum of the Eighth Central Committee*, August 2, 1966.

_____. *Speech at the Large Discussion Meeting of Work Group Heads of Tsinghua University*, August 4, 1966.

_____. *Speech at a Meeting of the Work Group Heads of Tsinghua University at which Ye and Lin Engaged in Self-Criticism*, August 4, 1966.

_____. *Comments on the Letter from Zhang Shizhao*, August 30, 1966.

_____. *Speech at the First Representative Gathering of the Capital University and Middle School Red Guards*, September 1, 1966.

_____. *Speech to Gathering of Red Guards from Beijing Universities and Schools*, September 13, 1966.

_____. *Speech to CCP Personnel and Party Committees of the Party Central and State Organizations*, September 22, 1966.

_____. *Speech at the Second Representative Gathering of the Capital University and Middle School Red Guards*, September 10, 1966.

_____. *Speech to the Fifth Small Group of the Central Work Conference*, October 13, 1966.

_____. *Speech to Meeting of Responsible Personnel from Central Party, Government, and Army Departments*, October 23, 1966.

_____. *Speech to the Central Work Conference*, October 26, 1966.

_____. *Speech to the Central Work Conference*, October 28, 1966.

_____. *Speech to the Closing Session of the Central Work Conference*, October 28, 1966.

_____. *Summary of Speeches (handwritten) to the Central Work Conference*, October 1966.

_____. *Speech when Meeting with Representatives of the Three Red Guard Headquarters of All Beijing-Area Universities and Schools*, November 8, 1966.

_____. *Speech to Enlarged Meeting of the Central Politburo*, December 15, 1966.

_____. *Speech to Working Personnel of Military Units*, February 1, 1967.

_____. *Markup Copies (handwritten notes) of the "Cherish Benevolence Hall Meetings" of February 16, 1967*, compiled by Zhang Chunqiao, Wang Li, and Yao Wenyuan, in Two-Case Materials from the Central Party Archives.

_____. *Markup Copies (handwritten notes) of the "Cherish Benevolence Hall Meetings" of February 16, 1967*, compiled by Zhang Chunqiao, Wang Li, and Yao Wenyuan, in Two-Case Materials from the Central Party Archives.

_____. *Speech to Representatives of Revolutionary Rebels from the Financial and Trade Departments*, February 17, 1967.

_____. *Speech to Rebel Representatives of the Financial and Trade Departments*, February 17, 1967.

_____. *Speech to Leading Cadres from Financial and Trade Departments and Bureaus*, February 18, 1967.

_____. *Speech to Representatives of Revolutionary Rebels from National Defense Industries*, February 18, 1967.

_____. *Extracts (handwritten) of Mao's Letter to Jiang Qing*, n.d.

_____. *Speeches to Representatives of Rebel Groups from the Foreign Ministry*, evenings of May 11 and 15, 1967; August 23, 1967; and September 16, 1967.

_____. *Speech at Meeting with the Staff of the Central Case Examination Group*, December 13, 1967.

_____. *Joint Report with Chen Boda, Kang Sheng, and Jiang Qing to Mao Zedong and Lin Biao on the Criminal Materials Detailing Treason and Treachery by Liu Shaoqi*, September 25, 1968.

_____. *Corrections to Ye Qun's Speech Delivered to a Group Meeting During the Twelfth Plenum of the Eighth Central Committee*, October 1968.

_____. *Conversations with Pakistan Ambassador*, December 12, 1969.

_____. *Speech to the State Economic Planning Commission*, February 20, 1970.

_____. *Original Report (handwritten) to Mao Zedong on the Situation in Cambodia*, March 20, 1970.

_____. *Talk with Minister of Interior, Albania*, June 16, 1970.

_____. *Speech to the Committee Drafting Changes in the Constitution*, August 22, 1970.

_____. *Speech to Enlarged Meeting of the Central Politburo*, August 29, 1970.

_____. *Speech to the Northeast, Central North, and Central South Groups at the Second Plenum of the Ninth Central Committee*, September 3 and 4, 1970.

_____. *Comments on Foreign Ministry Report*, April 4, 1971.

_____. *Comments on Report by the National Committee of Sports*, April 8, 1971.

_____. *Draft Report (handwritten) on CCP Politburo Meeting on China-America Talks*, May 29, 1971.

_____. *Speech to the Meeting of the Central Work Conference*, June 18, 1971.

_____. *Conversation with Mao Zedong when Meeting with the Vietnamese Premier*, November 22, 1971.

_____. *Speech at Meeting with High-Ranking Patriots in Beijing Organized by the CCP*, December 29 and 31, 1971.

_____. *Comments (handwritten) on Eulogy to Chen Yi*, January 8, 1972.

_____. *Personal Views on the Sixth Line Struggle of Our Party During the New Democratic Revolution*, June 10, 1972.

_____. *Talk with Returning Ambassadors and Responsible Personnel in the Foreign Ministry*, August 1 and 2, 1972.

_____. *Talk when Meeting with the Staff of People's Daily*, December 19, 1972.

_____. *Meeting with Henry Kissinger*, November 11, 1973.

_____. *Comments (handwritten) to Xinhua on "New Trends,"* January 1, 1974.

_____. *Comments (handwritten) on Foreign Ministry Report*, March 27, 1974.

_____. *Interjections During Speech by Mao Zedong to Members of the Central Politburo*, July 17, 1974.

_____. *Speech to Top Officials of the State Council*, February 1, 1975.

CHINESE LANGUAGE: PUBLIC BOOKS, NEWSPAPER ARTICLES, AND DOCUMENTARY COLLECTIONS

Beijing Daily, September 4, 1973.

Biography of Deng Yingchao (first draft).

Cao Weidong, *Red Medical Records* (Taiyuan: Shanxi People's Publishing House, 1993).

Central Research Office for Documentation, *Chronology of Zhou Enlai, 1949–1976*, vol. II (Beijing: Central Research Office Press, 1997).

_____. *Chronology of Zhou Enlai, 1898–1949*, ibid.

_____. *Compiled Materials from the Ten Year "Cultural Revolution,"* vol. II.

_____. *Chronology of Mao Zedong, 1893–1949*, vol. II, ibid.

Chen Xiaonong, *Chen Boda's Prison Memoirs: Personal Recollections and Other Materials* (Hong Kong: Tiandi Books, 1998).

Chinese Communist Party Information Reports, January 16, 1989.

CCP Party History Communications, vol. 10, 1987.

Collection of Documents on the Liping Meeting (Guiyang: Guizhou People's Publishing House, 1992).

Contemporary Chinese Foreign Relations (Beijing: China Social Sciences Publishing House, 1990).

Dong Baocun, *In the Whirlpool of History: Remembrance of Mao Zedong* (Beijing: Zhongwai Cultural Press, 1990).

Gao Zhenpo, *Memoirs of Zhou Enlai's Bodyguard* (Shanghai: Shanghai People's Publishing House, 2000).

Han Suyin, *Zhou Enlai and His Century, 1898–1998* (Beijing: Central Research Office Press, 1992).

Jin Chunming, *Historical Draft of "Great Cultural Revolution"* (Chengdu: Sichuan People's Publishing House, 1995).

Jin Feng, *Biography of Ye Qun*, People's Publishing House, n.d.

Jing Xizhen, *Beside Chief Peng: Memories of an Aide-de-camp* (Chengdu: Sichuan People's Publishing House, 1979).

Last Days of Zhou Enlai, 1966–1976 (Beijing: Central Research Office Press, 1995).

Li Haiwen, *Zhou Enlai's Family* (Beijing: China Youth Press, 1998).

Li Kefei, *Memoirs of Zhou Enlai's Chief Airplane Pilot* (Nanjing: Jiangsu Literary Publishing House, 1991).

Li Ping, *Life of Zhou Enlai* (Beijing: Central Research Office Press, 2001).

Li Rui, *True Record of the Mt. Lu Meeting (Revised)*, (Changsha: Hunan People's Publishing House, 1989).

Lin Ke, Xu Tao, and Wu Xujun, *Truth of History: Testimonials of Mao Zedong Staff* (Hong Kong: Liwen Publishing House, 1995).

Liu Yan, *Collection of Zhou Enlai's Early Writings* (Tianjin: Nankai University Press, 1993).

Liu Ying, *In the Tidal Waves of History* (Beijing: Central Party History Publishing House, 1992).

Lu Zaibing and Sun Zhirui, *Young Zhou Enlai* (Beijing: People's China Press, 1992).

Luo Diandian, *Dossiers on a Red Family* (Haikou: Nanhai Publishing Co., 1999).

Mao Mao (Deng Rong), *My Father During the Cultural Revolution Era* (Beijing: Central Research Office Press, 1993).

Mao Zedong and the Comintern (Beijing: Establishing the Party Publishing House, 1994).

Material Collections on Army-Party History, no. 6, 1984.

Military Science Institute, ed., *Biography of Ye Jianying* (Beijing: Contemporary China Publishing House, 1995).

Nie Rongzhen, *A Memoir* (Beijing: Warriors Press, 1983).

Pang Ruiyin, *Zhou Enlai's Early Years* (Nanjing: Jiangsu Educational Press, 1995).

People's Liberation Army Chief of Staff, *Biography of He Long* (Beijing: Contemporary China Publishing House, 1997).

Qian Jiang, *Origins of "Ping Pong Diplomacy"* (Beijing: Orient Publishing House, 1987).

Quan Yanchi, *Zhou Enlai: Coming Off the Alter* (Beijing: Central Party School Press, 1993).

_____. *Tao Zhu in the "Cultural Revolution"* (Beijing: Central Party School Press, no. 10, 1991).

_____. *Traveling Incognito—Yang Chengwu in 1967* (Guangzhou: Guangdong Travel Publishing House, 1997).

Records of Enlarged Central Politburo Meeting, September 12, 1935.

_____. November 3, 1935.

_____. December 6, 1966.

Research Staff, CCP Central Research Archives, *Biography of Zhou Enlai* (Beijing: People's Publishing House and Central Research Office Press, 1989).

Selected Works of Zhou Enlai's Correspondence (Beijing: Central Research Office Press, 1988).

Shao Yihai, *Lin Biao in the Throes of the September 13 Incident* (Chengdu: Sichuan Literary Press, 1996).

Shui Gong, *Chinese Marshal He Long* (Beijing: Central Party School Press, 1995).

Song Jialing et al., *The Great Man Zhou Enlai* (Beijing: Central Party School Press, 1996).

Study and Criticism, no. 4, 1973.

Sun Gang, *Beginnings of a Giant: Zhou Enlai* (Hangzhou: Zhejiang People's Publishing House, 1991).

Wang Dongxing, *Wang Dongxing Remembers Mao Zedong's Struggle Against Lin Biao's Counterrevolutionary Clique* (Beijing: Contemporary China Press, 1997).

Wang Haiguang, *Crash at Öndörkhan* (Shenyang: Liaoning People's Publishing House, 1997).

Wang Li, *Witness to the Cultural Revolution* (Hong Kong: Oxford University Press, 1993).

Wang Nianyi, *Years of Great Chaos* (Zhengzhou: Henan People's Publishing House, 1992).

When Zhou Enlai Was Young (Beijing: Wenwu Publishing House, 1988).

Yu Shicheng, *Mao Zedong and Deng Xiaoping* (Beijing: Central Party School Press, 1995).

Yang Guisong, *Love and Hate between Mao Zedong and Moscow* (Nanchang: Jiangxi People's Publishing House, 1999).

Zhang Guotao, *My Reminiscences*, vol. III (Beijing: Orient Publishing House, 1998).

Zhang Hanzhi, *Between the Wind and the Rain* (Hong Kong: Universal Publishers Ltd., n.d.).

Zhang Ning, *Dust from a Disaster* (Hong Kong: Mirror Books, 1997).

Zhang Yunsheng, *True Account of Maojiawan: Memoirs of a Secretary of Lin Biao's* (Beijing: Spring and Autumn Publishing House, 1988).

Zhang Zuoliang, *Memoirs of Zhou Enlai's Physician, 1966–1976* (Hong Kong: Sanlian Books, 1998).

Zheng Chaolin, *Remembering Yikuan* (Hong Kong: Chunyan Publishing House, 1997).

Zhou Bingde and Tie Zhuwei, *My Uncle Zhou Enlai* (Shenyang: Liaoning People's Publishing House, 2001).

Zhou Enlai's Childhood in Huai'an (Guiyang: Guizhou People's Publishing House, n.d.).

Zhu De, *A China History*, Compilation of Contemporary Historical Materials, n.d.

ARTICLES AND BOOK CHAPTERS

Central Party Research Office for Documentation, "Record of Meetings Involving Zhou Enlai During the Cultural Revolution," in Jing Feng, *Biography of Deng Yingchao* (Beijing: People's Publishing House, 1993).

"Comrade Zhou Enlai on his Personal and Revolutionary History—Conversation with an American Reporter," *CCP Archives*, no. 1, 1982.

Chen Zaidao, "Eyewitness to the July 20th Incident in Wuhan," *Revolutionary History Reference*, no. 2, 1980.

Da Ying, "The September 13 Incident: The Entire Story," in *Lin Biao After 1959* (Chengdu: Sichuan People's Publishing House, 1993).

Deng Xiaoping, "Speech at Meeting of the CCP Politburo, May 27, 1975," in Jia Sinan, *Records of Mao Zedong's Social Relationships* (Nanjing: Jiangsu Literary Publishing House, 1989); also Yu Shicheng, *Deng Xiaoping and Mao Zedong* (Beijing: Central Party School Press, 1995).

Deng Yingchao, "A Communist Party Member Who Strictly Followed Iron Discipline," *People's Daily*, June 30, 1982.

Du Xiuxian, "Lin Biao Departs from Mao Zedong Without So Much as a 'Goodbye,'" in *The Fall of the Lin Biao Counterrevolutionary Clique* (Beijing: Central Research Office Press, 1995).

Gu Baozi, "Ye Jianying: In and Outside the Ice Palace," in *Spotlight on Central South Lake* (Beijing: China Youth Press, 1998).

Hu Zhangshui, "Lin Biao and the Central Military Commission (Eight Orders)," in *Lin Biao After 1959* (Chengdu: Sichuan People's Publishing House, 1993).

Jia Lanxun, "Tragedy of [Liu] Shaoqi: Memoir of a Bodyguard," *Centenary Tides*, nos. 1–2, 2000.

Jiang Qing, "Written Letter of Self-Criticism to Mao Zedong and Members of the Politburo," June 28, 1975, in Yu Shicheng, *Deng Xiaoping and Mao Zedong* (Beijing: Central Party School Press, 1995).

Kan Min, "Phoenix and Nirvana: Mao Zedong and Guo Morou During the Cultural Revolution," in *Insiders: Truth for the World Left by Key Historical Figures* (Beijing: China Youth Press, n.d.).

Kang, "Xu Xiangqian: Group Leader of the 'Entire Cultural Revolution in the Military,'" in *Spotlight on Central South Lake* (Beijing: China Youth Press, 1998).

Ku Mu, "Remembrances of the Beloved Premier," in *Our Premier*, (Beijing: Central Research Office Press, 1990).

Li Desheng, "From the Mt. Lu Conference to the September 13 Incident," in Shao Yihai, *Wall-to-Wall Coverage of the Lin Biao September 13 Incident* (Chengdu: Sichuan Literary Publishing House, 1996).

Li Wenpu [Lin Biao Secretary], "True Story of the September 13 Incident," in *Chinese Sons and Daughters*, n.d.

Li Xuefeng, "Everything I Know About the Start of the 'Cultural Revolution,'" *Centenary Tides*, vol. 4, 1998.

Lin Biao, "Comments on *Cao Cao*," in Guan Weixun, *The Ye Qun I Knew* (Beijing: China Literary Press, 1993).

———. "Comments on the *Dictionary of Cultural Studies*," in Shao Hua and You Hu, *The Life of Lin Biao* (Wuhan: Hubei People's Publishing House, 1994).

Lin Liheng, "Recalling the September 13 Incident," in Shao Yihai, *Wall-to-Wall Coverage of the Lin Biao September 13 Incident* (Chengdu: Sichuan Literary Publishing House, 1996).

Liu Pingping, "Victorious Flower Dedicated to You," in *History in Remembrance*, no. 1.

Liu Yuan and He Jiatong, "Doubts and Suspicions about the 'Four Cleans,'" in *The Unknown Liu Shaoqi* (Zhengzhou: Henan People's Publishing House, 2000).

Mao Zedong, "Speech at the Opening Session of the CCP Ninth National Party Congress," April 1, 1969, in Xi Xuan and Jin Chunming, *A Concise History of the "Cultural Revolution"* (Beijing: Central Research Office Press, 1996).

———. "Directive Regarding Diagnosis of Bladder Cancer in Zhou Enlai," May 31, 1972, in Zhou Enlai Medical Team, *Supplementary Record of Zhou Enlai's Medical History*, n.p., n.d.

———. "Conversations with Wang Hairong," in *Red Revolution and Black Rebels: Research Papers on the Thirtieth Anniversary of the Cultural Revolution*, Twenty-First Century China Foundation Publishing House, n.d.

Shi Lei, "Geng Biao at the Crucible Moment of Our Party and Country," *Annals of the Chinese People*, no.4, 1994.

Su Caiqing, "Serious Battles in the Economic Front in the Early Cultural Revolution—Review of the Winter Seminar of Industrial and Transportation Sectors, 1966," in *Critique After a Decade* (Beijing: Central Party History Publishing House, 1987).

Tie Zhuwei and Li Haiwan, "Confidential Documents Signed Before Surgery," in *Spotlight on Central South Lake* (Beijing: China Youth Press, 1998).

Wang Dongxing, "Chairman Mao in the Days of Smashing Lin Biao's Counterrevolutionary Conspiracy," in *The Fall of the Lin Biao Counterrevolutionary Clique* (Beijing: Central Party Research Office Press, 1995).

———. "Conversation with Bian Zhiqiang and Zhang Zuoliang," May 31, 1972, in *Supplementary Record of Zhou Enlai's Medical History*.

———. *Telephone Directive to Wu Jieping*, February 7, 1973, in ibid.

Wei Shiyan, "Kissinger's Second Visit to China," in *Fluctuations in New China's Foreign Policy* (Beijing: World Knowledge Publishing House, 1994).

———. "Visit of the Advance Team Headed by [Alexander] Haig," ibid.

Wu De, "The Mt. Lu Conference and the Lin Biao Incident," in *Final Years of Zhou Enlai: 1966–1976* (Beijing: Central Research Office Press, 1995).

Wu Jieping, "Unforgettable Teachings," in *Endless Memories* (Beijing: Central Research Office Press, 1987).

Xiong Fei, "Footnotes to History," in *The Fall of the Lin Biao Counterrevolutionary Clique* (Beijing: Central Research Office Press, 1995).

Xu Xiangqiang, "Selfless Devotion, Unflagging Determination—Remembrance of Zhou Enlai During the Cultural Revolution," *Red Flag*, no. 3, 1978.

Xue Ming, "Zhou Enlai and He Long," in *Endless Memories* (Beijing: Central Research Office Press, 1987).

———. "Deep as the Ocean," *Zhou Enlai in My Eyes* (Shijiazhuang: Hebei People's Publishing House, 1993).

Yang Yinlu, "Jiang Qing and Lin Biao," *Centenary Magazine*, no. 4, 1999.

Yong Wentao, "At the Center of the 'Red Guard Movement,'" in *Final Years of Zhou Enlai: 1966–1976* (Beijing: Central Research Office Press, 1995).

Yu Qiuli, "A Pillar in the Turbulence, a Power to Halt the Roaring Waves," in *Our Premier* (Beijing: Central Research Office Press, 1990).

Zeng Minzhi, "The Ageing of Zhou Enlai's Career as a Diplomat," *Literary Digest*, no. 1, issue 31.

Zeng Zhi, "Last Days of Tao Zhu," *Biography of Tao Zhu* (Beijing: China Youth Press, 1992).

Zhang Yufeng, "Anecdotes from the Last Years of Mao Zedong and Zhou Enlai," *Annals of the Chinese People*, no. 1, 1989.

Zhao Wei, "Last Words," in *Zhou Enlai in My Eyes* (Shijiazhuang: Hebei People's Publishing House, 1993).

Zhou Enlai, "Suggested Notes on Studying the Theories and Workings of the Politburo," May 4 and 5, 1975, in Central Research Office for Documentation, *Biography of Zhou Enlai: 1949–1976*, vol. II (Beijing: Central Research Office Press, 1998).

Zong Daoyi, "Wang Li's Speech on August 7 and the Comedy of 'Seizing Power' at the Foreign Ministry," *Chinese Sons and Daughters*, no. 1, 2002.

ENGLISH LANGUAGE SOURCES

Burr, William, ed., *The Kissinger Transcripts: The Top Secret Talks With Beijing and Moscow* (New York: The New Press, 1998).

Chang Jung and Jon Halliday, *Mao: The Unknown Story* (New York: Knopf, 2005).

Kissinger, Henry, *White House Years* (Boston: Little, Brown, and Company, 1979).

———. *Years of Upheaval* (Boston: Little, Brown, and Company, 1982).

Lieberthal, Kenneth G., and Bruce J. Dickson, *A Research Guide to Central Party and Government Meetings in China, 1949–1986* (Armonk, NY: M.E. Sharpe, 1989).

Li Zhisui, *The Private Life of Chairman Mao: The Memoirs of Mao's Personal Physician* (New York: Random House, 1994).

Liu Siji, ed., *Mao Zedong in the Central Soviet* (San Francisco: China Books, 1993).

MacFarquhar, Roderick, and Michael Schoenhals, *Mao's Last Revolution* (Cambridge, MA: Harvard University Press, 2006).

Macmillan, Margaret, *Nixon and Mao: The Week that Changed the World* (New York: Random House, 2007).

Nixon, Richard M., *RN: The Memoirs of Richard Nixon* (New York: Grosset & Dunlap, 1978).

Short, Philip, *Mao: A Life* (New York: Henry Holt, 1999).

Wilson, Dick, *Zhou Enlai: A Biography* (New York: Viking, 1984).

Index

Index

PublicAffairs is a publishing house founded in 1997. It is a tribute to the standards, values, and flair of three persons who have served as mentors to countless reporters, writers, editors, and book people of all kinds, including me.

I.F. STONE, proprietor of *I. F. Stone's Weekly*, combined a commitment to the First Amendment with entrepreneurial zeal and reporting skill and became one of the great independent journalists in American history. At the age of eighty, Izzy published *The Trial of Socrates*, which was a national bestseller. He wrote the book after he taught himself ancient Greek.

BENJAMIN C. BRADLEE was for nearly thirty years the charismatic editorial leader of *The Washington Post*. It was Ben who gave the *Post* the range and courage to pursue such historic issues as Watergate. He supported his reporters with a tenacity that made them fearless and it is no accident that so many became authors of influential, best-selling books.

ROBERT L. BERNSTEIN, the chief executive of Random House for more than a quarter century, guided one of the nation's premier publishing houses. Bob was personally responsible for many books of political dissent and argument that challenged tyranny around the globe. He is also the founder and longtime chair of Human Rights Watch, one of the most respected human rights organizations in the world.

·   ·   ·

For fifty years, the banner of Public Affairs Press was carried by its owner Morris B. Schnapper, who published Gandhi, Nasser, Toynbee, Truman, and about 1,500 other authors. In 1983, Schnapper was described by *The Washington Post* as "a redoubtable gadfly." His legacy will endure in the books to come.

Peter Osnos, *Founder and Editor-at-Large*